T0132185

THE OTHER CHURCH

WALTER G. GUY

authorHOUSE®

AuthorHouse™
1663 Liberty Drive
Bloomington, IN 47403
www.authorhouse.com
Phone: 833-262-8899

Published by AuthorHouse 11/10/2023

ISBN: 979-8-8230-1574-5 (sc)
ISBN: 979-8-8230-1575-2 (hc)
ISBN: 979-8-8230-1573-8 (e)

Library of Congress Control Number: 2023919229

Print information available on the last page.

Scripture quotations marked KJV are from the Holy Bible, King James Version (Authorized Version). First published in 1611. Quoted from the KJV Classic Reference Bible, Copyright © 1983 by The Zondervan Corporation.

Any people depicted in stock imagery provided by Getty Images are models, and such images are being used for illustrative purposes only. Certain stock imagery © Getty Images.

This book is printed on acid-free paper.

Because of the dynamic nature of the Internet, any web addresses or links contained in this book may have changed since publication and may no longer be valid. The views expressed in this work are solely those of the author and do not necessarily reflect the views of the publisher, and the publisher hereby disclaims any responsibility for them.

There are two churches in the world; one that Jesus said He would build, and the other church that man is building. There is a separation coming of the other church from the Church of Jesus Christ.

CONTENTS

Scripture references are from the King James Bible; there are verses that are repeated throughout this book because the Word of God is so important that we need to be very familiar with it because it is the foundation for our faith.

THE PARABLE OF THE WHEAT AND THE TARES

Many years ago the Lord showed this author that there are two churches in the world, one that Jesus said He would build, and the one that man would build. This book deals with the differences between these two churches so they can be easily identified.

> Matthew 13:24-30 – *Another parable put he forth unto them, saying, The kingdom of heaven is likened unto a man which sowed good seed in his field: but while men slept, his enemy came and sowed tares among the wheat, and went his way. But when the blade was sprung up, and brought forth fruit, then appeared the tares also. So the servants of the householder came and said unto him, Sir, didst not thou sow good seed in thy field? from whence then hath it tares? He said unto them, An enemy hath done this. The servants said unto him, Wilt thou then that we go and gather them up? But he said, Nay; lest while ye gather up the tares, ye root up also the wheat with them. Let both grow together until the harvest: and in the time of harvest I will say to the reapers, Gather ye together first the tares, and bind them in bundles to burn them: but gather the wheat into my barn.*

The above passage of scripture tells that there is a counterfeit church, an imitation of the real church. The two continue to grow side by side, sometimes interwoven, until the time for the harvest. The first event in the harvest is the identification and separation of the counterfeit church from the true church.

This book consists of messages and a vision given to the author by the Holy Spirit. These messages tell, as a warning, what has begun to happen and will continue to happen to the church throughout history unto the time of the coming harvest that Jesus described.

It begins with the vision given to this writer in late 1988 signifying the coming separation of the two churches: the one church that man is building, and the true church that Christ said He is building.

> Matthew 16:18 – *And I say also unto thee, That thou art Peter, and upon this rock* (the statement that Peter made) *I will build my church; and the gates of hell shall not prevail against it.*

This identifies the separation of the "Tares" from the "Wheat". The vision in Chapter One is followed by a detailed description of the "other" church in the following chapters. Then the author presents a brief historical capsule of church history to reveal how the "other" church developed and became what it is today.

In order to easily identify the difference between the two churches, the author explains the divine, eternal purpose of the true church that Christ is building; the one that He is returning to receive unto Himself. Then, to better equip the reader to make his own decision about which church is Christ's and which to beware of, the author details the warning Christ and the apostle Paul gave about the deception in the last days: the deception brought about by "wolves in sheep's clothing", along with the false prophets, teachers and preachers. These will falsely speak about Christ claiming to be anointed and deceiving many.

> Matthew 24:24 – *For there shall arise false Christs, and false prophets, and shall shew great signs and wonders; insomuch that, if it were possible, they shall deceive the very elect.*

These two churches are identified along with God's plan for them. Keys to recognizing God's ordained and directed ministers are discussed to equip the reader to recognize the true servants of God as well as those of the "other" church. Also included is the next move of God within the church that is likely to occur. The final days of the true church are described that are to let you know that even though there are tumultuous times ahead for the saints, that the best is yet to come. This text incorporates a lot of scripture text since the Bible is the source of divine guidance and is what the Holy Spirit uses to reveal God's plan: in the scriptures we can have confidence. Several scriptures are repeated throughout the text because of their importance, and because repetition is a key to memorizing. The Holy Spirit gives us understanding of these scriptures revealing that we are now in the days approaching the fulfilment of the end-time prophecies.

The scriptures used are from the King James Bible version with some emphasis in parenthesis

Chapter 1

VISION OF CHRIST'S CHURCH AND THE OTHER CHURCH

Separation of the Wheat from the Tares

The following is a progressive vision that began in December, 1988, two weeks before Christmas and concluded Christmas Day.

It had been a year of financial leanness for my family. We were living by the grace of God at that time. After losing our business, I had taken a position that paid little more than minimum wage. I was doing what was in my hand to do, and God did the rest. We were living miracles as the Lord made a way where there was no way.

Facing the Christmas season with no money for shopping and the normal extras enjoyed by the season, I was feeling a little low—no, let me be honest: I was very low. It didn't feel like the normal Christmas season. We've been through this kind of trial twice before, and I did not like having to go through it again.

While driving to work one morning I decided to encourage myself in the Lord. I enjoyed the one-hour drive to and from work; it was a time of special prayer and communion with my Lord. In order to get into the Christmassy frame of mind, (I don't like to use the term "Christmas spirit"), so I began to pray about the birth of Jesus.

While in prayer, I began meditating on the birth of Jesus. I tried to picture in my mind the scene of the baby Jesus lying in the manger (the feeding trough used as a crib). As I imagined a view of the baby Jesus, these words came to me in my spirit: "Don't look down at a babe in a manger; look up at the King of Glory." When I looked up (in my spirit), the vision began. (Remember: I am still driving.)

I saw Jesus standing in full battle armor with His sword held high as though it was a call to go into action. His appearance was fierce, like a very mighty and determined warrior. He looked so totally awesome that words cannot describe His appearance. Such a fearsome sight, yet I had no sense of fear of Him.

As I gazed and marveled at Him, I heard the command, "Fall in, in rank!" In the spirit, a summons was given for His soldiers, and me, to get into position and stand at attention.

This first part of the vision focused on the fierceness of the army's commander, Jesus. He is coming back and He is ready to defeat His enemies; He is full of fury at His enemy. Never had I pictured Him this way. Then I remembered the description of Him in Revelation 19 when He leads His army of saints upon returning to the earth to set up His kingdom for a thousand years. What I saw was the same description of Him with fire in His eyes. You don't want to tangle with Him, get in His way, or be His enemy! Nothing and nobody can stand before Him when He comes as the absolute conqueror.

A couple days later I was meditating on this vision I had, then it resumed right where it left off. In response to the command to "fall in, in rank," I saw a frenzied scrambling of troops. This scrambling, bumping, running, and squaring off in ranks occurred over a period of time. They were rushing to find their proper place before Him.

Pondering on what I saw, I asked the question: How do you fall in and what does it mean? The answer was not spoken but revealed to me in my spirit. You must first have ears to hear the command: (as stated in Mark 4:9; Revelation 2:7, 11, 17, 29; and 3:6, 13, 22), then you must obey the command. Unfortunately, there are those who don't have ears to hear.

Those who are called must know and acknowledge their calling, their gifting, and their function. Then, knowing their call, they must find where their call, gift, and function fits. This is their position in the ranks. This isn't easy and results in the scrambling and bumping as the called ones seek where they fit in. The "fall in" is this time to find your position among the rest of the ranks, then get in that position and stand and await the next command.

Then I saw an anointing begin to flow from Christ the Commander down through the ranks. (Note: The anointing is the divine power and authority that comes from Christ, by His Holy Spirit, who was given it according to Matthew.)

Matthew 28:18-20 – *And Jesus came and spake unto them, saying, All power is given unto me in heaven and in earth. Go ye therefore, and teach all nations, baptizing them in the name of the Father, and of the Son, and of the Holy Ghost: teaching them to observe all things whatsoever I have commanded you: and, lo, I am with you always, even unto the end of the world. Amen.*

That anointing to minister the power and authority of Christ and His Word can't flow from the commander throughout the ranks if the troops are not in rank, out of their proper position, or in the wrong place. Being out of place leaves a gap that prevents the anointing from flowing through the ranks (of time or place) behind that position, like an open circuit. A person's proper position in rank fills a gap and completes a circuit from the one ahead to the one behind so the anointing can flow. (Note: a gap can also be a time period where there is no one in that position to function or pass on the anointing.)

Being in rank also means to be in fellowship and rightly related to those standing in adjacent ranks or positions so as not to hinder the flow of the anointing that comes from the chief. (So many are out of place today or assuming positions that they were not assigned to, meaning that flow of the pure gospel of truth from Christ is hindered.) I noticed that some, already in rank, have been standing in position for a long time. They were waiting for the ranks to be completed by those who have not yet found their proper position.

The following day, while in prayer, the vision resumed with Jesus standing at the head of His army, His church. The army in full rank before Him was standing in the formation of a triangle or wedge. The tip of that triangle was closest to Him and then fanned out. This indicated the expansion of His troops from the small beginning of the church to the present day.

Then it was as though I was viewing the vision through a zoom lens, and it was zooming back out to get a broader view. Then I could see that Christ and His army appeared to be standing on top of a mountain plateau. The sky all around was just black darkness, (as mentioned in Joel 2:1–2).

Suddenly, flashes of light punctuated the blackness; these flashes appeared to come from explosions that were striking against the mountain beneath Christ and His army. I observed that an intense warfare was being waged, but Christ and His troops were not moving, nor were they being hit by any of the weapons. The explosions were hitting the sides of the mountain and bringing chunks of it down.

The view zoomed out farther and I saw that the mountain had risen up out of a vast sea; it was the sea of humanity. The warfare against the mountain came from the sea of humanity, where sin abounds. I also noticed that there were a few people climbing up the side of the mountain trying to reach the mass of troops assembled above to join and get in the ranks, but the ranks seemed to be off limits to them, as they were not seeking access the proper way: the only access is through Jesus Christ, the Commander.

These climbers progress was being hindered by the attacks against the mountain. These blasts were knocking them down the mountain and back into the sea of humanity from which they came. This warfare against the mountain was so intense that it finally leveled the mountain and brought the whole thing down into the sea of humanity.

Yet Jesus and His church warriors were still standing in the same place, unmoved, untouched, and unharmed by the warfare against the mountain. They appeared to be standing in midair. It was as if they didn't need the mountain in the first place. The mountain was now completely gone.

On Christmas Day 1988, I decided to share this vision with my family. When I made this decision, I still did not know what the vision meant. As I prayed to ask the Lord if indeed I should share this with them, the Lord gave me the understanding of what this vision represented. Indeed, it was a different Christmas for us.

The mountain that the Lord and His army appeared to stand on—that some people were climbing to get to the top and that was being torn down—was the *other church*. It was the church that man built by man's ideas, methods, organizations, and denominations. It was the church that was filled with man's personalities, programs, and represented man. (I will refer to this other church of man as the IRS—the institutionalized religious system.)

The mountain was the *false church*, the church of human resources with success and prosperity, like the one described in Revelation 3:14–17, the Church of Laodicea. This is the church that left Jesus standing on the outside knocking to get in because they thought that they had everything – Revelation 3:20.

This false church, as a mountain, rose from the sea of humanity, or humanism. It had in it all of man's devices, designs, controls and authority. The mountain was the man made church; man built it and man governs it. It was not built by Christ, and yet it attempts to point to Him; it claimed Him; and it tries to represent Him. That is why He and His army appeared to stand on top of it.

This church of man is referred to as the harlot church and mystery Babylon, the religious system of man and of the world – the I.R.S. Those who were climbing the mountain to get into Christ's ranks represent man's efforts to qualify for service, or ministry, through man's system of recognition, credentialing and control. This church relies on human resources, methods, education, and programs rather than being led by the Holy Spirit.

This church has represented itself as the authority and the way of the Lord. However, it is not the way! Only Jesus is the way, the truth and the life – (John 14:6). People cannot work their way up the proverbial mountain, through the church of man's organization, to get into Christ's ranks to become part of His army. The other church cannot give you a true calling, your gifting, your rank, or your ministry. Man cannot give it to you, only Jesus can – (Ephesians 4:11). Man can only give you man's recognition in man's organizations. Denominational organizations do not ordain or make ministers in His church; only he does because it is His army. Man only does this in the I.R.S. type of false church.

It turns out that the false "other" church, which was the mountain in this vision, obscured humanities view of Christ and His true church. Satan, the thief, has used deceived man to build the "other" church which has gotten in the way of what Christ is building. After this false church, (the tares), was brought down back into the sea of humanity, all of humanity was now able to see Christ and His true church standing in plain unhindered view.

How is it that the other church of man obscures the world's view of Christ and His true church? The I.R.S. church of man wants people to put their trust, confidence of faith in their church, their pastor, their denomination or doctrines; but not really in Jesus Christ and His Word. Thus this other church is in the way. You can't get saved by the church – only by Jesus. The other church doesn't bring life, (the zoe), the eternal Spirit life of God.

Leadership, pastors and preachers of the other church, may use the name of Jesus, and use his Word, but they have no authority to do so. Thus they tend to mix their own ideas, doctrines and practices in their preaching. Jesus said He would reject such ministers:

> Matthew 7:21-23 – *Not every one that saith unto me, Lord, Lord, shall enter into the kingdom of heaven; but he that doeth the will of my Father which is in heaven. Many will say to me in that day, Lord, Lord, have we not prophesied in thy name? and in thy name have cast out devils? and in thy name done*

many wonderful works? And then will I profess unto them, I never knew you: depart from me, ye that work iniquity.

Also consider that everything that comes from God, our Heavenly Father, comes to us through the name and authority of Jesus Christ, and not by the church man has built.

John 16:23b – … *Whatsoever ye shall ask the Father in my name, he will give it you.*

The vision showed that the church that man built, (the mountain), will come under attack from the rest of humanity, those in the sea who are not part of the man-made church. These are the anti-god portions of humanity that promotes humanism, liberalism, communism, socialism, and woke-ism. The warfare includes infiltrating such policies and practices into the other church along with the corrupt doctrines, and pagan practices of the Roman Catholic Church. (A brief history of the Roman Catholic Church is covered in chapter 3.) The conclusion of all of this human effort will form the religion of the antichrist.

This vision did not show the destruction of the "other" church; instead, it showed the identification and separation of the false other church from the true church. This is parallel to the parable of the "Tares and the Wheat" in Matthew 13:36-43. This vision is only an excerpt in the scenario of major events that lay ahead, and it appears that as of 2023 it is already be in progress. The Lord, in His mercy, always forewarns His people through His servants using visions and prophecies.

The mountain, representing the church that man has built, does not reflect Jesus Christ. It may be possible that this mountain falling back down into the sea of humanity is likened to the "falling away" or time apostasy that is described by Paul.

2 Thessalonians 2:3 – *Let no man deceive you by any means: for that day shall not come, except there come a falling away first, and that man of sin be revealed, the son of perdition;*

The church Jesus is building represents and reflects Jesus Christ, having His character and nature. The carnal elements of man's flesh are the spots, wrinkles and blemishes that are removed so that Jesus can present His church spotless before Him and to His Heavenly Father.

> Ephesians 5:26 – *that he might sanctify and cleanse it with the washing of water by the word, that he might present it to himself a glorious church, not having spot, or wrinkle, or any such thing; but that it should be holy and without blemish.*

Christ's church will be just like Him:

> 1 John 3:2-3 – *Beloved, now are we the sons of God, and it doth not yet appear what we shall be: but we know that, when he shall appear, we shall be like him; for we shall see him as he is. And every man that hath this hope in him purifieth himself, even as he is pure.*

We are entering the prophesied time of the end-time harvest. The harvest is not simply the anticipated rapture of the church as some have assumed; that event comes when the harvest is complete. The harvest takes time and involves processing; it cannot occur "in the twinkling of an eye" as does the rapture.

> 1 Corinthians 15:51-52 – *Behold, I shew you a mystery; We shall not all sleep, but we shall all be changed, In a moment, in the twinkling of an eye, at the last trump: for the trumpet shall sound, and the dead shall be raised incorruptible, and we shall be changed.*

The identification and separation of the "Tares from the Wheat" is the first step in the harvest. This is what this vision is about. The second step in the harvest is the preparation of the harvested wheat. This is the thrashing and winnowing to separate the chaff from the kernel.

Just as it sounds, the thrashing and winnowing appears to be a period of persecution that will cause any worldliness in His people, (the spots, wrinkles and blemishes), to fall off and be blown away. The true church will cast off all things that soil it and hold it bound to this world. The end result of this "purification" process is that it will be like Jesus, as stated in 1 John 3:2-3 above.

When the wheat has been processed, it is ready to be taken into the storehouse, the place prepared for it. This is the time for the rapture of the church. The Holy Spirit is prompting the Body of Christ, His true Church, to prepare for the harvest, the ingathering of the crops, the saved souls. The Holy Spirit sounds the call of the Lord's approaching. This call is going out continually. Many people have heard it; it has been referred to as a coming harvest, or revival, that many have prophesied. However, with the harvest comes the opposition from the enemy – Satan.

We will see, and are seeing, an increasing warfare against the church. It will remove the other church, but it will strengthen and purge His true church. I suspect that the government, as the effort of man, will have much to do with the attack from the sea of humanity. After this identification and separation is complete, which has already begun, then comes the persecution of the true church. Not until the other church is able to see and recognize the true church, will it begin to oppose and oppress it along with the rest of the sea of humanity. This is the warfare that Jesus is ready to engage in along with His saints.

The conflict that I saw in this vision was rather one-sided: the attack came from the sea of humanity which brings down the false church back into its own ranks. This is why the true church Christ was untouched by that assault.

However, the enemy, Satan, will eventually use humanities false religions and governments to wage war against the true church. This will occur more intensely after the separation of wheat and tares is completed, when Christ and His church are more easily recognized. This time of persecution has happened before to the true church soon after it was formed by Christ. As it was in the beginning so shall it be at the end. The persecution will accompany a period of revival and soul winning; in fact, the persecution will be Satan's response to the revival, in order to try to stop it.

What is built by the Lord Jesus Christ and on His Word will stand. What is not will fall as Jesus stated:

> Matthew 7:24-27 – *Therefore whosoever heareth these sayings of mine, and doeth them, I will liken him unto a wise man, which built his house upon a rock: and the rain descended, and the floods came, and the winds blew, and beat upon that house; and it fell not: for it was founded upon a rock. And every one that heareth these sayings of mine, and doeth them not, shall be likened unto a foolish man, which built his house upon the*

sand: and the rain descended, and the floods came, and the winds blew, and beat upon that house; and it fell: and great was the fall of it. (Consider whose house is being built – His.)

I believe we will see great changes in what we call church in the near future as it should resemble much like it was when it began in the first century. The church of our Lord Jesus Christ will go full-circle to be as it was at the beginning by the power of the Holy Spirit to be a witness to the whole world. Keep your focus on the Lord Jesus Christ – the Commander of His army of true believers.

Chapter 2

CONFLICT WITH THE OTHER CHURCH

A Description Of The Other Church That Man Built

Two churches exist simultaneously in the world today; the true church that Christ is building, and the other church that man is building. The true church began with Jesus Christ who is the head and director. His church reflects His image, character and nature, and is thus filled with Him and functions as His Body on earth. His church is composed of the blood bought adopted children of God.

> 1 John 3:2 – *Beloved, now are we the sons of God, and it doth not yet appear what we shall be: but we know that, when he shall appear, we shall be like him; for we shall see him as he is.*

> 1 Corinthians 12:27 – *Now ye are the body of Christ, and members in particular.*

The false church, birthed out of the true church, came about when man took control, organized it, established his own rules and doctrines in it; including who is qualified to be a minister in it; and man functions as lord over it. And man claims he is doing it all in the name of Christ.

This false church also has false prophets, preachers and teachers who claim to come in Christ's name and in His authority, (like the Pope who is called the Vicar of Christ).

Matthew 7:15, 22-23 —*Beware of false prophets, which come to you in sheep's clothing, but inwardly they are ravening wolves. Many will say to me in that day, Lord, Lord, have we not prophesied in thy name? and in thy name have cast out devils? and in thy name done many wonderful works? And then will I profess unto them, I never knew you: depart from me, ye that work iniquity.*

The only power and authority they have is the ability to deceive.

Matthew 24:4-5 – *And Jesus answered and said unto them, Take heed that no man deceive you. For many shall come in my name, saying, I am Christ; and shall deceive many.*

Note: that "many" shall come to deceive; and many" shall be deceived; so this is not a rare case dealing with a few, but will occur on a wide scale. The apostle Paul addressed this issue in his letter to Timothy when he describes the corrupt condition of the false church in these last days.

2 Timothy 3:1-7 – *This know also, that in the last days perilous times shall come. For men shall be lovers of their own selves, covetous, boasters, proud, blasphemers, disobedient to parents, unthankful, unholy, without natural affection, trucebreakers, false accusers, incontinent, fierce, despisers of those that are good, traitors, heady, high-minded, lovers of pleasures more than lovers of God; having a form of godliness, but denying the power thereof: from such turn away. For of this sort are they which creep into houses, and lead captive silly women laden with sins, led away with divers lusts, ever learning, and never able to come to the knowledge of the truth.*

To verify that Paul is speaking about the condition of the false church, consider where you find a "form of godliness"; in a church that denies the power to change lives. He then issues the order, "from such turn away". Instead of reflecting Christ and His character within its people, the false church reflects man's carnal nature which is clearly identified in the above scripture because there is no repentance or change to righteousness. Paul also tells us that in the last days there would be an increase in false doctrines and departing from the true faith.

> 1 Timothy 4:1-2 – *Now the Spirit speaketh expressly, that in the latter times some shall depart from the faith, giving heed to seducing spirits, and doctrines of devils; speaking lies in hypocrisy; having their conscience seared with a hot iron;*

Thus there is no conviction of sin or repentance because such topics are avoided.

When you think of a church you think of a building, a name, a denomination, or the pastor/priest that is in charge. However, the true church is not a building, or any of the above. The word "church" means called out and assembled together, and does not require a building. Much of the true church in China meets "underground", out of sight of the public which is heavily monitored and controlled by the government. Jesus stated the simplicity of what is the true church. The fancy building with all its liturgy and ritual is man-made.

> Matthew 18:20 – *For where two or three are gathered together in my name, there am I in the midst of them.*

You don't need a building, a choir, stained glass windows, pews, an organ and piano to have a church; just people who assemble in His name. What is generally referred to as church is not really the true church of the Lord Jesus Christ. When many churches gather together, whose name are they gathering in: Catholic, Baptist, Methodist, or any other denominational name? Or do they gather together in the name of a pastor or preacher. Is the Lord's presence experienced when they gather, as Jesus stated in the above verse?

Jesus dwells by His Spirit in the hearts of His people who are referred to as His temple:

> Acts 7:48 – *"However, the Most High does not dwell in houses made with hands. As the prophet says:*

> 1 Corinthians 3:16-17 – *Know ye not that ye are the temple of God, and that the Spirit of God dwelleth in you? If any man*

defile the temple of God, him shall God destroy; for the temple of God is holy, which temple ye are.

Galatians 4:6 – *And because you are sons, God has sent forth into our hearts the Spirit of His Son, crying, "Abba, Father!"*

Jesus, Paul and others warned us that personalities would arise to gain followers after themselves so they could control and have preeminence in the church – thus creating a false church with false leadership.

Acts 20:28-31 – *Take heed therefore unto yourselves, and to all the flock, over the which the Holy Ghost hath made you overseers, to feed the church of God, which he hath purchased with his own blood. For I know this, that after my departing shall grievous wolves enter in among you, not sparing the flock. Also of your own selves shall men arise, speaking perverse things, to draw away disciples after them. Therefore watch, and remember, that by the space of three years I ceased not to warn every one night and day with tears.*

3 John 9-10 – *I wrote unto the church: but Diotrephes, who loveth to have the preeminence among them, receiveth us not. Wherefore, if I come, I will remember his deeds which he doeth, prating against us with malicious words: and not content therewith, neither doth he himself receive the brethren, and forbiddeth them that would, and casteth them out of the church.*

We see here that the apostle John says that there are those in leadership in the church that are self-centered and wicked, spiritually blind as to what God wants and who Christ has ordained to serve His church. These self-appointed, and man appointed, leaders are the basis for the establishment of the "other" church, regardless of what denomination or name they call themselves.

Throughout much of church history, some of those of the true church have existed within the false other church, and being under its control in varying degrees. Using its forms of control, the other church has been quenching and suppressing the true believers, choking the spiritual life (zoe) out of it and putting out the fire of the Spirit that has been kindled in their lives. Such believers will either be forced to leave that church or made to compromise and have their light go out, (like the five foolish virgins in Matthew 25).

The false other church is not actually headed by men, though they think they are. The false church is actually headed subtly by Satan. (This is covered in the following Chapter.) Man has been duped by Satan's manipulation, (as in the Garden), and the result is the false other church, as well as many other false religions. Thus we have the false church being a counterfeit trying to pass itself off as the church of the Lord Jesus Christ.

> 2 Corinthians 11:13-15 – *For such are false apostles, deceitful workers, transforming themselves into the apostles of Christ. And no marvel; for Satan himself is transformed into an angel of light. Therefore it is no great thing if his ministers also be transformed as the ministers of righteousness; whose end shall be according to their works.*

Man wants to be in control, but not as much as Satan does because of his lust for power and dominion over mankind: that dominion began in the Garden. Carnal man gets this desire from Satan; and therefore becomes a puppet to the enemy to do his bidding. If church leadership is not totally committed and yielded to the Holy Spirit and Christ, it will exert natural, human, carnal efforts in leadership that are likely under the influence of a powerful religious demonic spirit. Carnality, (*carnis* – flesh or carnivorous), is the wolf nature that seeks to satisfy its self. Those who are depending on human ability to lead the church are such that are duped by the enemy and operate under the influence of Satan or a religious spirit. There are preachers and ministers who are Satan's servants in disguise.

> 2 Corinthians 11:13-15 – *For such are false apostles, deceitful workers, transforming themselves into the apostles of Christ. And no marvel; for Satan himself is transformed into an angel of light. Therefore it is no great thing if his ministers also be transformed as the ministers of righteousness; whose end shall be according to their works.*

> John 8:44a – *Ye are of your father the devil, and the lusts of your father ye will do.*

A person can be a Christian, born-again, and still be carnally led, motivated, driven or controlled. This can happen to those who are not mature in the Lord, in His Word, through true discipleship and training.

> 1 Corinthians 3:1-3 — *And I, brethren, could not speak unto you as unto spiritual, but as unto carnal, even as unto babes in Christ. I have fed you with milk, and not with meat: for hitherto ye were not able to bear it, neither yet now are ye able. For ye are yet carnal: for whereas there is among you envying, and strife, and divisions, are ye not carnal, and walk as men?*

These are such as have not been taught to die to self and deny the carnal flesh.

> Luke 9:23 — *And he said to them all, If any man will come after me, let him deny himself, and take up his cross daily, and follow me.*

Jesus showed the apostle John the kind of church man builds: what man thinks is church, and what the Lord thinks of this kind of church.

> Revelation 3:15-17 — *I know thy works, that thou art neither cold nor hot: I would thou wert cold or hot. So then because thou art lukewarm, and neither cold nor hot, I will spue thee out of my mouth. Because thou sayest, I am rich, and increased with goods, and have need of nothing; and knowest not that thou art wretched, and miserable, and poor, and blind, and naked:*

The Laodicean Church is the example of what kind of church that man builds according to man's designs: it is the other church. This other church has been and will continue to be the source of persecution of the saints, the true church of the godly believers. The prophesied coming persecution will come from the various forms of the other church. The religious have always persecuted the righteous, just as was done to Jesus and the early church.

The prophesied revival in the church that so many speak of recently, will actually be the restoration of the true church. This is when it will return to be more like the church when it first began with the Holy Spirit of God directing it, and mankind depending on and obeying His leading. This will be the time of its identification and separation form the other church as referenced vision of Chapter One.

The word, revive means to re-make alive; awaking to alertness and activity from a state of being dormant, lethargic or apathetic. Revival may be possible in the other church in order to get people out of it to become part of the true church and awakened out of their lukewarm state and spiritual slumber.

> Ephesians 5:14-16 – *Wherefore he saith, Awake thou that sleepest, and arise from the dead, and Christ shall give thee light. See then that ye walk circumspectly, not as fools, but as wise, redeeming the time, because the days are evil.*

> Romans 13:11-14 – *And that, knowing the time, that now it is high time to awake out of sleep: for now is our salvation nearer than when we believed. The night is far spent, the day is at hand: let us therefore cast off the works of darkness, and let us put on the armour of light. Let us walk honestly, as in the day; not in rioting and drunkenness, not in chambering and wantonness, not in strife and envying. But put ye on the Lord Jesus Christ, and make not provision for the flesh, to fulfil the lusts thereof.*

The church under man's control is actually the exercise of a different and contrary religion; it can be called Humanism. The religion of man, Humanism takes this other church away from Christ and identifies it more with human government. Thus it adopts the efforts of globalism, New Age, wokeism and liberalism.

This Humanism moves God out and man in. This has not only occurred in the other church, but also in our educational institutions, governments, the media and entertainment. Man is acting as if he is god; running things his own way, based on his desires, his corrupted knowledge and political correctness.

There is no "hearing from God" in matters that God is concerned about; (abortion being a good example). Some may pray about things; they can't be pious without doing so: but do they hear; do they wait on God's answer or direction. NO! They prefer to ask God to bless their actions, if they pray at all. They govern by committee, popular vote, or hierarchical edict. The result is man's ways.

Proverbs 16:25 – *There is a way that seemeth right unto a man, but the end thereof are the ways of death.*

Man's dominion is strong in the other church. Humanism is man assuming the place of God; making decisions and taking on responsibilities that are God's. Humanism is actually the religion of the antichrist, man setting himself up as God; but it is actually under the influence and control of Satan. This will eventually be revealed soon.

2 Thessalonians 2:3-4 – *Let no man deceive you by any means: for that day shall not come, except there come a falling away first, and that man of sin be revealed, the son of perdition; who opposeth and exalteth himself above all that is called God, or that is worshipped; so that he as God sitteth in the temple of God, shewing himself that he is God.*

"By any means" includes using church doctrine to deceive people. This very thing has been going on in the other church since it began its infiltration into the church after its founding. This is the spirit of antichrist that is already at work.

1 John 4:3 – *and every spirit that confesseth not that Jesus Christ is come in the flesh is not of God: and this is that spirit of antichrist, whereof ye have heard that it should come; and even now already is it in the world.*

Revelation 13:18 – *Here is wisdom. Let him that hath understanding count the number of the beast: for it is the number of a man; and his number is Six hundred threescore and six.*

The infamous 666, the mark of the beast, is the number of man: the first 6 equals the body of man; the second 6 equals the soul of man; and the third 6 equals the spirit of man; thus 666 equals the sum total man. Man becomes a pawn of Satan; and this particular man exercises the abilities of Satan to whom he has submitted himself. This man may begin as a political figure, but will then assume a religious position assuming that he is as God. He will likely even be accepted and worshipped in the other church.

Before these very last day events occur, the other church will begin to react as a spiritual awakening begins to take place, and people start to pull out of the other church to become part of the true church; as the separation begins. The other church will see that it is losing control and influence and will fight to maintain that control over the people. Thus persecution expands as covered previously; religious leaders have always reacted this way.

> John 12:19 – *The Pharisees therefore said among themselves, Perceive ye how ye prevail nothing* (we have lost our influence over them)*? behold, the world is gone after him.*

As truth is revealed, some will withdraw as they recognize the deception and where the other church is heading. They will join with the true church as the Holy Spirit is again poured out in these last days, anointing His called and humble servants for anointed ministry as prophesied.

> Acts 2:16-21 – *But this is that which was spoken by the prophet Joel; And it shall come to pass in the last days, saith God, I will pour out of my Spirit upon all flesh: and your sons and your daughters shall prophesy, and your young men shall see visions, and your old men shall dream dreams: and on my servants and on my handmaidens I will pour out in those days of my Spirit; and they shall prophesy: and I will shew wonders in heaven above, and signs in the earth beneath; blood, and fire, and vapour of smoke: the sun shall be turned into darkness, and the moon into blood, before that great and notable day of the Lord come: and it shall come to pass, that whosoever shall call on the name of the Lord shall be saved.*

(Note: the "last days" referred to above are the last two millennial days, or two thousand years, that began at Pentecost and continue to the return of Christ. This is proof that it includes what still lays ahead are the last day signs mentioned.)

Throughout history there have been those who have pulled out of established church denominations because they have received more revelation of the truth. However, they end up forming new denominations reproducing the same manmade lethargy because they carried with them the same human traits and weaknesses that produced the other church that they left behind.

We have seen this over and over again which is why we now have so many different church denominations.

The weakness just addressed is the effort of man to control the church and set up a hierarchical order with conditions and control of who can be a minister, or is allowed to speak to the people. In addition, many of these new churches seek a unique form of identity to differentiate from the ones they left.

Their efforts in revival, though often proper, seem to always end up expanding the other church because it is only Jesus who can build His church, not man. Even those who start out purely motivated and led of the Holy Spirit, usually see that work go back in the control of man and thus become doomed to eventually go the way of the other church.

Finally, the other church will be aligned with the government and it will lobby for new laws aimed at outlawing the true church that has been separated from it. This harassment has already begun in our society and will greatly increase. The government will determine what constitutes a legal church at the direction and council of the other church. The I.R.S. (the tax people) has already set the parameters of what it defines as a legal and an illegal church; (which is contrary to the U.S. Code and the U.S. Constitution).

This period of persecution may very likely be during the period of the prophesied apostasy, the "falling away" or departing from the faith which will expose the nature of the other church.

> 2 Thessalonians 2: 3 – ... *for that day shall not come, except there come a falling away first, ...*

It is logical to conclude that hostility will result when the separation occurs. Human nature has a flaw that makes carnal people turn on those who hold strongly to opposing views.

The alignment of the other church with the liberal woke government will set the stage for the relationship of the false prophet with the antichrist; the false prophet being a religious figure allied with a political or government figure.

Jesus spoke of the two elements which constitute each church continuing to grow together through the ages until the harvest when they would be identified and separated; as in the parable of the Tares and the Wheat in Matthew 13:24-30.

The true church will live, practice and preach the Kingdom of God, just as Jesus did; as He instructed His disciples, which they did as listed in Matthew 4:17; 5:10; 24:14; Luke 10:10-11.

The *ZOE* (Spirit life) will be in the true church. It will be full of the Grace of God, which means acceptance, education and revelation of Jesus and His kingdom bringing forth the Fruit of the Spirit, as listed in Galatians 5:22-23, and which is the character and nature of God and Christ. This is what our Heavenly Father is looking for to be in the followers of Jesus Christ – (John 15:1-5).

The other church will continue to preach their version of the gospel; but it will be the social gospel, the soulish gospel, and some will even continue to preach in His name. Jesus said many would come in His name, preaching and performing in His name, but they would be deceivers.

> Luke 21:8 – *And he said, Take heed that ye be not deceived: for many shall come in my name, saying, I am Christ; and the time draweth near: go ye not therefore after them.*

> Matthew 7:22 – *Many will say to me in that day, Lord, Lord, have we not prophesied in thy name? and in thy name have cast out devils? and in thy name done many wonderful works? And then will I profess unto them, I never knew you: depart from me, ye that work iniquity.*

> Matthew 24:4-5 – *And Jesus answered and said unto them, Take heed that no man deceive you. For many shall come in my name, saying, I am Christ; and shall deceive many.*

Yes, they will preach the gospel and use His name. They will use the scripture skillfully also. They may preach it, but they will not live it or the principles of the kingdom, because their focus is on man, social issues, soulish issues (self), and building unto themselves, their organizations, their names, their buildings and their programs.

The other church has been and will continue to be full of laws, their laws. These are rules and regulations requiring compliance to man's religious standards for acceptance and conformity. There is no grace in this bunch; however different forms of the other church use greasy grace, which means, anything goes, because God loves you just the way you are and you don't need to repent or change.

The period of perceived revival and restoration, along with the accompanying persecution is typified and paralleled in Matthew 9:35 to 10:42. Yes, history repeats it-self, this is because the carnal nature of unredeemed man hasn't changed. Much of what is coming is very similar to what has happened in the past; (consider The Inquisition by the Roman Catholic Church).

The above mentioned scriptures appear to be prophetically representative of the experience of the true church in the last days, paralleling the ministry of the early church. It is a restoration or coming full cycle back to its beginning with the full glory of the Lord manifested in and through it.

Jesus Christ will be seen in His people as they are conformed to His image. This is the true and glorious church that He is returning for: full of His Glory; (which again is His character and nature, as listed in Galatians 5:22-23).

This end-time move of the Lord in His church is illustrated in what previously occurred in Matthew 9:35 thru Matthew 10:15. And the resultant persecution is typified in the continuing passages of Matthew 10:16-42. The prophetic scenario will be similar in these last days as what has already been recorded as follows:

> Matthew 9: 35 – *And Jesus went about all the cities and villages, teaching in their synagogues, and preaching the gospel of the kingdom, and healing every sickness and every disease among the people.*

Jesus provides the example of true ministry which is to be duplicated by His servants.

> John 14:12 – *Verily, verily, I say unto you, He that believeth on me, the works that I do shall he do also; and greater works than these shall he do; because I go unto my Father.*

Jesus is the embodiment of all of the five gift ministries, with all nine Gifts of the Spirit, as well as all of the Fruits of the Spirit, listed as follows:

Ephesians 4:11-12 – *And he gave some, apostles; and some, prophets; and some, evangelists; and some, pastors and teachers; for the perfecting of the saints, for the work of the ministry, for the edifying of the body of Christ:*

1 Corinthians 12:8-10 – *For to one is given by the Spirit the word of wisdom; to another the word of knowledge by the same Spirit; to another faith by the same Spirit; to another the gifts of healing by the same Spirit; to another the working of miracles; to another prophecy; to another discerning of spirits; to another divers kinds of tongues; to another the interpretation of tongues:*

Galatians 5:22-23 – *But the fruit of the Spirit is love, joy, peace, longsuffering, gentleness, goodness, faith, meekness, temperance: against such there is no law.*

John 15:4-5 – *Abide in me, and I in you. As the branch cannot bear fruit of itself, except it abide in the vine; no more can ye, except ye abide in me. I am the vine, ye are the branches: He that abideth in me, and I in him, the same bringeth forth much fruit: for without me ye can do nothing.*

(Note: it is the life of Christ, the vine, flowing through the branches, that produces this Fruit of the Spirit.)

The main requirement of this supernatural moving of the Lord, within His servants, is the manifestation this fruit of love and compassion for others to whom we are to minister.

Matthew 10:36 – *But when he saw the multitudes, he was moved with compassion on them, because they fainted, and were scattered abroad, as sheep having no shepherd.*

The apostle Paul tells us the best way to minister with the Gifts of the Holy Spirit to others. Note that the first listed Fruit of the Spirit is LOVE which is compassion in action.

1 Corinthians 12:31 – *But covet earnestly the best gifts: and yet shew I unto you a more excellent way.*

The proper motive for pure ministry is revealed here; it is the God kind of love. Without His love, Jesus is not properly represented, and the results of such ministry is shallow and empty, lacking the real power to change lives.

> Corinthians 13:1-3 – *Though I speak with the tongues of men and of angels, and have not charity, I am become as sounding brass, or a tinkling cymbal. And though I have the gift of prophecy, and understand all mysteries, and all knowledge; and though I have all faith, so that I could remove mountains, and have not charity, I am nothing. And though I bestow all my goods to feed the poor, and though I give my body to be burned, and have not charity, it profiteth me nothing.*

Note: the word charity is used here for love because real love means "giving" of what you have and what you are for the benefit of the other, just as Jesus stated.

> John 15:13 – *Greater love hath no man than this, that a man lay down his life for his friends.*

Thus, love or charity is the "*more excellent way*" that the true church is to show Jesus Christ to the world in these last days. This is the motive in humble servants of the true church that will turn the world upside down. God will use and elevate those who function in godly love, humble themselves and take on the role of true servants (bond-slaves of the master).

> 1 Peter 5:6 – *Humble yourselves therefore under the mighty hand of God, that he may exalt you in due time:*

It is the lack of this pure motive, love, humility and servitude that has prevented the other church from winning the world. In most cases, their prime motive is to build the size of their own congregation. Although you may find a semblance of love in the other church, that love is not the motive for its works. Instead, self-appeasement, achievement, success and building unto itself and a religious sense of duty are the motives found in the other church. Their goal is to venture into a building program for a larger church building.

Matthew 9:37 – *Then saith he unto his disciples, The harvest truly is plenteous, but the labourers are few;*

According to Jesus, the harvest is not about a bigger building but a greater number of souls brought into the kingdom of God through belief in Jesus as Savior and Lord. The harvest time is now and continues up until His return.

Matthew 9:38 – *pray ye therefore the Lord of the harvest, that he will send forth labourers into his harvest.*

Jesus is saying, "Pray, help me find and prepare them for the harvest". He is the one who finds the laborers that He has called, ordained and prepared to go out into the harvest. It is not man who calls, prepares and sends forth as is done in the other church – He does it. An obvious example of man doing this is seen in the Mormons and Jehovah's Witnesses, along with others that are less obvious.

Matthew 10:1 – *And when he had called unto him his twelve disciples, he gave them power against unclean spirits, to cast them out, and to heal all manner of sickness and all manner of disease.*

This is an example of His calling, choosing, anointing and sending into the harvest. We see and hear that this is what He is beginning to do again in recent days. Consider those who He chose and sent:

Matthew 10:2-4 – *Now the names of the twelve apostles are these; The first, Simon, who is called Peter, and Andrew his brother; James the son of Zebedee, and John his brother;[3] Philip, and Bartholomew; Thomas, and Matthew the publican; James the son of Alphæus, and Lebbæus, whose surname was Thaddæus; Simon the Canaanite, and Judas Iscariot, who also betrayed him.*

The personal identification shows that it is Christ who calls and empowers, giving an impartation of His ability to mortal men. Note also that these are men who the religious leaders, like those in the other church, would never consider for such a sacred work.

Another interesting note is the fact that the church did not even exist yet; it wasn't formed until three years later at Pentecost. Therefore, apostles are not merely leadership in the church, they are ambassadors of the Lord Jesus Christ; chosen ones sent out with the authority of Jesus, the sender. Also consider that there are many more apostles than the original twelve. Many more have been chosen and sent after Jesus rose from the grave and ascended to the Father in Heaven.

> Ephesians 4:10-11 – *He that descended is the same also that ascended up far above all heavens, that he might fill all things.) And he gave some, apostles; and some, prophets; and some, evangelists; and some, pastors and teachers;*

The other church refuses to accept that apostles and prophets are for today; (they prefer to be a non-prophet organization).

These that Jesus chose were a diverse group, having varied backgrounds, educations and character traits. Not likely the types who would be considered candidates for credentials in the other church or who could qualify to be among the order of the Pharisees and religious leaders. They lacked the self-righteousness to be sufficient for man to accept; but that is where Jesus comes in, because He became their righteousness as He imparted of Himself to them.

> Matthew 10:5-6 – *These twelve Jesus sent forth, and commanded them, saying, Go not into the way of the Gentiles, and into any city of the Samaritans enter ye not: but go rather to the lost sheep of the house of Israel.*

The first commission for evangelism and ministry of the kingdom was aimed at the Israelites. This commission was expanded by Christ once the example was given and the work was established. After Jesus ascended to The Father He sent the power of the Holy Spirit to equip His servants to carry on the same work He started.

> Acts 1:8 – *But ye shall receive power, after that the Holy Ghost is come upon you: and ye shall be witnesses unto me both in Jerusalem, and in all Judæa, and in Samaria, and unto the uttermost part of the earth.*

Jesus directs the path that His servants are to go and to whom they are to minister to. The other church is directed by men and they go where they have presumed to go rather than being directed by the Holy Spirit. When the true church is directed by the Holy Spirit they experience a true harvest of souls by the power of God, while the other church merely puts forth a form and effort, but without a valid spiritual harvest.

> Matthew 10:7-8 – *And as ye go, preach, saying, The kingdom of heaven is at hand. Heal the sick, cleanse the lepers, raise the dead, cast out devils: freely ye have received, freely give.*

Their ministry was performed just as Jesus Himself did it and commanded it to be carried on by His servants who would follow afterward.

> Acts 2:38-39 – *Then Peter said unto them, Repent, and be baptized every one of you in the name of Jesus Christ for the remission of sins, and ye shall receive the gift of the Holy Ghost. For the promise is unto you, and to your children, and to all that are afar off, even as many as the Lord our God shall call.*

By the time that Jesus gave His first apostles the power and command to go and minister to those to who He sent; He clearly demonstrated for them how to do each type of ministry. It will be done the same way by the true church in these last days. The Holy Spirit has patiently been preparing His people for this for many years, bringing us up to this time.

The other church rejects ministry being done in this fashion because they neither can understand it intellectually, nor can they control it; which they feel they must.

> Matthew 10:9-10 – *Provide neither gold, nor silver, nor brass in your purses, nor scrip for your journey, neither two coats, neither shoes, nor yet staves: for the workman is worthy of his meat.*

Christ's disciples were obedient and faithful. The purpose of the faith teaching of the past decades is to produce faithfulness; disciplined obedience that responds to a command without questioning, complaining or fussing about the impossibilities and lack of provision.

This particular command was changed later by Jesus because He would no longer be physically present with them.

> Luke 22:35-36 – *And he said unto them, When I sent you without purse, and scrip, and shoes, lacked ye any thing? And they said, Nothing. Then said he unto them, But now, he that hath a purse, let him take it, and likewise his scrip: and he that hath no sword, let him sell his garment, and buy one.*

Could the Lord require this again – most likely, as "the just shall live by faith and not by sight", and we operate in a hostile world that hates us as it hated Him. The importance of faith and faithfulness is not sufficiently understood. In many cases the faith teaching has been exaggerated, distorted and abused when taught by some preachers.

Faith comes from the Greek word *pistos,* which means confidence, assurance; but it also means fidelity or faithfulness; (which is how it should appear in Hebrews 11:6). Our faithfulness allows Him to do the miraculous that we, ourselves, are incapable of doing. Man does not perform the miraculous by his own faith. Man is not God, or a god, regardless of how famous those who teach such doctrines are. So Jesus' apostles went out faithfully as He commanded.

They went out and ministered the things of the kingdom freely; without charge, donations, love offerings, honorariums or fees. Yet they were able to be sent out without a purse or provision. The one whose work they performed in obedience to His commands would make sure they were provided for.

> Matthew 10:11-14 – *And into whatsoever city or town ye shall enter, enquire who in it is worthy; and there abide till ye go thence. And when ye come into an house, salute it. And if the house be worthy, let your peace come upon it: but if it be not worthy, let your peace return to you. And whosoever shall not receive you, nor hear your words, when ye depart out of that house or city, shake off the dust of your feet.*

Go where the doors are open! Do not waste time and energy on those wo are not receptive; time is too short. Go out to the highways and byways, out to the stranger and the poor, to those who know they are needy (in spirit) and looking for hope. (Consider also Luke 14:16-24.)

Matthew 10:15 – *Verily I say unto you, It shall be more tolerable for the land of Sodom and Gomorrha in the day of judgment, than for that city.*

Their rejection will usher them into the judgment of the wrath of God, which will be worse than what Sodom and Gommorrha experienced - they perished almost instantly. These who reject the gospel of Jesus Christ in the last days will wish they could die, but all they will get will be terrifying and painful torment. This is referenced in the Sixth Seal and the Fifth Trumpet of Revelation:

Revelation 6:15-17 – *And the kings of the earth, and the great men, and the rich men, and the chief captains, and the mighty men, and every bondman, and every free man, hid themselves in the dens and in the rocks of the mountains; and said to the mountains and rocks, Fall on us, and hide us from the face of him that sitteth on the throne, and from the wrath of the Lamb: for the great day of his wrath is come; and who shall be able to stand?*

Revelation 9:4-6 – *And it was commanded them that they should not hurt the grass of the earth, neither any green thing, neither any tree; but only those men which have not the seal of God in their foreheads. And to them it was given that they should not kill them, but that they should be tormented five months: and their torment was as the torment of a scorpion, when he striketh a man. And in those days shall men seek death, and shall not find it; and shall desire to die, and death shall flee from them.*

A revival and restoration of the true church has been covered in Matthew 10 up through verse 15. Now we see the persecution from the religious other church begins from verse 16 through verse 42.

Matthew 10:16 – *Behold, I send you forth as sheep in the midst of wolves: be ye therefore wise as serpents, and harmless as doves.*

Here we see Christ called, God ordained, ministers sent with a mighty anointing (verse 9-10) into the midst of so-called wolves, (refer to Matthew 7:15 and Acts 20:29). (This is covered in more detail in Chapter Six – THE WOLVES). True Holy Spirit led ministry is that which not only testifies of Christ, but also exemplifies Him in all His Godly nature. This is ministry that functions in gentleness, godly wisdom, taking full advantage of every situation and circumstance as Paul did in Acts 17:22-23.

> Matthew 10:17 – *But beware of men: for they will deliver you up to the councils, and they will scourge you in their synagogues;*

Many true ministers will attempt to serve in the other church which will object to such tactics, and will oppose their ministry, and have them removed. Thus we need to be discerning of man pleasers, those who ally with those who are of questionable character and motive; be led of the Holy Spirit, not the eye or ear. Church councils and religious organizations of the I.R.S. will slander, discredit, black list, excommunicate, defrock, and coerce such ministers in order to control.

They even send out enforcers to do dirty work to besmirch the integrity of God's anointed servants. The government won't do this; but, history shows that the other church does do such things to Christ's ministers, which includes beatings, torture, etc. whether physical or otherwise. The apostle Paul was a good example before his conversion. This was especially done by the Roman Church to those they called "heretics" who did not follow their particular dogma.

> Matthew 10:18 – *and ye shall be brought before governors and kings for my sake, for a testimony against them and the Gentiles.*

Government and the other church will work hand in hand in meeting out such demonic oppression. The other church blows the whistle on the true church, and uses their political connections to have laws passed in their favor to use against the true church. Then they will charge and persecute the true church, its leadership and individual outspoken believers. This is currently evident in their use of so-called "hate crimes" for preaching against the sins of abortion, same sex marriage and transgenderism.

With this type of mentality rising against the true church, it will not take much for the government accepted other church to sway legislation aimed at curtailing the so-called "extremism" of the true church. This will become more easily obtainable by the other church because of the true church's stand against the immoral direction of society and our liberal government.

In the near future we can expect to see more jockeying of moral, spiritual and ethical positions between the two churches. At present, both seem to be well mingled and not as easily defined as it will be that will result in the previously mentioned time of separation. The true church will draw closer to God and His Word while the other church will align more to man's fleshly qualities, fulfilling the humanist call which is the demonic religion of the other church.

> Matthew 10:19-20 – *But when they deliver you up, take no thought how or what ye shall speak: for it shall be given you in that same hour what ye shall speak. For it is not ye that speak, but the Spirit of your Father which speaketh in you.*

The empowerment poured out by the Holy Spirit upon the true saints will dumbfound them, and of course it will greatly disturb them. The true church will be greatly dependent on the leading and inspiration of the Holy Spirit. The opposition to this manifestation of Christ though His church will be on full display:

> Matthew 10:21 – *And the brother shall deliver up the brother to death, and the father the child: and the children shall rise up against their parents, and cause them to be put to death.*

This will begin the awaited manifestation of the true Sons of God, for God will be with them and His glory will be revealed through them. (This is covered in more detail in Chapter Ten – The Manifestation of His Presence).

> Romans 8:18-19 – *For I reckon that the sufferings of this present time are not worthy to be compared with the glory which shall be revealed in us. For the earnest expectation of the creature waiteth for the manifestation of the sons of God.*

Civil strife will result due to the intensity of the opposition; (as happened in past history under the Roman Catholic leadership, which is part of the other church). This opposition is already evident in our society. Child abuse laws allow children to turn in their parents for spanking them according to biblical discipline listed in – (Proverbs 22:15; 23:13 and 29:15). All we need are more laws aimed at curbing biblical principles of child rearing to see Matthew 10:21 fulfilled.

> Matthew 10:21-22 – *And the brother shall deliver up the brother to death, and the father the child: and the children shall rise up against their parents, and cause them to be put to death. And ye shall be hated of all men for my name's sake: but he that endureth to the end shall be saved.*

The religious strife will be elevated for society to see by the other church, by the government and the news media, so that even non-religious people will join in the persecution. When they do, it will bring open violence against the true believers.

> Matthew 10:23 – *But when they persecute you in this city, flee ye into another: for verily I say unto you, Ye shall not have gone over the cities of Israel, till the Son of man be come.*

Persecution will bring about a time of very mobile ministry in the true church as many will be forced to move about. This will continue right up until Christ returns.

Driven to mobile ministry, God sometimes uses the enemy to drive His people onward to spread the gospel; just as it did in the early church. The true church will accomplish what God ordained, even if we don't do it in a time of peace and affluence; we will achieve it in a time of adversity and opposition.

> Matthew 24:12-14 – *And because iniquity shall abound, the love of many shall wax cold. But he that shall endure unto the end, the same shall be saved. And this gospel of the kingdom shall be preached in all the world for a witness unto all nations; and then shall the end come.*

In the last days the world will be filled with sin and horrible iniquity, which is spiritual darkness; but the light of Christ will shine in and through His true church; thus the hatred aimed at the Lord's people.

Matthew 10:24-25 – *The disciple is not above his master, nor the servant above his lord. It is enough for the disciple that he be as his master, and the servant as his lord. If they have called the master of the house Beelzebub, how much more shall they call them of his household?*

As Jesus was recognized by religious leaders and government officials as a transgressor, so will His followers, the true church. Since His followers will not compromise, they will be forced by their godly conviction to violate the new laws that have been enacted against them.   Note how some of the other church is already endorsing conformity to corrupt government actions by wrongly referring to Scripture to endorse the government:

Romans 13:1-2 – *Let every soul be subject unto the higher powers. For there is no power but of God: the powers that be are ordained of God. Whosoever therefore resisteth the power, resisteth the ordinance of God: and they that resist shall receive to themselves damnation.*

Their error is that they fail to recognize that those who are evil in government violate what Paul recorded in the following verses. Those that God place in government are for "good works" and not the ungodly evil that is currently being promoted.

Romans 13:3-5 – *For rulers are not a terror to good works, but to the evil. Wilt thou then not be afraid of the power? do that which is good, and thou shalt have praise of the same: for he is the minister of God to thee for good. But if thou do that which is evil, be afraid; for he beareth not the sword in vain: for he is the minister of God, a revenger to execute wrath upon him that doeth evil. Wherefore ye must needs be subject, not only for wrath, but also for conscience sake.*

The dictates of ungodly leadership can be ignored as illustrated by the apostles Peter and John who defied the commands of the religious rulers.

Acts 4:18-20 – *And they called them, and commanded them not to speak at all nor teach in the name of Jesus. But Peter and*

John answered and said unto them, whether it be right in the sight of God to hearken unto you more than unto God, judge ye. For we cannot but speak the things which we have seen and heard.

Their defiance of commands of the religious leaders that are contrary to what Jesus instructed them to do, Peter and John were again brought before the council.

Acts 5:27-29 – *And when they had brought them, they set them before the council: and the high priest asked them, saying, Did not we straitly command you that ye should not teach in this name? and, behold, ye have filled Jerusalem with your doctrine, and intend to bring this man's blood upon us. Then Peter and the other apostles answered and said, We ought to obey God rather than men.*

You notice that the disciples spoke the truth, even when it came to identifying the errors of the false religious leaders. When the true saints do the same thing in pointing out and identifying the false church for their practices, doctrines, and encouraging people to leave such, there definitely will be persecution. To defy man's laws, commands and doctrines, one will be judged and punished by man; but not by God.

Acts 5:40b-42 – *and when they had called the apostles, and beaten them, they commanded that they should not speak in the name of Jesus, and let them go. And they departed from the presence of the council, rejoicing that they were counted worthy to suffer shame for his name. And daily in the temple, and in every house, they ceased not to teach and preach Jesus Christ.*

On the other hand, to defy God's commands, one will be judged and punished by God. Many will have the opportunity to choose who they will obey! Will it be possible that the saints may also have to defend themselves from violence or be prepared to thwart it?

Luke 22:35-38 – *And he said unto them, When I sent you without purse, and scrip, and shoes, lacked ye any thing? And they said, Nothing. Then said he unto them, But now, he that hath a purse, let him take it, and likewise his scrip: and he that hath no sword, let him sell his garment, and buy one. For I say unto you, that this that is written must yet be accomplished in me, And he was reckoned among the transgressors: for the things concerning me have an end. And they said, Lord, behold, here are two swords. And he said unto them, It is enough.*

Obviously Jesus' instruction to carry a sword was not for offensive purposes, nor to win converts, or gain financial support. The swords were for self-defense and to appear to hostile men that they will not be taken advantage of. To be weaponless is a form of piety that is scripturally unfounded. This piety is seen in the other church. They even want our nation to be weaponless and defenseless. The other church will take offense when the true church takes measures to defend its self in various ways. (Much of the liberal other church is anti-Second Amendment.)

Matthew 10:26-27 – *Fear them not therefore: for there is nothing covered, that shall not be revealed; and hid, that shall not be known. What I tell you in darkness* (night), *that speak ye in light* (day): *and what ye hear in the ear* (of your spirit), *that preach ye upon the housetops* (any place where you can be heard).

Pray for boldness and speak openly with it; do not hide your light under a bushel at this opportune time' God can use you mightily.

Acts 4:23-33 – *And being let go, they went to their own company, and reported all that the chief priests and elders had said unto them. And when they heard that, they lifted up their voice to God with one accord, and said, Lord, thou art God, which hast made heaven, and earth, and the sea, and all that in them is: who by the mouth of thy servant David hast said, Why did the heathen rage, and the people imagine vain things? The kings of the earth stood up, and the rulers were gathered together against the Lord, and against his Christ. For of a truth against thy holy child Jesus, whom thou hast anointed, both Herod, and Pontius Pilate, with the Gentiles, and the people of Israel, were gathered together, for to do whatsoever thy hand and thy counsel determined before to be done. And now, Lord, behold their threatenings: and grant unto thy servants, that with all boldness they may speak thy word, by stretching forth thine hand to heal; and that signs and wonders may be done by the name of thy holy child Jesus. And when they had prayed, the place was shaken where they were assembled together; and they were all filled with the Holy Ghost, and they spake the word of God with boldness. And with great power gave the apostles witness of the resurrection of the Lord Jesus: and great grace was upon them all.*

Be sensitive in your spirit so you can hear what the Spirit is saying. He will warn of entrapments of the enemy, advise you of opportunities to share the gospel, and give directions for provision.

Matthew 10:28 – *And fear not them which kill the body, but are not able to kill the soul: but rather fear him which is able to destroy both soul and body in hell.*

Before the return of Jesus there will be fearful days, full of worry and anxiety; God has always told His people not to give in to fear. Fear is one of Satan's greatest weapons against God's children. Fear will stop you cold; it will cause you to back up and yield ground to the enemy that is yours which you were commanded to take and hold firm.

Ephesians 6:10-13 – *Finally, my brethren, be strong in the Lord, and in the power of his might. Put on the whole armour of God, that ye may be able to stand against the wiles of the devil. For we wrestle not against flesh and blood, but against principalities, against powers, against the rulers of the darkness of this world, against spiritual wickedness in high places. Wherefore take unto you the whole armour of God, that ye may be able to withstand in the evil day, and having done all, to stand.*

Yes it is possible that there are some who may probably be hurt or even killed; but consider this – everyone dies. Those who die in Christ's service receive a special reward and recognition.

> Revelation 12:11 – *And they overcame him by the blood of the Lamb, and by the word of their testimony; and they loved not their lives unto the death.*

True believers are to take a STAND, and that is on and with the Word and promises of God.

> Romans 8:31-32 – *What shall we then say to these things? If God be for us, who can be against us? He that spared not his own Son, but delivered him up for us all, how shall he not with him also freely give us all things?*

We in the true church must recognize God's great loving care for us!

> Matthew 10:29-31 – *Are not two sparrows sold for a farthing? and one of them shall not fall on the ground without your Father. But the very hairs of your head are all numbered. Fear ye not therefore, ye are of more value than many sparrows.*

Don't worry about provision to sustain you and your family during this time; (refer also to Matthew 6:25-34). Such worry can cause you to take your eyes off the Lord and His kingdom and focus your attention on this vile world with its troubles causing you to lose your effectiveness for Him.

> Matthew 13:22 – *He also that received seed among the thorns is he that heareth the word; and the care of this world, and the deceitfulness of riches, choke the word, and he becometh unfruitful.*

> 1 Peter 5:7-10 – *casting all your care upon him; for he careth for you. Be sober, be vigilant; because your adversary the devil, as a roaring lion, walketh about, seeking whom he may devour: whom resist stedfast in the faith, knowing that the same afflictions are accomplished in your brethren that are in the*

world. But the God of all grace, who hath called us unto his eternal glory by Christ Jesus, after that ye have suffered a while, make you perfect, stablish, strengthen, settle you.

The gospel will go forth in spite of the opposition of the world and the false other church.

Matthew 10:32-33 – *Whosoever therefore shall confess me before men, him will I confess also before my Father which is in heaven. But whosoever shall deny me before men, him will I also deny before my Father which is in heaven.*

Faithfulness without compromise is needed. Jesus gave the command to "Come out of Babylon" which is the wicked other church – (Revelation 18:4). For those who are still in the other church, trying to evangelize and bring truth into it, will be told to leave. Jesus didn't continue ministering to the Pharisees; He gave His Word where it would be welcomed. He told us not to cast our pearls before swine – (Matthew 7:6).

It is also important to recognize that many, so-called, Christians who do not deny Christ with their mouth, do so with their actions or behavior. Such is the character of many in the other church. They live a double standard that is totally unacceptable to God. Your lifestyle, both public and private, should reveal and confess Christ as being His representative.

This coming time of persecution will tempt many to be two-faced, or double minded; depending on where they are and who they are with. Many are experiencing this persecution now in other parts of the world. Too many people fail to realize the serious conflict between the world with the other church that are in opposition to the true church; it can become violent at times.

Matthew 10:34-36 – *Think not that I am come to send peace on earth: I came not to send peace, but a sword. For I am come to set a man at variance against his father, and the daughter against her mother, and the daughter in law against her mother in law. And a man's foes shall be they of his own household.*

This is a time of extreme opposition for the sake of the truth in Christ. An example of this has already occurred in history and will continue up to the return of Christ. Some of the most hateful and bitter arguments within families occurs over differences in beliefs of doctrines or churches attended by family members. (Much like the differences in political opinions also.)

We should all be working at this time to acquire unity of the faith and spiritual knowledge of the truth of God's Word into your family members now while we still have peaceful times. Work at building Christ into your family's lives. The family has always been the target of the enemy; his object is to divide and conquer that which God has ordained and put together.

> Matthew 10:37 – *He that loveth father or mother more than me is not worthy of me: and he that loveth son or daughter more than me is not worthy of me.*

Don't put family relationships ahead of your relationship with God and Christ. This writer spent time ministering in Africa where I encountered a major problem called "tribalism". One tribe could not have any relationship with another tribe. This I found to also be a fact between different churches and denominations which tended to be very tribal; they refused to work together and considered the Christians of another tribe to be an enemy. They put their tribal heritage ahead of their Christian relationship. (This was evidence of being part of the other church.) Such preferred relationships could force you into a spiritually deadly compromise in the time of persecution. Keep God and His kingdom first in your life, and God will take care of everything else in your life.

> Matthew 6:33 – *But seek ye first the kingdom of God, and his righteousness; and all these things shall be added unto you.*

A true Christian will submit his will and desires to God and be willing to deny all selfish pursuits.

> Matthew 19:38-39 – *And he that taketh not his cross, and followeth after me, is not worthy of me. He that findeth his life shall lose it: and he that loseth his life for my sake shall find it.*

True discipleship is needed; and it will be tested and proven. Your will, your desires, your ways, all have to die and be yielded to His will, His desires and His ways so He can use you for His Glory.

Matthew 10:40-42 – *He that receiveth you receiveth me, and he that receiveth me receiveth him that sent me. He that receiveth a prophet in the name of a prophet shall receive a prophet's reward; and he that receiveth a righteous man in the name of a righteous man shall receive a righteous man's reward. And whosoever shall give to drink unto one of these little ones a cup of cold water only in the name of a disciple, verily I say unto you, he shall in no wise lose his reward.*

Faithfulness will be rewarded. God's people of the true church, those fleeing persecution, will need help from the rest of the people of the true church. Be ready and willing to help, even if you have to go underground to do so. Some leaders in the true church have to relocate, even often, to flee persecution yet continuing to spread the Word.

Acts 8:1b & 3-4 – *And at that time there was a great persecution against the church which was at Jerusalem; and they were all scattered abroad throughout the regions of Judæa and Samaria, except the apostles. As for Saul, he made havock of the church, entering into every house, and haling men and women committed them to prison. Therefore they that were scattered abroad went every where preaching the word.*

The Bible does not direct us to stay put and be silenced, but to move and continue to speak with boldness, (as in Matthew 10:23). Those who travel will need help, shelter, provisions, aid and encouragement – (Acts 4:32). Doing so will be rewarded by God.

There is coming a time of great turmoil in the church, especially in America, because we are not used to such conditions. Everything will seem to fall apart as every institution of man will be shaken.

Hebrews 12:26-27 – *whose voice then shook the earth: but now he hath promised, saying, Yet once more I shake not the earth only, but also heaven. And this word, Yet once more, signifieth the removing of those things that are shaken, as of things that are made, that those things which cannot be shaken may remain.*

Unfortunately, persecution is promised for the righteous of the true church.

> 2 Timothy 3:10-12 – *But thou hast fully known my doctrine, manner of life, purpose, faith, longsuffering, charity, patience, persecutions, afflictions, which came unto me at Antioch, at Iconium, at Lystra; what persecutions I endured: but out of them all the Lord delivered me. Yea, and all that will live godly in Christ Jesus shall suffer persecution.*

Much persecution will come from the other church because it is filled with the ungodly, even though it tries to portray itself as being godly; it merely has a form. Its behavior identifies it as the false church.

> 2 Timothy 3:1-5 – *This know also, that in the last days perilous times shall come. For men shall be lovers of their own selves, covetous, boasters, proud, blasphemers, disobedient to parents, unthankful, unholy, without natural affection, trucebreakers, false accusers, incontinent, fierce, despisers of those that are good, traitors, heady, highminded, lovers of pleasures more than lovers of God; having a form of godliness, but denying the power thereof: from such turn away.*

The other church has a form of godliness; you do not see a form of godliness in the world, so we know this speaks of the other church and not the true church. These character traits are part of the means of identification. It is not what they confess, or believe, or where they go to church, it is what they are and what they do!

There are also two kinds of Christians: those who have head knowledge because they know who Jesus is; then there are those who have heart experience because they have a personal relationship with Jesus. Those with head knowledge are the some of the ones in the other church because they are still conformed to the world.

> Romans 12:2 – *And be not conformed to this world: but be ye transformed by the renewing of your mind, that ye may prove what is that good, and acceptable, and perfect, will of God.*

Galatians 2:20 – *I am crucified with Christ: nevertheless I live; yet not I, but Christ liveth in me: and the life which I now live in the flesh I live by the faith of the Son of God, who loved me, and gave himself for me.*

Galatians 4:6 – *And because ye are sons, God hath sent forth the Spirit of his Son into your hearts, crying, Abba, Father.*

Colossians 1:27 – *to whom God would make known what is the riches of the glory of this mystery among the Gentiles; which is Christ in you, the hope of glory:*

Those with heart experience are those in who the Spirit of Christ is in, they are the true church as they are conformed to Him: thus the conflict between the two churches.

God has been preparing a leadership for these last days that He has called and trained to serve the separated true church. He has not allowed most of them to have a place in the I.R.S. other church that man has built. He has been keeping them from being entangled and entrenched it, yet they are able to recognize it as false and problematic.

God has been using a few of those in the other church, but they are transitional. They try to represent the true light in the other church of man; however, if they continue to be the true light they will eventually be forced out as the separation occurs.

God has used the church in almost every form and fashion in which it has existed throughout history because, in most cases, it is all He has had to work with. However, it depends on how much of God's Word is used, because God honors His Word, not the minister who preaches it.

Ephesians 5:25b-27 – ... *as Christ also loved the church, and gave himself for it; that he might sanctify and cleanse it with the washing of water by the word, that he might present it to himself a glorious church, not having spot, or wrinkle, or any such thing; but that it should be holy and without blemish.*

The other church that man is building is full of spots, wrinkles and blemishes. To be prepared for His Glory, the church will have to be purged, purified and perfected for Christ's coming for it. This is part of the process of the separation of the two churches. Jesus is returning for a church that looks like Him, in which His character and nature is revealed.

> 1 John 3:1-3 – *Behold, what manner of love the Father hath bestowed upon us, that we should be called the sons of God: therefore the world knoweth us not, because it knew him not. Beloved, now are we the sons of God, and it doth not yet appear what we shall be: but we know that, when he shall appear, we shall be like him; for we shall see him as he is. And every man that hath this hope in him purifieth himself, even as he is pure.*

Any true believers who are still in the other church shall withdraw or be expelled from it during this time of separation. This will be God's doing, so be prepared. Heed the warning given by Jesus.

> Revelation 18:4 – *And I heard another voice from heaven, saying, Come out of her, my people, that ye be not partakers of her sins, and that ye receive not of her plagues. For her sins have reached unto heaven, and God hath remembered her iniquities.*

The withdrawal is now underway in part. Some have recognized the spiritual religious whore and pulled out. They seek to be part of the true church of Christ. Others sense the need but haven't moved out, still others have yet to see the truth, and likely will not.

The other church is the mystery, or mystical, Babylon the great whore, the false church that man has built. The one that God will destroy, even by the one with whom she commits whoredom, the Anti-Christ. Please read Revelation 17 through Chapter 19 to see for yourself.

This other church already has a history of persecuting the saints of the true church; but it isn't over yet.

> Revelation 17:4-6 – *And the woman was arrayed in purple and scarlet colour, and decked with gold and precious stones and pearls, having a golden cup in her hand full of abominations and filthiness of her fornication: and upon her forehead was a name written, MYSTERY, BABYLON THE GREAT, THE MOTHER OF HARLOTS AND ABOMINATIONS OF THE EARTH. And I saw the woman drunken with the blood*

of the saints, and with the blood of the martyrs of Jesus: and when I saw her, I wondered with great admiration (at how people were deceived by her).

No one ruler, no nation, no war has killed more Christians than that harlot other church. This is why the apostles and prophets rejoice in heaven when they see her destruction.

Revelation 18:20 – *Rejoice over her, thou heaven, and ye holy apostles and prophets; for God hath avenged you on her.*

The False Prophet will be a product of the other church; and very likely he will be the head of it at that time. The main portion of the harlot is the Roman Catholic Church; however this whore has other churches that are spin offs called "daughters". Thus the other church is composed of many denominations and independent churches that are made by man and are not being led of the Holy Spirit.

They have some of the same doctrines and practices as Rome; and even though they have dispensed with some of the erroneous doctrines, rituals and practices, but they still maintain a lot of Rome's Pagan beliefs and observances. Examples are: Lent; Good Friday; Easter instead of Resurrection Day; Infant Baptism; Catechism; an elevated class of Clergy and Hierarchy; Christmas, as well as others; instead of God's Ordained Holy Days.

Religion dictates that man works out of a sense of duty, and thereby earns stature, reputation, etc. But this only works in man's eyes and in man's organizations. Man cannot earn anything from God, nor can he produce anything for Him. We are His workmanship (Ephesians 2:10), and we can only walk obediently in what He has ordained for us. Everything else is wood, hay and stubble that will be burned up – (1 Corinthians 3:12-13).

It is not our works that please God; it's our fellowship, love and devoted obedience as shown in the Lord's rebuke of the church at Ephesus.

Revelation 2:1-5 – *I know thy works, and thy labour, and thy patience, and how thou canst not bear them which are evil: and thou hast tried them which say they are apostles, and are not, and hast found them liars: and hast borne, and hast patience, and for my name's sake hast laboured, and hast not fainted. Nevertheless I have somewhat against thee, because thou hast left thy first love. Remember therefore from whence thou art fallen, and repent, and do the first works; or else I will come unto thee quickly, and will remove thy candlestick out of his place, except thou repent.*

Christ is returning for the church that He built!

Matthew16-18 – (upon Peter's declaration of who Jesus is, Jesus said)*: ... ... and upon this rock I will build my church; and the gates of hell shall not prevail against it.*

All else is done in vain!

Psalm 127:1a – *Except the LORD build the house, they labour in vain that build it:*

The other church is built in vain and a description of it is clearly given.

Revelation 3:14-19 – *And unto the angel of the church of the Laodiceans write; These things saith the Amen, the faithful and true witness, the beginning of the creation of God; I know thy works, that thou art neither cold nor hot: I would thou wert cold or hot. So then because thou art lukewarm, and neither cold nor hot, I will spue thee out of my mouth. Because thou sayest, I am rich, and increased with goods, and have need of nothing; and knowest not that thou art wretched, and miserable, and poor, and blind, and naked: I counsel thee to buy of me gold tried in the fire, that thou mayest be rich; and white raiment, that thou mayest be clothed, and that the shame of thy nakedness do not appear; and anoint thine eyes with eyesalve, that thou mayest see. As many as I love, I rebuke and chasten: be zealous therefore, and repent.*

Jesus was left standing outside this church seeking to come in.

Revelation 3:20 – *Behold, I stand at the door, and knock: if any man hear my voice, and open the door, I will come in to him, and will sup with him, and he with me.*

Jesus is desiring the same entrance with the other church, but they won't allow Him in! This is the last church that Jesus Christ spoke of; it is the one that made Him so sick that He would vomit to rid it out from Himself. Yet He still calls for them to change, repent and be made alive unto Him, as in verse 18, because He does not want any to perish, verse 19.

Whatever man builds reflects man's character, abilities and personality. The same applies to the church that man builds. What Christ builds reflects His character, nature, ability and personality.

It may be time to evaluate your church and your own life in view of what lies ahead. May you not be found lacking when He arrives. May you be found in His church when He comes: and may you be fully prepared for the days between now and then.

Chapter 3

HOW THE OTHER CHURCH DEVELOPED

A HISTORICAL OVERVIEW OF HOW THE TARES DEVELOPED

We need to look back at church history to see the departure from what was already established by Jesus' apostles and their successors. In so doing we need to recognize that much of early church history is not accurate. This is because much of early church history was written by the Roman Church which adjusted historical truth to justify its own existence. We will begin at the time when significant change began to take place in what has become recognized as the church.

In 313 A.D. Constantine became emperor, with the title of Caesar of Rome; and he claimed to be a Christian. Rome's subjects usually followed in the ways of their Caesar. So now, under Constantine, "Christianity is in", and paganism is out. In fact, Constantine established Christianity as the official State Religion. So now Christianity is not only acceptable, but it is now fashionable. This opens the door for all manner of compromise and moral ills to enter – thus the Tares.

Prior to Constantine, the Caesars made sport of Christians as history has recorded. Nero has long been considered the most notorious of the degenerate Caesars, but there were others far worse than he was: such as Caligula and Domition, who both severely persecuted the early church.

In an attempt to annihilate Christianity, Domition killed off all those who provided leadership in the church in Rome; thus godly influence was removed from the church. His technique was quite effective, although it did not wipe out Christianity as intended; it did stop its spiritual growth and development.

When the qualified, skilled in the Spirit, and the knowledgeable leaders were eliminated, there was no one to teach, preach and instruct people in the deeper truths and ways of God. Eliminated were those who were able to rightly divide the Word of Truth, to discern what was of God and what was not of God, and to hear in the spirit what God wanted to communicate with His believers.

A new age has begun for the church. It now has acceptance, but no knowledgeable, spiritual leadership. With a brand new generation of Christians ushered into the church came a new generation of church leaders. However, these new leaders have a great void in knowledge of the Word and the kingdom of God. Also lacking were the gifted and called God ordained ministers to the church.

This new generation of church leadership came from those who were the pagan priests of the former Roman religion who now transferred into the new religion of the state. Their old jobs no longer existed, especially when paganism was later outlawed under Constantine's son.

With this new order of leadership, in the now socially acceptable church, came all the pagan rituals and observances that have been the practice of the pagan priests for generations before. They merely changed the names to fit in with church norms. These were incorporated in the church as doctrines and rituals at that time and much of it is still observed in the other church today. This new leadership were paid professionals; paid by the state government; the first time such a thing existed in the church. They also became an elite class called the Clergy.

In 323 A.D. Constantine built the city of Constantinople in what is now known as the nation of Turkey. This city became the eastern version of Rome; an eastern capitol from which he could rule his expanded empire. As a result, this city became the seat of the Eastern Orthodox Church while Rome remained the seat of the Roman Catholic Church.

Constantine commissioned houses of worship to be built in his new city. Some were built for pagan worshippers in this very strong pagan stronghold, that is, until paganism was outlawed; and some houses of worship were built for the Christians. Many of these houses of worship were built next to each other as religious centers for both Christians and pagans.

Christians had never seen anything like this before because church meetings were either held in people's houses, in public meeting places, or in secret locations during the persecution. This was the beginning of the use of church buildings. Constantine went back to Rome and did the same thing there with establishing houses of worship; thus church buildings.

Constantine named these worship buildings after great Christians like Peter, Paul, Luke, Mary, etc. Years later, when sainthood was initiated in the Roman Church, these names became what we see now on Rome's churches – St. Mary's, St. Peter's, St. Luke's, etc.

When first introducing Christianity as the State Religion, Constantine bribed his soldiers to become Christians. He offered a silver nugget to everyone in his army who would be baptized as a Christian, so guess what? The Roman Church was filled with converts and not believers, (much like it is today). Also this meant that the church was not only run by the State, but was also being supported by the State.

Paganism eventually dries up financially. Money is now going to the church and not the pagan temples and their priests. In fact their temples became deserted as the pagan, especially their leadership, moved to where the money and the attention was – the church. So they brought all their superstitions and rituals with them into the Roman Church.

Much of what is in the Roman Catholic Church today can be traced all the way back through to the paganism that was in ancient Babylon under Nimrod and his wife Semaremis. This is where the worship of the "Holy Mother and Child" originated.

The Roman Senate, composed of seventy Senators, was the model for the Roman Church's College of Cardinals who determine who is to be the next Pope, (or acting Caesar). The Roman Empire changes from a political entity into a religious entity. The demise of political Rome began about 377 A.D. and fully culminated around 500 A.D.

In the Book of Daniel, Chapter 10:13-14 & 20 we discover that every empire that had influence on earth, especially on Israel, had one of Satan's prince angels influencing it. They work against God's people to hinder answers to prayers as written here in these verses in Daniel. This spirit-being, a fallen angel, worked as an evil motivator behind the kings and rulers in their empires. Through this means, Satan has tried to rule the world by being the evil power behind the scenes. Daniel's prayers were hindered by such evil forces, and God sent His angel to Daniel in response to his prayer and fasting.

> Daniel 10:11-14 – *And he said unto me, O Daniel, a man greatly beloved, understand the words that I speak unto thee, and stand upright: for unto thee am I now sent. And when he*

had spoken this word unto me, I stood trembling. Then said he unto me, Fear not, Daniel: for from the first day that thou didst set thine heart to understand, and to chasten thyself before thy God, thy words were heard, and I am come for thy words. But the prince (satanic angel) of the kingdom of Persia withstood me one and twenty days: but, lo, Michael, one of the chief princes (angels of God), came to help me; and I remained there with the kings of Persia. Now I am come to make thee understand what shall befall thy people (Israel) in the latter days: for yet the vision is for many days.

The angel explains the spiritual warfare that Israel will experience even unto the very last days.

Daniel 10:20 – *Then said he, Knowest thou wherefore I come unto thee? and now will I return* (to the spirit realm) *to fight with the prince* (satanic angel) *of Persia: and when I am gone forth, lo, the prince (satanic angel) of Grecia shall come;* (who will influence the leader of the next empire). (Refer to Ephesians 6:12 regarding the spiritual warfare that Christians are engaged in.)

This indicates to us that every civilization, society, culture, nation and government has one of Satan's angels appointed to guide it into the evil opposition of the devil against God' people. That is why we see so much evil in the world. Spiritual warfare is the battle that is going on in the realm of the spirit where we cannot see or enter except by prayer and faith, applying the spiritual forces that God has provided for us.

Daniel was exerting such spiritual force when one of God's angels, Gabriel, broke through the warfare into this material realm and delivered the message to Daniel. He said he would return to the spiritual dimension to resume the battle against Satan's angel, who was the evil prince over that nation. He also said that after that prince of Babylon was defeated, another one from another nation, (Persia), would arise. Then he would have to fight that one until it was defeated.

It appears that when one of Satan's prince angels was defeated, it meant the demise of that empire that it ruled over in the spirit realm. It would then be followed by another. Same battle, new warriors; and so it continues until the King of Kings defeats the head of the enemy forces; when Jesus Christ rids the earth of Satan and his cohorts.

The spiritual satanic Prince of Rome was never defeated as were his predecessors. Instead he transferred his rule from the political entity, which he saw die out from under him, to the thriving new religious entity – the Roman Church. Having never been defeated, the Roman Empire continues to this day, only it is disguised as the Church of Rome.

Thus political Rome has never been defeated or succeeded by a conquering empire. King Nebuchadnezzar's dream of the image tells of each empire being defeated by another empire, up until the last empire being Rome, which Christ the Rock, comes to destroy.

> Daniel 2:31-33 – *Thou, O king, sawest, and behold a great image. This great image, whose brightness was excellent, stood before thee; and the form thereof was terrible. This image's head was of fine gold, his breast and his arms of silver, his belly and his thighs of brass, his legs of iron, his feet part of iron and part of clay. Thou sawest till that a stone was cut out without hands, which smote the image upon his feet that were of iron and clay, and brake them to pieces.*

From Daniel's time there were four empires that would rule the earth: Babylon being the head, Media-Persian being the torso, Greece being the groin and Rome being the legs, feet and toes. Note that Rome has a split into two entities, the Eastern Orthodox and the Roman branch, thus the two legs. Then other developments within the empire form feet and toes of mixed components that do not blend together; this represents the many divisions and sects of the Protestant church. Thus the Roman Empire, as it exists today, and does not need to be revived as many end-time preachers teach.

The Roman Empire still continues right up to the time that Jesus returns and destroys the entire thing and sets up His own divine eternal Kingdom. Of particular note is the fact that Nebuchadnezzar's image is all one unit from the head to the feet. Thus Rome has within it the same elements that were in the head – Babylon. This is why the Roman Catholic Church still maintains much of the corrupt religious practices that were begun in Babylon by Nimrod and his wife, Semaremis.

The objectives of the Roman Catholic Church have been the very same as those objectives of the Caesars of Rome. Those objectives have been pursued then on. Since the demise of political Rome, the plans of the Caesar's for world conquest and dominion have been the objective of the Roman Catholic Church.

Through the history of the Roman Catholic Church the kings of the nations would bow before the Pope and kiss his ring as a sign of subservience. The Pope often told the kings what to do since He ruled over them. As Rome's Caesar, the Pope of Rome's church, wants the entire world to be in subjection. Many wars have been fought over this very purpose, but some kings object to the Pope's rule over them. Few people seem to realize that the Roman Church was behind such wars. This is because many people were locked up in this church system and blinded by it. (Note: the Jesuits are the Vatican's covert operatives behind assassinations and intrigue that start these wars and have worked to manipulate governments.)

So it appears that the satanic Prince of Rome still rules in the spirit realm within the Roman church today in various degrees. Much of the world today is under the influence of the Roman Empire (church). Many people can see this, especially under the current Pope Francis, (the first Jesuit to be made a Pope), who is even defying traditional Catholic norms and promoting Communism, the LGBT+ movement and globalism.

The current Pope is clearly under the influence of this powerful, high ranking "religious" spirit of Satan's angels. It appears that he may actually be aligned with the "spirit of antichrist"; the same spirit that will motivate and possibly even inhabit the Antichrist. The Roman church and its offspring, the man-made elements of some of the Protestant Church, will likely form the harlot referred to as the great whore of Revelation Chapter 17 and 18.

Since Rome was the seat of power politically, it automatically became the seat of power religiously. The Church of Rome began to dictate to other churches all over the world since most of the civilized world was used to Roman rule since before the time of Christ.

Roman Church exerted so much influence that it changed the time and day of Jesus' birth and His crucifixion. Could it be that the leadership of the Roman Church is referred to in Daniel 7?

> Daniel 7:25 – *And he shall speak great words against the most High, and shall wear out the saints of the most High, and **think to change times** and laws: and they shall be given into his hand until a time and times and the dividing of time.*

A study of scripture shows Jesus was not born on December 25, but in late September or early October during God's appointed Holy Feast Days: Trumpets, Atonement and Tabernacles. Consider where the sheep and shepherds were when Jesus was born – out in the fields, not in the winter stalls; which is why a feeding trough, called a manger, was available to be used as a cradle for the baby Jesus.

Easter is pagan festival day celebrating sex and fertility, (thus eggs and bunny rabbits), and was a product of ancient Babylon. They even designated the resurrection as Easter; but Easter is the English (Saxon) name of Eastre, who was the Saxon goddess of sex and fertility. This same goddess has also been identified in different societies as the "Queen of Heaven", the Babylonian goddess Ashtoreth (aka Asheroth), the goddess Venus of the Romans, the goddess Astarte of the Assyrians, the goddess Aphrodite of Greece and Isis of Egypt. The Roman Church even changed the day of Jesus crucifixion; Jesus was not crucified on Good Friday as established.

Scripture tells us that Jesus had to spend three days and three nights in the grave, and you can't get three days and three nights from Friday sunset to Sunday sunrise. (We need to understand that Hebrew days and nights go from sunset to sunset.) Jesus was crucified on a Wednesday, the Day of Preparation when Israel killed the Passover Lamb: Jesus became our sacrificial "Passover Lamb". He had to be off the cross before sunset because the next day, which began after sunset, was Passover, which is the High Holy Sabbath of Israel: it was not the weekly Sabbath of Sunday. Jesus arose sometime after sunset Saturday which then began the first day of the week – Saturday.

The leadership of the Roman Church changed times and seasons to accommodate their pagan Babylonian ceremonial observations in an attempt to "Christianise" them.

Dominion by man in the church, led by a religious spirit, is the operation of the spirit of antichrist as described by the apostle John.

> 1 John 4:1-3 – *Beloved, believe not every spirit, but try the spirits whether they are of God: because many false prophets are gone out into the world. Hereby know ye the Spirit of God: Every spirit that confesseth that Jesus Christ is come in the flesh is of God: and every spirit that confesseth not that Jesus Christ is come in the flesh is not of God: and this is that spirit of antichrist, whereof ye have heard that it should come; and even now already is it in the world.*

This religious spirit operates through mankind, and will especially operate in the future through a particular man.

> Revelation 13:18 – *Here is wisdom. Let him that hath understanding count the number of the beast: for it is the number of a man; and his number is Six hundred threescore and six.*

We are told that 666 is the number of man: there are three 6's and each 6 represents a part of man, who has three parts. So 6 = man's spirit, 6 = man's soul, and 6 = man' body, thus 666 = the number of man.

Originally God gave dominion of the earth to man, as listed in Genesis 1:26. Man lost that dominion when he submitted to the trickery of the devil in the garden. Satan took over dominion of the earth since then and has delegated his dominion to his evil angels to run rough shod over mankind ever since. Jesus had to become a man, whom God had given original dominion, in order to bring redemption to mankind and restore God's initial plan.

The devil thus tries to direct man to organize for control and dominion in every sphere of human activity which is why he so opposes true Christians in their lives and works. In the Roman other Church, the leadership set themselves up as exclusive and professional. Their leaders were now identified by elite titles and Clerical garments. There was now an air of prestige and high recognition for them as individuals which never existed in the early church.

About 500 A.D. the Roman Catholic Church is fully set up and in power to control nations and peoples. Gregory becomes Pope, and in order to maintain man's control and authority over Kings and their people, he claims direct succession to the apostle Peter. With no knowledgeable leaders to refute this doctrine, we find that God's ordained apostles and prophets are done away with. They are no longer needed because they have been replaced by the Pope and the Cardinals.

Man has to eliminate God given authority to supplant it with man-made authority. This is where the Roman Church got the doctrine of Apostlolic Succession, and where the Protestant Church got the idea that the apostles and Prophets were not for today.

Pope Gregory was a mad man who was crazed with superstition and paganism. He loved mysterious, dark and spooky things, and so he incorporated them in the church as forms of worship: thus were developed the spooky Gregorian Chants in the Catholic Church. Regardless of how pious or spiritual some of the chants may be, (which were later further developed by studious monks), their origin and purpose was to add the sense of mystique to the church services.

With the demise of political Rome, the civilized world entered into the age of "barbarianism". This was actually due to the crazed advance of the corrupt religion of Islam and its demon inspired leader Mohamed. With barbarianism, education dies, along with numerous arts and craftsmanship and especially Biblical scholarship. (Note: church history at this point is written by the Roman Church in order to justify its existence and thus is full of errors.) With no intellect or study of the scriptures, the door is left open to extreme superstition and pagan rituals in society as well as in the church: that is until the "Reformation" began.

This is why the Roman Church places credence in their traditions rather than knowledge of the scriptures. This is because the scriptures reject the things that the Roman Church brought into Christianity and claims that their church is based on their fundamental "tradition" rather than scripture.

These traditions and rituals become Holy and Sacred. This plunges the church and society into the "Dark Ages". The age when there is very limited spiritual light; when Christ is not recognized, and illumination of the scriptures is absent. Instead, every form of human darkness and religious superstition takes its place.

Early church history was falsified by the Roman Catholic Church. True church history did not begin to be recorded until well after 500 A.D. All church history recorded prior to that time was contrived by the Roman church's history writers in order to justify their existence and prove that the Roman Church was a continuation of the original church; which it is not.

The writings of revered men like Ambrose, Augustine, Tertullian, Ignatius, Jerome, Irenaeus and Origian became considered as divinely inspired, and thus studied more than the scriptures. These men were the last of the intellectuals and literates at that time. Each of them had been influenced by the pagan philosophers Aristotle and Plato. Today their writings are studied and revered in most seminaries. This is part of the source of "liberalism" in today's Bible Schools.

The Reformation brings light into the situation and brings an end to the long road of the Dark Ages. The Reformation's beginning is credited to Martin Luther and his 96 thesis in 1517 A.D. The Protestant movement begins, but its foundation is still in Roman Catholicism; but the reformers now reject the Pope, and Jesus Christ is presented again as the Savior and

Head of the true church by faith and not by works. However, many of the same traditions are carried on as before in these off-spring churches of Rome.

The Protestant Reformation was a reaction to Rome but not a full return to the tenants of the early church. This return to the purity of early church Christianity is still going on; the reformation isn't over yet, not until we are fully restored to the way Christ wants us to be. Since the 1970's I have taught that the church is going to go "full circle" and will return to be like the church was when it was first formed.

Revelation always brings division. Over the course of time, independent thinkers searching the scriptures find more truth and see more errors in way we have church. They bring discoveries forth, get rejected by the established leadership, so they go out and start a new group with a fresh revelation. This is how new denominations have started. The former then begins to discredit the new movement; then opposes the new reformers. It remains the same today.

Qualification for leadership in the other church remains in the hands of man. The establishment seeks to preserve itself, so it sets up qualifications designed to procreate itself through its new incoming initiates who desire to move up the ranks within that denomination.

Views differing from those of the established churches are considered to be heresies which must be eliminated in the most expedient fashion. This was done many times in a very forceful and fearful fashion in order to discourage others from the pursuit of further revelation. This is where saints of old were martyred by the harlot church because of their efforts in the reformation. This even happened within the Protestant Church; (consider the life and works of John Calvin who had those who disagreed with his doctrine burned at the stake – murdered.)

Martin Luther was an intellectual of his day, so emphasis on church leadership went to intellectualism and educational qualifications rather than on quality of spirit, a call of God, and Godly preparation for the ministry. The same conditions continue today in traditional churches; the traditional church views the credentials of man as more significant than a gifting and calling of God on one's life.

Drawn in the writings of Augustine, Tertullian, Jerome, etc. who were the highly respected intellectuals of their day, meant that you studied those who followed Socrates and Plato, (both of whom were pagan philosophers). Thus pagan philosophy was further entrenched in the "Christian" educational programs for leadership qualifications in the church.

During the early days of the reformation the role of the Roman Catholic Priest now became the Protestant Pastor. The Roman Catholic tradition of a one-man priest presiding over a congregation has become the one-man Pastor after the tradition of Rome, and not after the pattern of the early church that had multiple Elders. There were no preeminent personalities because they tend to gain followers after themselves and hinder believers from following God. Eldership, providing multiple leaders provides checks and balances of the men who are truly called of God and led of the Holy Spirit.

Scripture identifies one preeminent personality who presented a problem to that particular church.

> 3 John 9-10 – *I wrote unto the church: but Diotrephes, who loveth to have the preeminence among them, receiveth us not. Wherefore, if I come, I will remember his deeds which he doeth, prating against us with malicious words: and not content therewith, neither doth he himself receive the brethren, and forbiddeth them that would, and casteth them out of the church.*

Man ordained leadership tries to promote and preserve that which is of man, and what man wants; consider the following when the religious leaders of Jerusalem tried to figure out what to do about Jesus:

> John 11:47-48 & 53 – *Then gathered the chief priests and the Pharisees a council, and said, What do we? for this man doeth many miracles. If we let him thus alone, all men will believe on him: and the Romans shall come and take away both our place and nation. … Then from that day forth they took counsel together for to put him to death.*

> John 12:19 – *The Pharisees therefore said among themselves, Perceive ye how ye prevail nothing? behold, the world is gone after him.*

The efforts of man's religion fail when they come against that which God has ordained. Motives need to be discerned by the wise and mature. God ordained leadership will promote and preserve that which is of God; they also recognize or discern those who are not ordained of God; those who are imposters, as well as those of the enemy – wolves in sheep's clothing.

Let's look at the early church and see the differences with what we see in the church today. Emphasis was on teaching and making disciples, not on preaching sermons. The lack of teaching keeps the church ignorant and spiritually immature. Loving care and fellowship was also encouraged.

> *Matthew 28:19-20 – Go ye therefore, and teach all nations, baptizing them in the name of the Father, and of the Son, and of the Holy Ghost: teaching them to observe all things whatsoever I have commanded you: and, lo, I am with you alway, even unto the end of the world. Amen.*

> *Ephesians 1:17-19 – that the God of our Lord Jesus Christ, the Father of glory, may give unto you the spirit of wisdom and revelation in the knowledge of him: the eyes of your understanding being enlightened; that ye may know what is the hope of his calling, and what the riches of the glory of his inheritance in the saints, and what is the exceeding greatness of his power to us-ward who believe, according to the working of his mighty power,*

Preaching was for outside the church; note the word "sent" as it refers to going out to preach the gospel elsewhere and not within the four walls of a church building.

> *Romans 10:13-15 – For whosoever shall call upon the name of the Lord shall be saved. How then shall they call on him in whom they have not believed? and how shall they believe in him of whom they have not heard? and how shall they hear without a preacher? and how shall they preach, except they be sent? as it is written, How beautiful are the feet of them that preach the gospel of peace, and bring glad tidings of good things!*

The Bible contains no mention of a church building: meetings were in homes and public meeting places and fellowship was significant among believers.

> *Acts 2:46-47 – And they, continuing daily with one accord in the temple, and breaking bread from house to house, did eat*

their meat with gladness and singleness of heart, praising God, and having favour with all the people. And the Lord added to the church daily such as should be saved.

Acts 20:20 – *and how I kept back nothing that was profitable unto you, but have shewed you, and have taught you publickly, and from house to house,*

There was no local church membership as it is currently used to reinforce man's organizational control to demand loyalty to that unit. It is also used for financial purposes in maintaining support as well as acquiring mortgage loans for their expensive buildings. True membership in the church was actually the result of being included in the universal Body of Christ, which is the sum of those who belong to Jesus.

Romans 12:5 – *so we, being many, are one body in Christ, and every one members one of another.*

1 Corinthians 12:12 & 27 – *For as the body is one, and hath many members, and all the members of that one body, being many, are one body: so also is Christ. … Now ye are the body of Christ, and members in particular.*

Churches were not locked into specific address locations, but tended to be mobile within the various cities and able to move about from location to location as needed. Today churches are locked into specific locations by their permanent structures. They can't and won't get up and move, even when persecution comes. Instead they will have to compromise their beliefs and practices in order to be maintained in their place.

A pastor over a church is not mentioned in scripture as the head of an assembly of believers. Elders are listed as the overseers of local assemblies. A pastor is one of the Gift ministries to function as a Shepherd. A Shephard's job is to protect the flock, tend to needs and injuries (healing), and to provide them with the proper spiritual food so they can mature. That leading and provision means they can use other resources and Gift ministries to see that the sheep get the proper spiritual nutrition; they don't spoon feed the sheep all by themselves.

Elders are referred to as the leadership of a church. They are the governing body of the local assembly. A pastor is not mentioned as the leader of a church. However, a Pastor can be included among the elders, but he is not the sole leader.

> Acts 14:23 – *And when they had ordained them elders in every church, and had prayed with fasting, they commended them to the Lord, on whom they believed.*

> 1 Timothy 5:17 – *Let the elders that rule well be counted worthy of double honour, especially they who labour in the word and doctrine.*

> Titus 1:5 – *For this cause left I thee in Crete, that thou shouldest set in order the things that are wanting, and ordain elders in every city, as I had appointed thee:*

> James 5:14 – *Is any sick among you? let him call for the elders of the church; and let them pray over him, anointing him with oil in the name of the Lord:* (Note: the plural term "elders" means not a single leader.)

The functions of apostle and prophet that were principles in the early church were deleted by the "other" church in order for them to create and maintain their church hierarchy. The role of apostle and prophet are not understood in today's church, primarily due to their absence as well as the rise of the false prophets that Jesus warned us about.

An apostle can best be described as an Ambassador of Christ to the church in general. He is one sent with the authority of the sender. The prophet is a spokesperson of Christ with specific words for specific people at a specific time.

The Lord will send in His prophets when His people begin to lose their identity as His people. Prophecy has two forms: forth telling, giving a significant message; and foretelling, describing what lies ahead. The message of the prophet is generally "repent and return to God". Failure to do so will lead to consequences which may be foretold; obedience to the warning will lead to the blessing of His presence with those people, also foretold.

Specific messages may be given by prophets to certain groups of people, or to individuals, because those people have not been in tune enough with the Lord to hear from Him for themselves. People fail to understand just how important it is to hear in the spirit what the Lord speaks. Most Christians don't even know that the Lord does speak to them today because they have not been taught to listen, and thus, they don't have spiritual ears to hear. Some people do not have ears to hear or discern, some hear but cannot discern what is spoken by the Lord.

> John 12:28-30 – *Then came there a voice from heaven, saying, I have both glorified it, and will glorify it again. The people therefore, that stood by, and heard it, said that it thundered: others said, An angel spake to him. Jesus answered and said, This voice came not because of me, but for your sakes.*

> Revelation 2:7 – *He that hath an ear, let him hear what the Spirit saith unto the churches; To him that overcometh will I give to eat of the tree of life, which is in the midst of the paradise of God.* (This is so important that it is repeated in Revelation 2:17, 29 and 3:6; 13: and 22.)

True leadership in the church comes from Christ, and is ordained by Him.

> Ephesians 4:10-12 – *He that descended is the same also that ascended up far above all heavens, that he might fill all things.) And he gave some, apostles; and some, prophets; and some, evangelists; and some, pastors and teachers; for the perfecting of the saints, for the work of the ministry, for the edifying of the body of Christ:*

Note: when was it that Jesus provided these ministry gifts to His church? It was after He ascended back to the Father in Heaven. In other words, these gift ministries are for the church age which has not ended yet. The Lord does the choosing and commissioning, not man.

> Acts 13:1-3 – *Now there were in the church that was at Antioch certain prophets and teachers; as Barnabas, and Simeon that was called Niger, and Lucius of Cyrene, and Manaen, which*

had been brought up with Herod the tetrarch, and Saul. As
they ministered to the Lord, and fasted, the Holy Ghost said,
Separate me Barnabas and Saul for the work whereunto I have
called them. And when they had fasted and prayed, and laid
their hands on them, they sent them away.

Human appointments, ordinations and elections develop into man-made organizations with human control. The result is the professional clergy that we have in most churches today.

There are those today that are hearing the Spirit say it is time for the five-fold ministry gifts of Ephesians 4 to be fully restored. This is a revelation from the Lord. However, implementing these gift ministries back into proper function must be accomplished by the Lord and not by man or human organizations. When men try to do this on their own the results are another man-made organization that is ineffective and exists for its own benefit.

Psalm 127:1a – *Except the* LORD *build the house, they labour*
in vain that build it:

There are many in ministry today that are working for God but not allowing God to work through them. They are doing their own thing; their own way and are not hearing the Lord's directions for building His Church the way He wants. Jesus spoke of these ministers.

Matthew 7:21-23 – *Not every one that saith unto me, Lord,*
Lord, shall enter into the kingdom of heaven; but he that doeth
the will of my Father which is in heaven. Many will say to me
in that day, Lord, Lord, have we not prophesied in thy name?
and in thy name have cast out devils? and in thy name done
many wonderful works? And then will I profess unto them, I
never knew you: depart from me, ye that work iniquity.

Jesus went on to say that in building His house, the true church, it must be done His way in obedience to Him.

Matthew 7:24-27 – *Therefore whosoever heareth these sayings*
of mine, and doeth them, I will liken him unto a wise man,
which built his house upon a rock: and the rain descended, and

the floods came, and the winds blew, and beat upon that house;
and it fell not: for it was founded upon a rock. And every one
that heareth these sayings of mine, and doeth them not, shall
be likened unto a foolish man, which built his house upon the
sand: and the rain descended, and the floods came, and the
winds blew, and beat upon that house; and it fell: and great
was the fall of it.

Building the church in obedience to Christ makes a church that is strong, built on the rock, and able to stand against the storms of life and anything the enemy throws at it. Those who attempt to build the Lord's house (the church) man's way, using human organization and intellect, fail to do so in obedience to the Lord. The end result is, when the storms of life and efforts of the enemy attack, it will fall because it is built on human effort which is like unstable and shifting sand.

What we need to do is not only to wait on the direction from the Lord, but also wait for the implementation and means to come from Him. He will usually do it differently than man will. In fact, He will usually use different people than man would chose to use. This is a big reason why man tries to do the building; it is so that he can control it.

Man's efforts in establishing the five-fold ministry results in establishing false apostles, prophets, etc. Some are even self-appointed and thus are interfering with God's sovereign plans, drawing away from the work God has planned for those He has chosen and ordained for the work.

2 Corinthians 11:13 – *For such are false apostles, deceitful workers, transforming themselves into the apostles of Christ.*

Man forms an organization; God forms an organism. Human organization tends to oppose the God made organism (the true church); this is because it cannot control it, nor understand how it works and operates. The other church of man opposes any budding new move of God for spiritual revival because it takes control out of man's hands, and they don't like that.

For example: this author observed multiple times how a wonderful move of God in a church ended because man wanted to control it. It happened to a church that I was a part of. I watched the spiritual deterioration from what the Holy Spirit brought forth, as man's leadership basically said, "Thank you

Lord, we'll take it from here". When they did that, I saw the Spirit of the Lord leave as man took over.

Historically, a similar thing has happened in many church denominations. They began as a fresh move of the Holy Spirit brought a new awakening. The original organization did not accept the new move of God forcing the "awakened" to separate in order to continue with the new movement. After a period of time this new became organized by man and eventually, the fire died out. That movement then became much like the organization they previously moved out of.

One example is the Nazarene Church. When they first began they had a powerful move of the Holy Spirit in their midst with the Pentecostal Gifts of the Holy Spirit in operation, (as listed in 1 Corinthians 12:8-10). After a period of time the leadership of this denomination determined that they wanted more control over their services, because they did not like the "gifts" operating randomly among the congregants. They wanted all active and spoken ministry to come from the pulpit. So they changed their perspective on their church services, and shut down the people operating in the Gifts of the Holy Spirit which they were not in control of.

So the leadership determined that the move of the Holy Spirit was no longer as the Pentecostals accept, but now they called it, Sanctification. It is interesting to note that the logo of the Nazarene Church still features the Dove representing the Holy Spirit, just as many Pentecostal churches do; but they dismissed His operating of His gifts among the people. Man's control quenches the Holy Spirit; when that happens, the Holy Spirit leaves and that church is left to their own resources rather the divine assistance that comes from the Lord.

> 1 Thessalonians 5:16-20 – *Rejoice evermore. Pray without ceasing. In every thing give thanks: for this is the will of God in Christ Jesus concerning you. Quench not the Spirit. Despise not prophesyings. Prove all things; hold fast that which is good.*

Super religious people, like the Pharisees, are zealots who try to preserve their place of recognition in society or in religious order. Many of today's clergy become like the Pharisees to the true move of God in the church. Because a new move of God does not fit their particular form of religious practice they will oppose what God is doing; just as happened during Jesus" ministry. They refuse to move on with what God is doing, even when God proves it is His work by the miraculous that was done. They prefer to hold onto and reinforce the traditions of the past, where they were secure and comfortable, rather than follow the leading of the Holy Spirit.

> Mark 7:9 – *And he* (Jesus) *said unto them, Full well ye reject the commandment of God, that ye may keep your own tradition.*

Note: not all traditions of man are wrong; there are Godly traditions that should be carried on; that which is scriptural.

> 2 Thessalonians 2:15 – *Therefore, brethren, stand fast, and hold the traditions which ye have been taught, whether by word, or our epistle.*

The only pattern that existed for church form for centuries was the Roman one. As a result, at the time of the reformation, which is not finished yet because we need to return to the pattern of church as it was when it began, the reformers eliminated many man-made traditions of Rome, but still carried out a lot of its form. Therefore it is important for us to follow the leading of the Holy Spirit and learn what the Spirit is saying to the church today.

The apostle Paul warned about corrupt leadership in the church when he addressed the elders of the church in Ephesus.

> Acts 20:28-30 – *Take heed therefore unto yourselves, and to all the flock, over the which the Holy Ghost hath made you overseers, to feed the church of God, which he hath purchased with his own blood. For I know this, that after my departing shall grievous wolves enter in among you, not sparing the flock. Also of your own selves shall men arise, speaking perverse things, to draw away disciples after them.*

The man-made organization controls and lives off of the church, and it will not relinquish its power of control and position within it, but maneuvers to solidify their influence.

Godly leadership builds the church as a living, functioning and maturing organism. God provides the organization as He raises up its leaders and gift ministries, then places them in their proper places (in rank) where He wants them.

1 Corinthians 12:27-30 – *Now ye are the body of Christ, and members in particular. And God hath set some in the church, first apostles, secondarily prophets, thirdly teachers, after that miracles, then gifts of healings, helps, governments, diversities of tongues. Are all apostles? are all prophets? are all teachers? are all workers of miracles? have all the gifts of healing? do all speak with tongues? do all interpret?*

Then He is in control, and those who submit to and depend on Him know it as the results become evident. God knows how to organize, and He sets the parameters for those He can use that can be depended on to be faithful and obedient. That is why He gives the qualifications for leadership positions in the church that He builds.

1 Timothy 3:2-13 – *A bishop* (leaders or overseer) *then must be blameless, the husband of one wife, vigilant, sober, of good behaviour, given to hospitality, apt to teach; not given to wine, no striker, not greedy of filthy lucre; but patient, not a brawler, not covetous; one that ruleth well his own house, having his children in subjection with all gravity; (for if a man know not how to rule his own house, how shall he take care of the church of God?) Not a novice, lest being lifted up with pride he fall into the condemnation of the devil. Moreover he must have a good report of them which are without; lest he fall into reproach and the snare of the devil.*

(Notice the "*husband of one wife*", which excludes women from positions of church leadership which is now being done in some parts of the other church. This does not prevent a woman from bring forth the Word of God to others; but prevents leadership positions only. The reason is mentioned in 1 Timothy 2:14.)

Likewise must the deacons be grave, not double tongued, not given to much wine, not greedy of filthy lucre; holding the mystery of the faith in a pure conscience. And let these also first be proved; then let them use the office of a deacon, being found blameless. Even so must their wives be grave, not slanderers, sober, faithful in all things. Let the deacons be the husbands of one wife, ruling their children and their own houses well. For they that have used the office of a deacon well purchase to themselves a good degree, and great boldness in the faith which is in Christ Jesus.

The following illustration compares the appearance of the kind of church that man builds with the church that Jesus builds. Man's control and organization of a church is like a crustacean; a creature whose skeletal structure is external as a shell. The supporting structure is external, highly visible and functions to contain, bind up, hold and control the body. The supporting structure is all that shows, not the actual body.

What do you see when you look at a typical man-made church? You see a man, (usually in clerical or priestly apparel), highly visible personalities, churchy ornamentations, organizational hierarchy, programs and unique ornate buildings. Do you see a representation of the Lord Jesus Christ? What are you supposed to see in a true Jesus built church.

> Galatians 2:20 – *I am crucified with Christ: nevertheless I live; yet not I, but Christ liveth in me: and the life which I now live in the flesh I live by the faith of the Son of God, who loved me, and gave himself for me.*

The character and nature of Jesus is seen in the people of the church that He is building; and is exemplified by the leadership that undergirds such an organism. Leadership in the true church resembles a human skeletal structure; which is all internal, not like the external of a crustacean. Christ's leadership will not contain, bind up, hold in and control the body; nor is it highly visible. It provides support from within, allowing the body to mature and expand naturally while having the continued support it needs to maintain its stature. This internal structure allows the body to grow without the restraint that is imposed by an external crustacean support structure.

> Ephesians 4:11-13 – *And he gave some, apostles; and some, prophets; and some, evangelists; and some, pastors and teachers; for the perfecting of the saints, for the work of the ministry, for the edifying of the body of Christ: till we all come in the unity of the faith, and of the knowledge of the Son of God, unto a perfect man, unto the measure of the stature of the fulness of Christ:*

In a Jesus built church you see the exterior of the body, the people, and they represent Him to whom they belong. The true church is in His image.

1 John 3:1 – *Beloved, now are we the sons of God, and it doth not yet appear what we shall be: but we know that, when he shall appear, we shall be like him; for we shall see him as he is.*

When you consider the skeletal structure in the human body you notice that there are numerous and diverse bones required in order to create this support system. Each bone has a specific location with a vital function. If one bone were out of place, or missing, the whole body would know it and would have a debilitating effect. This is referenced in 1 Corinthians 12:27 where it says, *"and members in particular".*

A crustacean can live and grow; but for it to grow, it must break out of its skeletal shell, expand, then form a new external skeletal structure to contain it just like the one it broke out of and discarded. This is illustrative of a church that man builds when it grows.

As mentioned previously, this author believes that the true church of the Lord Jesus Christ is to be restored to its original form and ready for His return; and it will be like Him with His character and nature which is the Fruit of the Spirit – Galatians 5:21-22. This means it has to be rid of man-made spots, wrinkles and blemishes that are the result of the false doctrines and pagan practices that were brought into it from Rome, and whose roots go all the way back to ancient Babylon.

Ephesians 5:26-27 – *that he might sanctify and cleanse it with the washing of water by the word, that he might present it to himself a glorious church, not having spot, or wrinkle, or any such thing; but that it should be holy and without blemish.*

In Ezekiel Chapter 37 we read about the valley of dry bones; this speaks of revival. This is about God restoring His people Israel, but it is also a parallel to re-awakening the true church back to the form in which it began; the church that Jesus is returning for.

Revive means to re make alive, to restore back to life. Note the process that begins after the wind of the Holy Spirit begins to stir the dry bones. It is the bones first that come together which means the structural leadership is raised up first. This is the supporting skeletal structure that must be set in order because all the rest of the body depends on it and is supported by it.

What is written in Ezekiel preceding the revival in Chapter 37; it is recognizing the need to deal with false leadership and their failure to be the proper support structure. This is dealt with in Ezekiel Chapter 34, the prophecy against the false shepherds, (pastors, prophets and leadership).

We need to be able to recognize God's true leadership! True leaders are the guardians of truth, builders and shepherds of His Holy Habitation – His Church, which is the Body of Christ on the earth. Jesus told us how to identify His true ministers; they manifest the Fruit of the Spirit, which is the character and nature of God and fully manifested in Jesus. This is the key to identifying the true leaders from the false ones.

> Matthew 7:15-16 & 20 – *Beware of false prophets, which come to you in sheep's clothing, but inwardly they are ravening wolves. Ye shall know them by their fruits. … Wherefore by their fruits ye shall know them.*

The fruits mentioned here are not man's works but the character and nature of the Lord that is formed in them. It is the life of the vine, the Spirit of Christ, in them that produces this divine fruit.

> John 15:1-5 – *I am the true vine, and my Father is the husbandman. Every branch in me that beareth not fruit he taketh away: and every branch that beareth fruit, he purgeth it, that it may bring forth more fruit. Now ye are clean through the word which I have spoken unto you. Abide in me, and I in you. As the branch cannot bear fruit of itself, except it abide in the vine; no more can ye, except ye abide in me. I am the vine, ye are the branches: He that abideth in me, and I in him, the same bringeth forth much fruit: for without me ye can do nothing.*

True leadership in His church works to bring forth this divine fruit in each member of His church. This fruit shows that the people are being conformed to the image of Christ. This is what pleases Christ, and also is what our Heavenly Father is looking for.

> John 15:8 – *Herein is my Father glorified, that ye bear much fruit; so shall ye be my disciples.*

IMPORTANT NOTE: GOD'S MINISTERS ARE NOT TO BE RECOGNIZED BY THEIR SIGNS, WONDERS, GIFTS OR

PROPHECIES, BUT BY THIS DIVINE FRUIT – GOD'S CHARACTER
AND NATURE THAT MANIFESTS IN THEM.

The reason for this is that signs, wonders and supernatural gifts can
be counterfeited by Satan and his servants. But they cannot duplicate the
character and nature of God, (the Fruit of the Spirit), because they have the
inward character and nature of Satan; they are the devil's ministers in disguise
that have infiltrated the church creating the other church.

> John 8:44 – *Ye are of your father the devil, and the lusts of
> your father ye will do. He was a murderer from the beginning,
> and abode not in the truth, because there is no truth in him.
> When he speaketh a lie, he speaketh of his own: for he is a liar,
> and the father of it.*

> John 10:10 – *The thief* (Satan and his allies) *cometh not, but
> for to steal, and to kill, and to destroy:* (which is what he does
> in forming the false "other" church).

Jesus knows who the false ministers are even though they declare they
speak for Him.

> Matthew 7:22-23 – *Many will say to me in that day, Lord,
> Lord, have we not prophesied in thy name? and in thy name
> have cast out devils? and in thy name done many wonderful
> works? And then will I profess unto them, I never knew you:
> depart from me, ye that work iniquity,* (doing your own thing).

The traits and works of the false leaders contrast greatly with the true
leaders of His church. False leaders guard their traditions and doctrines and
refuse correction; they also seek to build, protect and reinforce their group
or organization. They also have to constantly reinforce their pet doctrines,
because that is where their security is. And, of course, money is the most
important emphasis in their ministry; and they usually have lots of it because
they spend a lot of their ministry preaching on prosperity, (theirs).

> 1Timothy 6:5-6 – *perverse disputings of men of corrupt minds,
> and destitute of the truth, supposing that gain is godliness: from*

such withdraw thyself. But godliness with contentment is great gain.

The wealth and prosperity doctrine draws many because it is what people want to hear. The error is that it focuses people's attention on the material things of creation rather than on the Creator who promised to provide all things.

Matthew 6:33 – *But seek ye first the kingdom of God, and his righteousness; and all these things shall be added unto you.*

They draw followers unto themselves, and they are threatened by those who show any kind of spiritual discernment or prowess to expose them. They fear loss of their sheep of which they live off of. They build physically instead of spiritually; in fact, they stifle true spiritual development in their sheep because it becomes a threat to them. They cultivate an organizational growth demanding devotion and loyalty to it and to themselves. They are just the opposite of the character that was in John the Baptist as he said:

John 3:30 – *He must increase, but I must decrease.*

True leadership carries on Christ's commission with His leadership and Holy Spirit anointing on them.

Luke 4:18-19 – *The Spirit of the Lord is upon me, because he hath anointed me to preach the gospel to the poor; he hath sent me to heal the brokenhearted, to preach deliverance to the captives, and recovering of sight to the blind, to set at liberty them that are bruised, to preach the acceptable year of the Lord.*

His servants are secure in Him, and are thus able to face all manner of organized opposition from the false other church. The God ordained leaders will bring the true church out of the false church, the "Great Whore", the mystical religion of Babylon, where the pagan practices of Rome originated. Here is a look at the whore of Revelation 18:1-24, examined:

- vs 2 describes the harlot church
- vs 3 describes her influence as being world wide

- vs 4 the call of God to His people to get out
- vs 5-7 describes her position & influence
- vs 8 … describes the lamentation of the world over her end
- vs 20 describes God's true servants of past rejoicing
- vs 22-23 describes the false church services & activities
- vs 24 describes her fruit

There is a war in the spirit realm, (in the heavens); and God's army, the true church, is being raised up for this warfare along with God's angles who fight against Satan's prince angel over Rome. This is the religious spirit, which is likely the spirit of antichrist mentioned by the apostle John in his first epistle. The battle is to bring people out of the bondage of the false other church with its false worship and practices.

The warfare is described in Revelation 17 and it occurs in the spirit realm, and is also mentioned in Ephesians 6:12-13.

> Revelation 17:14 – *These shall make war with the Lamb, and the Lamb shall overcome them: for he is Lord of lords, and King of kings: and they that are with him are called, and chosen, and faithful.*

Since this warfare occurs primarily in the spirit realm, but manifests results in our physical realm, supernatural displays of power will need to be employed, which are the supernatural Gifts of the Spirit listed in 1 Corinthians 12:8-11. However, the enemy will also use supernatural powers to try to counter and deceive people with lying signs and wonders to keep people from the truth.

> 2 Thessalonians 2:9-10 – *even him, whose coming is after the working of Satan with all power and signs and lying wonders, and with all deceivableness of unrighteousness in them that perish; because they received not the love of the truth, that they might be saved.*

> Matthew 24:24 – *For there shall arise false Christs, and false prophets, and shall shew great signs and wonders; insomuch that, if it were possible, they shall deceive the very elect.*

This is an intense warfare, and Jesus will be using those whom He has personally called, trained and prepared; tested by fiery trials, proven and found faithful. These are the godly leaders whom He has been raising up for years; most of who have been hidden or obscure during their time of preparation. They will be recognized by their spiritual fruit, their faithfulness and obedience in the face of opposition. They will also be known by their anointing, (the empowerment of the Holy Spirit upon them), and His authority that shall be given them as well as the manifestation of His presence in their ministry. It will be as though Jesus Christ Himself was ministering and not a mere man.

Chapter 4

THE HEADSHIP OF THE LORD JESUS CHRIST

JESUS IS THE HEAD THE TRUE CHURCH – MAN IS THE HEAD OF THE OTHER CHURCH

Part One – DECAPITATION

Scripture tells us that Jesus is the head of the church and the church is identified as His Body here on earth. Removing the head from the body is known as decapitation.

> Ephesians 1:22-23 – *and hath put all things under his feet, and gave him to be the head over all things to the church, which is his body, the fulness of him that filleth all in all.*

> Ephesians 4:15-16 – *but speaking the truth in love, may grow up into him in all things, which is the head, even Christ: from whom the whole body fitly joined together …*

> Ephesians 5:23 – *For the husband is the head of the wife, even as Christ is the head of the church: and he is the saviour of the body.*

> Colossians 1:18 – *And he is the head of the body, the church: who is the beginning, the firstborn from the dead; that in all things he might have the preeminence.*

Jesus, as Head of His church, is the rightful authority who provides His leadership from which flows His guidance, anointing and divine power. This authority is called "The Headship of Christ". His Body, the church, is to be in direct submission under Him as the head in order to receive His doctrines, the leading of the Holy Spirit, His directives, as well as His character and nature, (the life of the vine which is the Fruit of the Spirit).

The other church is not joined to Jesus as its Head. It became separated from Jesus as the head during the fourth century when man set himself up as the head of the church; as when the Pope declared himself to be the Vicar of Christ. This formed the "other" church; thus it was decapitated. This was done through man elevating himself to a position as master and created an organization, (and later denominations), that are totally under man's control and not led by the Lord. They think they work for Him, but fail to allow Him to work through them.

Man's rule over the church is not Spirit led, but soulish led; it is man's ideas of what he thinks the Lord wants rather than hearing from Jesus to do things His way.

> Isaiah 55:8-9 – *For my thoughts are not your thoughts, neither are your ways my ways, saith the Lord. For as the heavens are higher that the earth, so are my ways higher than your ways, and my thoughts than your thoughts.*

The Lord does things in ways that we don't even imagine. He accomplishes what He has determined if we obey Him and follow His way. This is what is described in building His house – the true church.

> Matthew 7:24-27 – *Therefore whosoever heareth these sayings of mine, and doeth them, I will liken him unto a wise man, which built his house upon a rock: and the rain descended, and the floods came, and the winds blew, and beat upon that house; and it fell not: for it was founded upon a rock. And every one that heareth these sayings of mine, and doeth them not, shall be likened unto a foolish man, which built his house upon the sand: and the rain descended, and the floods came, and the winds blew, and beat upon that house; and it fell: and great was the fall of it.*

When built His way, in obedience to Him, the house (or church) will stand against whatever the enemy, and the world, throws against it. Failure to build it His way, and instead do it man's way, means the house, (the other church) will not stand when the trials of life hit.

When man relies on his own abilities and resources then the enemy is able to beguile the human mind with errors and thoughts that are misleading and even totally contrary to the truth of God's Word. Thus we see false doctrines and observances enter into the church; this has happened gradually through history, (as is demonstrated in Appendix A).

Leadership in the other church does not govern by divine directives, but by the will of man as expressed in popular vote, committees of religious hierarchy, spiritual bigots, or by doctrinal dogmas.

Although there are likely true believers in the other church, they are not being properly discipled since the leadership is of man and not of Christ. Therefore such believers are not maturing in the Lord. They are also subject to a variety of false doctrines and errors. Jesus is concerned for those who believe in Him, thus the call to "come out" of this Babylonian religious system that has become the other church.

> Revelation 18:4 – *And I heard another voice from heaven, saying, Come out of her, my people, that ye be not partakers of her sins, and that ye receive not of her plagues.*

With man's leadership over the other church, Satan has opportunity to influence since such leadership is not operating under Christ's leadership. These are those that Jesus referred to as "wolves" in Matthew 7:15-22, (cited in the previous chapter), saying their works were not of Him, and He did not know them. Thus the spirit of antichrist is able to operate in and through them.

> 1 John 2:18-19 – *Little children, it is the last time: and as ye have heard that antichrist shall come, even now are there many antichrists; whereby we know that it is the last time. They went out from us, but they were not of us; for if they had been of us, they would no doubt have continued with us: but they went out, that they might be made manifest that they were not all of us.*

Such religious leadership is actually of Satan. From the beginning, Satan has tempted mankind to take upon himself the role of God, just as Satan himself attempted.

> Genesis 3:4-5 – *And the serpent said unto the woman, Ye shall not surely die: for God doth know that in the day ye eat thereof, then your eyes shall be opened, and ye shall be as gods,*

The apostle Paul warned of such a condition arising in the church at Colosse:

> Colossians 2:8-10 – *Beware lest any man spoil you through philosophy and vain deceit, after the tradition of men, after the rudiments of the world, and not after Christ.*

Paul continues in his warning that such false leadership is responsible for the decapitation of the head from the body.

> Colossians 2:18-19 – *Let no man beguile you of your reward in a voluntary humility and worshipping of angels* (and other false doctrines), *intruding into those things which he hath not seen, vainly puffed up by his fleshly (soulish) mind, and not holding the Head, from which all the body by joints and bands having nourishment ministered, and knit together, increaseth with the increase of God.*

Here Paul warns of the false worship he sees entering into the church. This foretells of the entry of the mystical Babylonian rituals which he sees man brining into the church through Rome. In verse 19, Paul tells that this mystical worship will result in the dismemberment of the Head from the Body. This means the loss of true spiritual nourishment which emanates from the Head; thus the loss of the "zoe" life of Christ, (the vine), to and through the Body. (Note: *Zoe* is the Greek word for life, that is life as God has it; eternal life, as found in John 10:10.).

The next three verses tell of the human ordinances, rituals and practices that will be established by the leadership of man over the other church. All of this which is foretold is exactly what we now have and still experience in many churches today.

Colossians 2:20-23 – *Wherefore if ye be dead with Christ from the rudiments of the world, why, as though living in the world, are ye subject to ordinances, (touch not; taste not; handle not; which all are to perish with the using;) after the commandments and doctrines of men? which things have indeed a shew of wisdom in will worship, and humility, and neglecting of the body; not in any honour to the satisfying of the flesh.*

Here, Paul asks why a person would return to the bondage of man-controlled religion and doctrines which permeate many churches today. Although these things sound good, and make sense to men, and look very pious and self-debasing, they are all vain forms of religious pretense. They are man's attempt to attain holiness which is not humanly possible. These are referred to as "dead works" in Hebrews 6:1, from which we need to repent.

Holiness is a product of the Spirit of Christ in us, and living our life led by the Spirit, which is the life (*zoe*) that flows from His Headship over us. With the head decapitated from the body, the body can no longer receive input from that head on how to carry on living in His life (*zoe*). An artificial, man-made life-support system is then needed to sustain the body. This is exactly what has happened to the other church as it has existed on artificial life support for so long that it thinks this is natural.

When you look at the headless body of the other church, dismembered from its true head, Christ, you are actually looking at two bodies, not one. It is as though one were overlaid on top of the other so that in the physical realm the natural eye sees one body referred to as the church.

The second body is that of the false other church, which is referred to as the great whore of Revelation Chapter 17 & 18. This second body appears to contain, or hold captive, much of the true Body of Christ. This second body is frequently described as a female body, referred to as the Bride of Christ. However, the Body of Christ is properly portrayed as a male body, an extension of Him, whose body true believers belong to.

Ephesians 2:15b – ... *for to make in himself of twain one new man*, (not a woman or a bride).

The Body of Christ is composed of those who believe in Jesus as Savior and Lord; those in whom His Spirit dwells. They are called in many scriptures, "sons of God". (Note: God's sons are not a bride, but His adopted children referred to as "sons".)

> John 1:12 – *But as many as received him, to them gave he power to become the sons of God, even to them that believe on his name:*

> Romans 8:14 & 16-17 – *For as many as are led by the Spirit of God, they are the sons of God. ... The Spirit itself beareth witness with our spirit, that we are the children of God: and if children, then heirs; heirs of God, and joint-heirs with Christ;*

> Galatians 4:6-7 – *And because ye are sons, God hath sent forth the Spirit of his Son into your hearts, crying, Abba, Father. Wherefore thou art no more a servant, but a son; and if a son, then an heir of God through Christ.*

> Philippians 2:14-15 – *Do all things without murmurings and disputings: that ye may be blameless and harmless, the sons of God, without rebuke, in the midst of a crooked and perverse nation, among whom ye shine as lights in the world;* (His light shining through us.)

> 1 John 3:1-3 – *Behold, what manner of love the Father hath bestowed upon us, that we should be called the sons of God: therefore the world knoweth us not, because it knew him not. Beloved, now are we the sons of God, and it doth not yet appear what we shall be: but we know that, when he shall appear, we shall be like him* (not like her); *for we shall see him as he is. And every man that hath this hope in him purifieth himself, even as he is pure;* (purified from false doctrines so His light can shine through us without hindrances so that He can be seen in us.)

Imagine a male head on a female body. This sounds like an abomination; yet this is exactly how many Christians view the church. They see Jesus as the male head on a female body. They call this body "the bride of Christ".

Nowhere in the Bible is the church actually called His bride; it is only called His Body.

The other church gets the idea that the church is His bride comes from the misapplication of Ephesians 5:23-27 which is used only as an allegory for illustrative purpose: "as a bride", (not "is the bride"). The only scripture reference to the visible Bride of Christ is in Revelation 21 which refers to the heavenly city, the New Jerusalem as being the Bride of Christ, not the church.

> Revelation 21:9-10 – *And there came unto me one of the seven angels which had the seven vials full of the seven last plagues, and talked with me, saying, Come hither, I will shew thee the bride, the Lamb's wife. And he carried me away in the spirit to a great and high mountain, and shewed me that great city, the holy Jerusalem, descending out of heaven from God,*

Some argue that since the New Jerusalem is the future dwelling place of the saints, that the city also refers to the church. We must also recognize that "saints" are not exclusively the church of the New Testament. There are numerous saints of the Old Covenant, and they do not constitute the church. They also are to be citizens of the New Jerusalem, but they are not His Body here on earth. However, they do have the rights to the marriage supper as Old Testament believers do along with Abraham, the father of faith.

> Hebrews 11:13-16 – *These all died in faith, not having received the promises, but having seen them afar off, and were persuaded of them, and embraced them, and confessed that they were strangers and pilgrims on the earth. For they that say such things declare plainly that they seek a country. And truly, if they had been mindful of that country from whence they came out, they might have had opportunity to have returned. But now they desire a better country, that is, an heavenly: wherefore God is not ashamed to be called their God: for he hath prepared for them a city.*

The following is presented for consideration: note that in Revelation 21 the heavenly city is also referred to as "The Lamb's Wife", why? After Jesus ascended to the Father in heaven, and sat down at His right hand; where are the thrones located where they are seated? Most likely they are enthroned in the Holy City meaning Jesus is already there, thus it is called the Lamb's Wife. However this Holy City is designated to be our place after we are resurrected and taken to be with Him. The marriage supper of the Lamb is when we, the true church and the O.T. saints, are united with Him; then He leads us to enter into the Holy City. When Christ with His full body of believers enter into the city then the marriage is consummated.

The female body appears to be the false other church called the great whore and mystery (mystical or religious) Babylon that the Lord calls for His people to come out of. (Note: a whore is an immoral female.)

> Revelation 18:4 – *And I heard another voice from heaven, saying, Come out of her, my people, that ye be not partakers of her sins, and that ye receive not of her plagues.*

Who are "My people" that the Lord has issued this call to? It has to be none other than those believers in Him who are still bound up in the false other church. Revelation 17 and 18 tells us about his harlot other church, the religious system, that actually descended from the ancient Babylonian religion that was formed under Nimrod and Semaremis, and likely continued into Nebuchadnezzars's Babylon of Daniel's time.

The pagan doctrines and observances of the Babylonian religion have been preserved and maintained through the Roman Catholic Church to this day, and some of which remains in the Protestant Churches which are the spin-offs of the Roman church.

Much of what Rome established is still carried on and observed in many main-line Protestant, Bible believing, Evangelical churches, including Pentecostal and Independent churches. This is the religious system that has continued through all the major empires from Nimrod to this present day; that is, until Jesus returns to destroy the entire system, as represented in Daniel 2:36-45. The end of these empires and their religious systems occur with the return of Jesus to set up is Kingdom on earth.

> Daniel 2:44-45 – *And in the days of these kings shall the God of heaven set up a kingdom, which shall never be destroyed: and the kingdom shall not be left to other people, but it shall break in pieces and consume all these kingdoms, and it shall stand for ever. Forasmuch as thou sawest that the stone was cut out of the mountain without hands, and that it brake in pieces the iron,*

the brass, the clay, the silver, and the gold; the great God hath made known to the king what shall come to pass hereafter: and the dream is certain, and the interpretation thereof sure.

It is Jesus Christ, the Rock, that will crush this political and religious system with all of its tentacles that reach into all political and mercantile corners of the world. The sphere of influence of these empires covers the entire world and is referred to by the ships, sailors and merchants that trade by sea to places "afar off" in Revelation18:17.

Since the Rock has not yet crushed the iron and clay of the image, we must realize that we are still under the influence of this whorish religion from ancient Babylon. This woman, the false other church, is not the expected beast or the antichrist; but she rides along on top of the beast system which carries her along.

> Revelation 17:3 & 7 – *So he carried me away in the spirit into the wilderness: and I saw a woman sit upon a scarlet coloured beast, full of names of blasphemy, having seven heads and ten horns. ... ... And the angel said unto me, Wherefore didst thou marvel? I will tell thee the mystery of the woman, and of the beast that carrieth her, which hath the seven heads and ten horns.*

This beast is the religion of man which is inspired by Satan, (as in Genesis 3:5). She utilizes the beast nature to achieve her goals. This beast nature is that of the base, carnal sin nature derived by mankind from his submission to Satan.

> Revelation 17:5 – *and upon her forehead was a name written, MYSTERY, BABYLON THE GREAT, THE MOTHER OF HARLOTS AND ABOMINATIONS OF THE EARTH.*

Mystery Babylon is actually "Mystical Babylon". The word "mystery" means: secretive religious rites, (per Strong's Concordance and Thayers Greek Lexicon). She uses her mysticism, and what the Bible calls "sorceries", (which includes witchcraft and Pharmacia, drugs and potions), to deceive and control this other form of church. This other church will be judged and brought down.

> Revelation 18:23 – *and the light of a candle shall shine no more at all in thee; and the voice of the bridegroom and of the bride shall be heard no more at all in thee: for thy merchants were the great men of the earth; for by thy sorceries were all nations deceived.*

This woman is also symbolically called a city because of the immense number of people that dwell in this religious system. She represents the ancient Babylonian religious system, so this is the name given her; Mystery Babylon.

She is actually the false church who has always tried to claim Christ as being hers. She claims it from the position of being the mother of God, and thus, the Queen of Heaven. This is the woman usurping authority over man,

> 1 Timothy 2:12 – *But I suffer not a woman to teach, nor to usurp authority over the man, but to be in silence.*

There are multiple forms of Babylon referred to in Revelation; one is the "mystical" religious system and others are the political, financial and social systems of Babylon. Please do not confuse each as being one and the same. Read Revelation 17:1-6 and 15-18:5; and 18:20-24, as these passages describe the religious impact as well as the political and social activities of this Babylonian system.

PART TWO: THE APOSTOLIC AND PROPHETIC ROLES IN RESTORING CHRIST'S HEADSHIP OVER THE CHURCH

Bible scholars agree that national Israel and the New Testament church are parallel; that is, they both endure similar experiences. Some teachers believe that the church is a spiritual form of Israel, and thus a parallel. Warning; some go too far and say that the church is now literal Israel using "replacement" theology. They believe that the church has replaced natural Israel in God's plan; this is not true!

Just as physical Israel was taken captive by its enemy, Babylon, so it is with the church; it has been taken captive by spiritual (mystical) Babylon.

The prophets who foretold of Israel's captivity and later their return were all persecuted or killed by the false religious leaders of their day. Those same religious leaders were responsible for their nation going into captivity: and later, those same type of religious leaders were responsible for the crucifixion of Jesus Christ.

The physical city/nation of Babylon did not kill the prophets; it was the spiritual (mystical) Babylon, the false religious system in Israel and Jerusalem that did. So it is today that the prophets of God are declaring the same about much of the church which is held captive in spiritual Babylon's religious system, the other church. It is the same with mystical Babylon that has killed the saints of the New Testament church for centuries.

> Revelation 18:24 – *And in her was found the blood of prophets, and of saints, and of all that were slain upon the earth.*

(The book, FOXES BOOK OF MARTYERS, gives a great amount of information as to how the other church has killed and persecuted the true saints; especially since the Reformation.)

So it is today with God's prophets in the true church; prophets which much the other church denies even exist, saying they are not for today. Such prophets declare the truth to set the captives free, but their words go against the established institutionalized religious system, (the I.R.S.), so they are rejected and persecuted.

Fortunately our society is civilized enough to forgo murdering the prophets; (at least for the present time). However, they are still subject to character assassination when books and magazine articles are written about them.

The prophets and the apostles will rejoice when they finally see the end of the false religious system that has deceived the other church system and held them captive for so long.

> Revelation 18:20 – *Rejoice over her, thou heaven, and ye holy apostles and prophets; for God hath avenged you on her.*

Why will the apostles of Jesus Christ also rejoice? What is an apostle and what does he do? As covered in a previous chapter, an apostle is an ambassador; one sent with the authority of the sender.

2 Corinthians 5:19-20 – *Now then we are ambassadors for Christ, as though God did beseech you by us: we pray you in Christ's stead, be ye reconciled to God.*

The apostle is Christ's representative to set in order the things of the church so that it serves Christ by guiding it into full maturity. Jesus Christ is called an apostle because He was sent by God, His Father, as His representative to man, having God's divine authority and power.

Hebrews 3:1-2 – *Wherefore, holy brethren, partakers of the heavenly calling, consider the Apostle and High Priest of our profession, Christ Jesus; who was faithful to him that appointed him,*

True apostolic ministry is to reveal Christ in His fullness to the church so that Christ is fully formed in the saints. The other church denies that apostles are for today. Apostles are ordained by Jesus and the Father for a particular task – to reveal Jesus with power and authority.

Galatians 1:1& 15-16 – *Paul, an apostle, (not of men, neither by man, but by Jesus Christ, and God the Father, … But when it pleased God, who separated me from my mother's womb, and called me by his grace, to reveal his Son in me, that I might preach him among the heathen;*

Galatians 4:19 – *My little children, of whom I travail in birth again until Christ be formed in you,*

Ephesians 4:12-13 – *for the perfecting of the saints, for the work of the ministry, for the edifying of the body of Christ: [13] till we all come in the unity of the faith, and of the knowledge of the Son of God, unto a perfect man, unto the measure of the stature of the fulness of Christ:*

The apostles grieve at the state of the church for being separated from its head. They will rejoice when they see the Body restored to the Head and separated from the false female body of the Babylonian religious system. The modern day apostles work to restore His Headship to the church so that the

Body of Christ may come to the full stature it is supposed to have. They labor with the other gift ministries to have man removed as the head of the church so that Christ may have His rightful position. Jesus Christ is always prominent in the ministry of true apostles.

> 1 Corinthians 2:2 – *For I determined not to know any thing among you, save Jesus Christ, and him crucified.*

Please understand that the Lord, by His Spirit, still moves in and through His church even though His headship is lacking over His Body at present. This is because He still honors His Word to the extent that it is used in the other church. When we see His Headship is restored, we shall see a mighty move of His Spirit in His church because the hindrance of man is gone. This will be a move not seen since the early church in the Acts of the Apostles. We will enter a new time of the Acts of the Last Day Apostles as His Spirit is poured out; this can only flow from Him as the Head.

Christ will truly be the Head of the church only when church leadership learns to seek and receive His divine directives in how to govern and lead, rather than relying on man's ways.

> Matthew 20:25-27 – *But Jesus called them unto him, and said, Ye know that the princes of the Gentiles exercise dominion over them, and they that are great exercise authority upon them. But it shall not be so among you: but whosoever will be great among you, let him be your minister; and whosoever will be chief among you, let him be your servant:* (Note: you certainly do not see this in the "other" church.)

This will happen when the church submits to His divine order and authority; under all of the five Gift Ministries working together. The Gift Ministries will also have to be in proper ranks, that is, in proper relationship to one another.

Christ, as Head, is all authority over the church, (and over everything else also). His authority is conveyed to the church through His selected Gift Ministries who apply His name and operate in the order or rank which was established by God, the Father.

1 Corinthians 12:27-28 – *Now ye are the body of Christ, and members in particular. And God hath set some in the church, first apostles, secondarily prophets, thirdly teachers, after that miracles, then gifts of healings, helps, governments, diversities of tongues.*

The Lord's set divine order of spiritual authority is: 1) the apostles; 2) the prophets; 3) the teachers; 4) the evangelists, who manifest miracles and healings; then last in rank; 5) the pastors, or elders who are the administrators of the church government, helps and related shepherding tasks.

Under the current headship of man in the Babylonian system, we see the pastor as the sole authority in the church; yet this is not God's plan. This comes from the tradition of the Babylonian priesthood which was adopted by the Church of Rome. From this the Roman Catholic (pagan style) priest became the pattern for the Protestant pastor.

The biggest obstacle to God's divine order in the church is from those who hold the position of pastor. They oppose the divine authority of the other Gift Ministries because they view these other ministries as a threat to their influence and control over the people. They do not want to submit to the authority of the other Gift ministries; they prefer the authority and control for themselves or their man made denominational authorities who place them in their positions. In most cases it is the security of their position and income that they fear losing. This may sound harsh, but it is true none-the-less.

Control and influence over the people is what the harlot church and the Babylonian I.R.S. system is all about; it is man's control over what belongs to God. This was the opposition Jesus faced that led to His crucifixion.

John 12:19 – *The Pharisees therefore said among themselves, Perceive ye how ye prevail nothing? behold, the world is gone after him.*

John 11:47-48 – *Then gathered the chief priests and the Pharisees a council, and said, What do we? for this man doeth many miracles. If we let him thus alone, all men will believe on him: and the Romans shall come and take away both our place and nation.*

In these last days, the Lord is raising up His apostles who will work to separate the true Body of Christ from the Great Whore of Babylon religious system, the other church. They will operate in divine order with His authority and power to reconnect His Body to His Headship. They will labor so that the saints will finally be perfected, completely matured in the image and likeness of the Lord Jesus Christ.

> Ephesians 4:13-16 — *till we all come in the unity of the faith, and of the knowledge of the Son of God, unto a perfect man, unto the measure of the stature of the fulness of Christ: that we henceforth be no more children, tossed to and fro, and carried about with every wind of doctrine, by the sleight of men, and cunning craftiness, whereby they lie in wait to deceive;* (by the "other" church), *but speaking the truth in love, may grow up into him in all things, which is the head, even Christ: from whom the whole body fitly joined together and compacted by that which every joint supplieth, according to the effectual working in the measure of every part, maketh increase of the body unto the edifying of itself in love.*

> Ephesians 5:26-27 — *that he might sanctify and cleanse it with the washing of water by the word, that he might present it to himself a glorious church, not having spot, or wrinkle, or any such thing; but that it should be holy and without blemish.*

There is coming a time of "apostolic anointing". Some in ministry are already sensing its coming and have recognized this apostolic calling in the lives of a few. This is quite new to most of us. Some who have this calling to apostleship are trying to move in the calling prematurely, not having received the commissioning which carries with it the anointing with His authority.

This is what happened to Paul when he was called and tried to minister but produced no results, but only chaos. He was commissioned eight to fourteen years later in the city of Antioch after enduring a period of frustration knowing his call but not permitted to function in that calling.

> Acts 3:1-2 — *Now there were in the church that was at Antioch certain prophets and teachers; as Barnabas, and Simeon that was called Niger, and Lucius of Cyrene, and Manaen, which*

had been brought up with Herod the tetrarch, and Saul. As
they ministered to the Lord, and fasted, the Holy Ghost said,
Separate me Barnabas and Saul for the work whereunto I have
called them.

The I.R.S. Babylonian system will try to hinder this move of God by establishing false, man-appointed apostles. Their purpose is to deceive and thwart the work of the Lord's true apostles. This is already beginning to happen because man appointed apostles do not have to wait on Christ's appointed time for their commissioning as do the true apostles. So we have some of the false ones out there misleading and deceiving parts of the church even now. We need to test and prove them!

Revelation 2:2b – *... and how thou canst not bear them which*
are evil: and thou hast tried them which say they are apostles,
and are not, and hast found them liars:

Jesus warned of a great deception in the last days by false preachers, prophets and ministers of all sorts. Jesus said many would be deceived by them. This deception would not be limited in size or scope, but would be on such a large scale that many would fall for their misleading and fraudulent doctrines. How could this happen? Jesus said they would come in His name, showing supernatural signs and wonders, declaring that he is "anointed". Note that "Christ" is the Greek word for Messiah which means "anointed"; and they will deceive and lead people deeper into the mystical Babylonian religion.

How can the church avoid being so deceived? Jesus stated very clearly how to recognize these false pretenders; "By their fruit ye shall know them".

Matthew 7:15-16 & 20-23 – *Beware of false prophets, which*
come to you in sheep's clothing, but inwardly they are ravening
wolves. Ye shall know them by their fruits. ... Wherefore by
their fruits ye shall know them. Not every one that saith unto
me, Lord, Lord, shall enter into the kingdom of heaven; but
he that doeth the will of my Father which is in heaven. Many
will say to me in that day, Lord, Lord, have we not prophesied
in thy name? and in thy name have cast out devils? and in thy
name done many wonderful works? And then will I profess unto
them, I never knew you: depart from me, ye that work iniquity.

Jesus declares that He never knew them or called them to be His ministers. This fruit that we must recognize is not their works but the Fruit of the Spirit, which is His character and nature, and can only be produced by His Spirit life flowing in and through His ministers.

> John 15:4-5 – *Abide in me, and I in you. As the branch cannot bear fruit of itself, except it abide in the vine; no more can ye, except ye abide in me. I am the vine, ye are the branches: He that abideth in me, and I in him, the same bringeth forth much fruit: for without me ye can do nothing.*

This fruit is described in Galatians 5 and comprises the character and nature of God that was in full manifestation in Jesus Christ, and is to be in all of His followers. This fruit is contrasted with the works of the flesh of unregenerate man.

> Galatians 5:19-23 – *Now the works of the flesh are manifest, which are these; Adultery, fornication, uncleanness, lasciviousness, idolatry, witchcraft, hatred, variance, emulations, wrath, strife, seditions, heresies, envyings, murders, drunkenness, revellings, and such like: of the which I tell you before, as I have also told you in time past, that they which do such things shall not inherit the kingdom of God. But the fruit of the Spirit is love, joy, peace, longsuffering, gentleness, goodness, faith, meekness, temperance: against such there is no law.*

Christ's true apostles work to see the Fruit of the Spirit produced in the saints. This was Paul's burden which he repeated over and over to the church at Galatia:

> Galatians 5:21b – *of the which I tell you before, as I have also told you in time past, that they which do such things **shall not inherit the kingdom of God**.*

True apostolic anointing will also be recognized by His authority being seen and experienced in and through His apostles. Most Bible scholars understand that the word apostle means, "one sent"; however, this is only part of the meaning. The full definition of an apostle is, "one sent with the full authority of the one sending". It means for one to go as a full representative of the sender as if the sender himself was going.

Only the Lord Jesus Christ can make true apostles; and even then it is only by the will of God the Father:

> Ephesians 1:1 – *Paul, an apostle of Jesus Christ by the will of God, to the saints which are at Ephesus, and to the faithful in Christ Jesus:*

False apostles are made by man, not by the Lord.

> Galatians 1:1 – *Paul, an apostle, (not of men, neither by man, but by Jesus Christ, and God the Father, who raised him from the dead;)*

False apostles can only go out with the authority of a church, (denomination or man's organization). Many consider missionaries to be apostles because they are sent out; however they are sent by a church or organization of man and can only operate with the authority of that church or organization of man. They do not have the true apostolic authority of Christ; however they have the apostolic authority of that church that sent them. Instead they operate more as evangelists to preach the gospel where it has not gone before.

False apostles need to be recognized for what they are because they can mislead the church. False apostles introduce false doctrines. They also can form new cults as they gather people as a following unto themselves. The importance of this is in fact that the true apostles are the guardians of true doctrine. They are concerned with having people follow Christ as they set the example of how to live.

The reason we have so many diverse doctrines and denominations today in the Babylonian or (I.R.S.) system is that the apostles were "done away with" by the Roman Church. The Roman Church had to do this in order to deny the spiritual authority of Christ over the church. This was done so that man could make claim to that authority instead, via the Pope.

True apostles will clear the air of false doctrine. And will restore sound doctrine universally. They are the guardians of true doctrine, along with the true prophets. With apostles and prophets eliminated by mystical Babylon, man's doctrines took over. These doctrines divided many into multiple groups, thus we have multiple denominations. (See Appendix A for a partial list of false doctrines that were progressively added to the Babylonian church system.)

All five Gift Ministries are to work toward the purpose of perfecting the saints to be full and properly mature children of God.

> Ephesians 4:13-15 – *till we all come in the unity of the faith, and of the knowledge of the Son of God, unto a perfect man, unto the measure of the stature of the fulness of Christ: that we henceforth be no more children, tossed to and fro, and carried about with every wind of doctrine, by the sleight of men, and cunning craftiness, whereby they lie in wait to deceive; but speaking the truth in love, may grow up into him in all things, which is the head, even Christ:*

The work for the true apostles will be complete when Jesus returns for His Body, the true church. Until that time the apostles will labor with the prophets, for the restoration of His Headship and the completion of the saints to spiritual maturity. Theirs is a ministry founded in love: love for Christ and love for His Body, the church.

They have a jealous love for the Body of Christ and are highly incensed at those who malign it, deceive it, abuse it or in any way hinder it from its relationship with the Head, Jesus Christ. They are especially incensed with the female Babylonian religious system that masquerades as the church, calling itself the Queen of Heaven.

They will function as the true servants, the bond-slaves of Jesus Christ. They will be rightly motivated. God will have tested and proved them through many years of trials and wilderness experiences. They will be proven to be faithful and patient having learned to endure many things for Christ's sake without fighting back or becoming resentful.

> 1 Corinthians 13:7 – (Love/Charity) … *beareth all things, believeth all things, hopeth all things, endureth all things.*

> 2 Corinthians 4:8-12 – *We are troubled on every side, yet not distressed; we are perplexed, but not in despair; persecuted, but not forsaken; cast down, but not destroyed; always bearing about in the body the dying of the Lord Jesus, that the life also*

of Jesus might be made manifest in our body. For we which live are alway delivered unto death for Jesus' sake, that the life also of Jesus might be made manifest in our mortal flesh. So then death worketh in us, but life in you.

2 Timothy 4:5 – But watch thou in all things, endure afflictions, do the work of an evangelist, make full proof of thy ministry.

Jesus Christ wants to make sure there is nothing impure in their hearts. Their message is Christ and Him Crucified in us; that we are transformed from this vile world and conformed to His image; that Christ is seen and revealed in us. This is so that when Christ returns we will be ready; we will be like Him.

1 John 3:2-3 – Beloved, now are we the sons of God, and it doth not yet appear what we shall be: but we know that, when he shall appear, we shall be like him; for we shall see him as he is. And every man that hath this hope in him purifieth himself, even as he is pure.

So that we will be ready to rule and reign with Him in His Kingdom.

PART THREE: THE STATE OF THE CHURCH WITHOUT THE HEADSHIP OF CHRIST

While in prayer one day, the Spirit of the Lord put a question in my mind. He queried, "What do you see when you look at the church"? I took the question quite seriously, and I knew He was referring to what everyone calls church; but more specifically, the other church. I thought intently for an honest and accurate answer. My response was, "When I see the church, I see buildings, programs, personalities, organizations, all man-made."

A few moments later the Spirit of the Lord posed another question to me. This time He asked, "When you look at the church, do you see me, (referring to Jesus Christ)?" I almost felt like that question was a "set up" based on the first answer I gave. My response to this second question was heartbreaking; I had to say, "No, I don't see Christ in the church".

Basically, He was pointing out to me that the headship of man in the church was an unacceptable substitute for Christ's Headship over the church. The answers to the questions bore the proof that the Life of Christ, (the "zoe" form of life; life as God has it), was not evident in the typical church. The church was getting along on a religious "form" of life. The true church has this life in the spirit realm by faith unto salvation, but it is not visibly manifesting the "zoe" life for the world to see.

This "zoe" life comes from Christ being made "alive" in the believer; being seen in us; being formed in us; thus being seen in His church. This life comes only from the Head of the church. If Christ is not revered in individual lives and in the position of Head over the church, then that life, which He is, cannot flow from the Head through the Body as Jesus stated.

> John 15:4-5 – *Abide in me, and I in you. As the branch cannot bear fruit of itself, except it abide in the vine; no more can ye, except ye abide in me. ⁵ I am the vine, ye are the branches: He that abideth in me, and I in him, the same bringeth forth much fruit: for without me ye can do nothing.*

Instead, with man as head of the church, the only life seen in the church is that of carnal, fleshly man. With man as Head of the church all that is seen are man's human frailties, weakness and carnal character traits that the apostle Paul identified would be seen in the church of the end-times.

> 2 Timothy 3:1-5 – *This know also, that in the last days perilous times shall come. For men shall be lovers of their own selves, covetous, boasters, proud, blasphemers, disobedient to parents, unthankful, unholy, without natural affection, trucebreakers, false accusers, incontinent, fierce, despisers of those that are good, traitors, heady, highminded, lovers of pleasures more than lovers of God; having a form of godliness, but denying the power thereof: from such turn away.*

Paul is obviously referring to the condition of the church in the last days because where else do you find a "form of godliness"; certainly not in the world. Thus there is no drawing power whatsoever to bring in the lost to come to Christ. The other church looks and acts just like the rest of the world; and it has no power to bring repentance and change lives to Christ.

The world needs to see Christ, and in fact, has a hunger to see Him; but the church hasn't been able to reveal Jesus in real life, only in the words preached by the pastor. Church people have become "dull of hearing" from so many words and from no overt action or evidence of what is preached. There is too much preaching and no real living of what is preached.

The world has a practical saying; "action speaks louder than words". The *zoe* form of life of Christ is to be seen in the church, but it isn't seen because the people of the other church don't show it or live it. They don't show it or live it because, in general, they haven't even been taught it or seen it. Most people in the other church don't even know what the *zoe* life is.

Is it no wonder that the media was publishing articles in the mid 1960's stating that "God is dead". The other church could not show that He is alive. This media campaign proved that the world is watching the church, looking for the hope that we preach about, but they didn't see it. Thus the world does not take the church seriously. Therefore, since that time the world has been mocking and making fun of the church and its TV preachers.

Watch TV and you will see what the world thinks of church and Christians. Yes, we get angered over it; but we need to ask "why do they do it"? It is not the attack of the enemy assaulting the believers, as I have heard many preach. No, in fact it is the result of our own behavior. The world is playing back to us exactly the way they see us; mostly as hypocrites.

In 1999, a horrible motion picture was released that raised the ire of Christians across the nation. Universal Pictures made a film called "THE LAST TEMPTATION OF CHRIST". Indeed, it was an abomination. Church leaders were calling for demonstrations, boycotts and other campaigns against Universal and their parent company M.C.A.

Friends of mine were very active in these demonstrations. They asked me to join in this "holy" cause against the "evil" Universal Studios. Universal was building their new theme park in Central Florida, so they had an ideal place to hold rallies and demonstrations.

I know that my friends could not understand me when I declined to become involved. They may have felt I was ashamed to show my Christianity in a public demonstration. Ashamed, I was; but not for what they thought was cowardice. I was ashamed of the church! I was ashamed that they had to resort to such a behavior of a worldly type of demonstrations. I was ashamed because they were treating the situation as though they were "closing the barn door after the horses got out". They were dealing with a situation after the fact, rather than dealing with what could have prevented it.

Finally, I expressed what God had laid on my heart about the situation. Those I shared it with could not really grasp it at the time. I think it was because they were so caught up with their "cause" that their state of frenzy would not allow real reasoning to get through to them.

I told them that I blame the church for the production of the film, THE LAST TEMPTATION OF CHRIST. "Why", they asked in a horrified expression. I told them that I hold the church responsible for that movie because IF THE CHURCH HAD BEEN THE CHURCH THAT CHRIST INTENDED IT TO BE, THAT MOVIE COULD NEVER HAVE BEEN MADE.

If the church was showing Christ to the world as He really is, there is no way that anyone could have perceived Jesus Christ to be what the movie portrayed. Even if the idea of making such a movie were brought up, nobody would go to the expense of producing it because the credibility of Christ in the church would belay any idea of potential profitability. Making that film would never have even entered the mind of its producers.

My comments did not do much to enhance my relationship with my friends, but I had to respond by the Spirit of the Lord which is in me and not by my human feeling, intellect or ideas, as they were doing. Believe me, I hurt for the church in this polluted condition, and I labor to purify it and prepare it for our Lord at His coming.

It was the church that made the movie possible by its lack of having the Life of Christ seen in it. Then we had the nerve to blame others for our own failure. Our holy warriors went out, in the Lord's name, to work against, and pray against, Universal Studios, while refusing to recognize their own failure. This whole thing grieved me and I am sure it grieved our Lord Jesus Christ. What a Shame! May God forgive us of doing this wrong. We only made ourselves look even worse in the eyes of the world. We even made enemies because of it which makes it harder to bring them to the Lord.

Over the years such conditions have continued to grow even worse in our society. Recently we have seen the promotion of "wokeism", the emergence of the LGBT+, the gay agenda, transgenderism and same-sex marriages. There are even churches that are embracing these abominations. Such churches fail to recognize that they are under the influence of the spirit of antichrist, and as such, they are preparing themselves to submit to the Antichrist when he comes on the scene.

All of this is actually the fulfillment of the prophetic word given through the apostle Paul, as cited three pages previous, in 2 Timothy 3:1-5. The result of man being the head of the church produces the "other" church that is full of man's ways, reason, programs, organization and carnality. The life of man is seen in such a church, not the Life of Christ.

People think the wickedness described by Paul in the referenced scripture is about those in the world; WRONG! As stated previously; this behavior is in those who have a "form of godliness"; and what did Paul say how we are to react to them? "From such turn away"!

The problem of the church in which man is the Head is, "denying the power thereof". The true power in the church is that which comes down from the Head – Christ; and by His Spirit that He gives to His true called and ordained servants.

> Matthew 28:18-20 – *And Jesus came and spake unto them, saying, All power is given unto me in heaven and in earth. Go ye therefore, and teach all nations, baptizing them in the name of the Father, and of the Son, and of the Holy Ghost: teaching them to observe all things whatsoever I have commanded you: and, lo, I am with you alway, even unto the end of the world. Amen.*

When man is Head of the church, then Christ's power and authority is denied the ability to flow, hindered or prevented. With Christ as the Head of the Church, His power and authority is evident. His power is His Life (zoe), and His Life changes our lives by conforming us to His image. His Headship supplies that life changing power. (I am not referring to the salvation experience; you can't be in the true church unless you are "born-again". I'm talking about the transformation and conforming to Him which is to occur as we live our life according to His Word after being "saved" as a new creation.)

> 2 Corinthians 7:15 – *Therefore if any man be in Christ, he is a new creature: old things are passed away; behold, all things are become new.*

This is what the "other" church needs now: His life in it, by His headship over it. Without His Headship all we have to work with is what man can provide. Thus we have man's fleshly weaknesses evident which is what the apostle Paul described in His second letter to Timothy.

An indictment of the other church can be made in these last days, charging it with gross sin and the carnal ways of man. Consider what Paul wrote to the church in Rome; it sounds similar to what he wrote in his second letter to Timothy.

> Romans 13:11-14 – *And that, knowing the time, that now it is high time to awake out of sleep: for now is our salvation nearer than when we believed. The night is far spent, the day is at hand: let us therefore cast off the works of darkness, and let us put on the armour of light. Let us walk honestly, as in the day; not in rioting and drunkenness, not in chambering and wantonness, not in strife and envying. But put ye on the Lord Jesus Christ, and make not provision for the flesh, to fulfil the lusts thereof.*

It appears that much of the other church missed the purpose and meaning of repentance and water baptism. Baptism in water is the symbolic representation of death to self (the fleshly carnal nature), burial of that old nature, and resurrection unto a new life. Water baptism is not for babies, nor is it sprinkling, as is done in the other church. True baptism requires that we repent of our sins, deny self with its sinful carnal nature and burying it; thus immersion fully under water which is symbolic of burying it. Then we arise from the water into a changed new (zoe) life that is now under the Lordship of Jesus Christ whose life now flows through us.

> Galatians 2:20 – *I am crucified with Christ: nevertheless I live; yet not I, but Christ liveth in me: and the life which I now live in the flesh I live by the faith of the Son of God, who loved me, and gave himself for me.*

> Colossians 3:1-3 – *If ye then be risen with Christ, seek those things which are above, where Christ sitteth on the right hand of God. Set your affection on things above, not on things on the earth. For ye are dead, and your life is hid with Christ in God.*

Water baptism is a public acknowledgment of repentance. Repentance means change. If there is no change then there is no repentance; then any ceremonial baptism is an ineffective show. Then there is no new life, no Zoe life of Christ! As a result the old life of the natural carnal man remains to be seen; as in the other church. Does this sound harsh? Check scripture, it says that a new life, a changed life, is the evidence of Jesus Christ in a person. The evidence of a changed life must be seen.

> 2 Corinthians 5:17 – *Therefore if any man be in Christ, he is a new creature: old things are passed away; behold, all things are become new.*

Church! It's time to repent! Repent of playing church with man's artificial copy – the other church. Repent of having man's headship over the church. We need to get man, and ourselves, out of the way and let CHRIST BE THE HEAD OVER ALL THINGS TO THE CHURCH.

> Ephesians 1:19-23 – *and what is the exceeding greatness of his power to us-ward who believe, according to the working of his mighty power, which he wrought in Christ, when he raised him from the dead, and set him at his own right hand in the heavenly places, far above all principality, and power, and might, and dominion, and every name that is named, not only in this world, but also in that which is to come: and hath put all things under his feet, and gave him to be the head over all things to the church, which is his body, the fullness of him that filleth all in all.*

We need to humble ourselves before Him and seek Him for His divine directives on how to build and run His church. We need leadership in our churches that will not do anything until they seek Him and hear from Him!

Jesus said he would build His church; so let's let Him do it. We need to hear from Him, and then do what He commands. Many Christians today do not even believe that the Lord speaks to His people. They have not been taught that He speaks into our spirit; and many don't have spiritual ears to hear; neither does their leadership.

Now it is time to "hear what the Spirit says to the churches". Now it is time to repent of being the other church. Now it is time to allow Him to be the HEAD OF HIS CHURCH!

PART FOUR: THE PATTERN OF DIVINE ORDER FOR LEADERSHIP IN HIS CHURCH

> 1 Corinthians 11:3 – *But I would have you know, that the head of every man is Christ; and the head of the woman is the man; and the head of Christ is God.*

Since the church is the Body (or family) of Christ, and is composed of men and women, Christ's headship in relation to each individual must be established before it can be experienced in the church corporately. The family unit of husband and wife is the basic unit of what composes the church. Christ's headship must be established and maintained in the family unit or it cannot possibly exist in the church. The family unit, of a believing husband and wife, is the Body of Christ in its most finite detail.

> Matthew 18:20 – *For where two or three are gathered together in my name, there am I in the midst of them.*

It is in the family unit where Christ wants to manifest Himself and be seen by others, particularly by their children. The family unit is the starting place for all ministry; for all practicing of our faith; for proving the truth of God and His Word in trials and testing; and for living out the commands and the Will of God.

The starting place for the family is the recognition of who is in charge, who has the authority, and who has the final responsibility. This is divine order that is to prevail throughout all eternity. The Body of Christ needs to live and show this to the world in this present day.

If any one position in the order is out of place, missing, or in the wrong place, it interrupts or short circuits the flow of divine authority with all of its divine benefits. The things of God are then hindered from being experienced in our lives when the divine order is violated. We then suffer from the consequences; the loss of the loving, caring, providing, protecting and blessed covering that emanates from the father that is to flow to his children.

This same loss is experienced in the corporate Body of Christ, the church. I have heard pastors preach that the church is to build strong families; however, it is strong families that actually form the church. The church, which is the assembly of families, can only reflect what the families have in Christ.

Divine order is very simple. It all stems from God the Father; He is the Head of Christ. It is to Him that His Son is submitted. The Son did nothing but what He sees the Father do; likewise He says only what He hears the Father say.

> John 5:19 & 30 – *Then answered Jesus and said unto them, Verily, verily, I say unto you, The Son can do nothing of himself, but what he seeth the Father do: for what things soever he doeth, these also doeth the Son likewise. ... I can of mine own self do nothing: as I hear, I judge: and my judgment is just; because I seek not mine own will, but the will of the Father which hath sent me.*

> John 8:28 – *Then said Jesus unto them, When ye have lifted up the Son of man, then shall ye know that I am he, and that I do nothing of myself; but as my Father hath taught me, I speak these things.*

Jesus demonstrated to us how to be in submission to the Head of divine authority. "The Head of Christ is God, His Heavenly Father". "The head of every man is Christ". This is the Word of God! This means that men are to have a relationship with Christ as Christ had with His Father.

Just imagine how wonderful family life would be if every husband did nothing but what they saw Jesus do; if they said nothing but what they heard Jesus say. Just imagine how wonderful the church would be if every man followed this pattern. This is the Will of God, yet we don't do it. We still live as though it's "every man for himself", even in the church.

Then we see that "the head of the woman is the man". This sure does not fit in our society today. We even have laws that dictate just the opposite to the divine order of God. Just imagine how wonderful marriages would be if divine order was followed; if every woman would do nothing but what she saw her husband did as an example for her, or said nothing but that which he set the example of what to say.

In the natural we see this as dictatorship, but it is no such thing if actual divine headship is followed. A woman's submission to her husband should be just like that of her husband's submission to Christ; just as Christ's to His Father. (Note: submission is earned by love. When a husband truly loves his wife, she recognizes his love and willingly submits to him because of that love.) The divine qualities of God's love, care, protection, guidance and provision would flow through each down to the children. What LOVE! What JOY! What divine qualities would be experienced and evident for all in the world to see.

We must also recognize that when we practice true headship and divine order, then we pass on the responsibility to the next higher level. This takes much burden off of each of us and ultimately places it on to the next higher in rank, and ultimately to our Heavenly Father.

> 1 Peter 5:7 – *casting all your care upon him; for he careth for you.*

The burdens, cares and responsibilities go up through the headship, and the blessings come back down from the Head to us. This is God's way. Can you see what we are missing by not doing it God's divine way in obedience to Him.

The very first quality that divine headship passes down the ladder is love. God is love; and His love gets passed to Christ, from Christ to man, from man to the woman, and falls on the children. What a life for all of us to experience and walk in God's kind of love. Then we also become recipients of the rest of God's character and nature as described in the Fruit of the Spirit.

> Galatians 5:22-23 – *But the fruit of the Spirit is love, joy, peace, longsuffering, gentleness, goodness, faith, meekness, temperance: against such there is no law.*

All of these virtues are passed on by following the principle of headship as laid out in the beginning of this Section in 1 Corinthians 11:3.

Operating under divine headship offers the best of life that could be possibly obtained. Yet natural man thinks of it as being in bondage, enslaved, forced to be under an oppressive hand. God's hand is not oppressive but uplifting and upholding.

The divine order of headship extends to the children in every believer's family.

> Colossians 3:20 – *Children, obey your parents in all things: for this is well pleasing unto the Lord.*

Ephesians 6:1-3 – *Children, obey your parents in the Lord: for this is right. Honour thy father and mother; (which is the first commandment with promise;) that it may be well with thee, and thou mayest live long on the earth.*

This proves that divine order and headship is best for everyone. So why don't we practice it? Satan, our enemy, rejects this divine headship, and instead, fosters rebellion, iniquity and doing your own thing; after the pattern he established in defiance of God. Thus we have the other church that man is building, out of divine order, but under Satan's influence.

We need to instruct the church how to recognize divine order of headship and practice it as was demonstrated by Jesus. Thus our families will be in divine order and blessed by God; then also will our churches begin to walk in the glory of the Lord as His Headship begins to direct us. What a beautiful Body of Christ we will see when we obey His Word and walk in the divine order of the Headship of Christ.

Most of the other church is lacking God's divine order of leadership. The requirements for leadership in the church are clearly spelled out.

1 Timothy 3:1-7 – *This is a true saying, If a man desire the office of a bishop, he desireth a good work. A bishop then must be blameless, the husband of one wife, vigilant, sober, of good behaviour, given to hospitality, apt to teach; not given to wine, no striker, not greedy of filthy lucre; but patient, not a brawler, not covetous; one that ruleth well his own house, having his children in subjection with all gravity; (for if a man know not how to rule his own house, how shall he take care of the church of God?) Not a novice, lest being lifted up with pride he fall into the condemnation of the devil. Moreover he must have a good report of them which are without; lest he fall into reproach and the snare of the devil.*

The Roman Church doesn't allow its priests to have a wife, which means that he has no children or a family unit in which to demonstrate his qualification for leadership. He lacks a family unit! Thus he is not qualified to be in leadership of a true church; but he can be in leadership of the other church that man is building.

The following is another example of "out of order" leadership that can be found a few of the other churches: a woman as a pastor of a church is totally out of divine order. This is totally contrary to the views of our current society and social norm. However, consider the qualifications listed in God's Word:

> 1 Timothy 3:2 – *A bishop then must be blameless, the husband of one wife,*

The question now is, why can't a woman be considered for leadership over a church? This goes back to what happened in the Garden and the divine role that God placed in women.

> 1 Timothy 2:11-15 – *Let the woman learn in silence with all subjection. But I suffer not a woman to teach, nor to usurp authority over the man, but to be in silence. For Adam was first formed, then Eve. And Adam was not deceived, but the woman being deceived was in the transgression. Notwithstanding she shall be saved in childbearing, if they continue in faith and charity and holiness with sobriety.*

Here we see that the original sin was ascribed to the woman who allowed herself to be deceived by Satan. Adam, her husband, was not deceived: his was a deliberate act that most do not understand. We need to consider what Adam was like before sin destroyed the life they had. Adam was made in the image and likeness of God. He had all of God's character and nature, which included God's kind of love for his wife. Adam also knew that God had a plan of redemption because it was established before the foundation of the world, (human society).

> Ephesians 1:4 – *according as he hath chosen us in him before the foundation of the world, that we should be holy and without blame before him in love:*
>
> 1 Peter 1:19-20 – *but with the precious blood of Christ, as of a lamb without blemish and without spot: who verily , but was manifest in these last times for you,*

We need to understand that Eve committed an act of lust which results in sin.

> James 1:15 – *Then when lust hath conceived, it bringeth forth sin: and sin, when it is finished, bringeth forth death.*

However, Adam committed an act of love as he took upon himself her act of defiance knowing that God already has a plan of redemption. Thus Adam can be referred to as a shadow of, or a type of Christ being a figure of His that was to come.

> Romans 5:14 – *Nevertheless death reigned from Adam to Moses, even over them that had not sinned after the similitude of Adam's transgression, who is the figure of him that was to come.*

Here is something to consider: most preachers blame Adam, the husband, for the entrance of original sin into the world. What we fail to realize that the woman was also called Adam: it was she that brought sin into the world. God referred them both as Adam because God considered them to be one, as husband and wife.

> Genesis 5:1-2 – *This is the book of the generations of Adam. In the day that God created man, in the likeness of God made he him; male and female created he them; and blessed them, and called their name Adam, in the day when they were created.*

God named her Adam: this is the Adam that is blamed for original sin. God did not name her Eve, it was Adam who named her Eve.

> Genesis 3:20 – *And Adam called his wife's name Eve; because she was the mother of all living.*

People also fail to realize that it was God who shed the first blood for the first atonement for sin when He made coats of animal skins to over their nakedness.

Genesis 3: 21 – *Unto Adam also and to his wife did the* LORD *God make coats of skins, and clothed them.* (Note: God refers them as husband and wife.)

Thus, it was God who initiated the shedding of blood for sin, as established before the foundation of the world. This was carried on until Jesus was placed on the cross to put an end to the animal blood sacrifice for sin. Adam and Eve taught this to their children, Cain and Able, but Cain refused and did his own thing.

So we see that in proper divine order, women are not to take, or usurp authority, or assume leadership over man or the church due to original sin. Consider this: it was a woman who was the first to see spiritual death; but it was also a woman who was the first to see spiritual life; that was Mary at the tomb. However, women are permitted to teach, preach and even to prophecy as enabled by the Holy Spirit.

Acts 2:17-18 – *And it shall come to pass in the last days, saith God, I will pour out of my Spirit upon all flesh: and your sons and your daughters shall prophesy, and your young men shall see visions, and your old men shall dream dreams: and on my servants and on my handmaidens I will pour out in those days of my Spirit; and they shall prophesy:*

Acts 21:8-9 – *And the next day we that were of Paul's company departed, and came unto Cæsarea: and we entered into the house of Philip the evangelist, which was one of the seven; and abode with him. And the same man had four daughters, virgins, which did prophesy.*

Thus we see that women are able to speak and serve as the Lord directs, but they are not to *"usurp authority over the man"*, or be in positions of leadership over man, but to be in submission in divine order. As a result of original sin, women are not to be head over man, or a church, because it would defy God's divine order of authority.

Too many churches are conforming to the whims of our corrupted society, educational system and demonically inspired political environment. The standard for living is the Word of God and conformity to Jesus Christ! Church – WAKE UP!

Romans 13:11-14 – *And that, knowing the time, that now it is high time to awake out of sleep: for now is our salvation nearer than when we believed. The night is far spent, the day is at hand: let us therefore cast off the works of darkness, and let us put on the armour of light. Let us walk honestly, as in the day; not in rioting and drunkenness, not in chambering and wantonness, not in strife and envying. But put ye on the Lord Jesus Christ, and make not provision for the flesh, to fulfil the lusts thereof.*

Note that the apostle Paul wrote this passage to the church in Rome addressing carnal behavior that needed to be put off.

Chapter 5

WHAT IS THE TRUE CHURCH AND WHAT IS ITS PURPOSE

THE CHURCH THAT CHRIST IS RETURNING FOR

Most believers understand that the church is the "gathered", "called together" or "the assembled unto God", which is the meaning of the Greek word *ekklesia* and translated *church* in the Bible. So by definition we see that the church is the meeting together of the followers of the Lord Jesus Christ. They are called out from the world, separated from it, (meaning they are holy); and gathered or assembled unto Him for worship, and the building themselves up to spiritual maturity in His image.

What the church is can more easily be understood if we know its purpose. When the question is asked of people, "What is the purpose of the church", there are different answers given depending on the beliefs and practices of each individual church. One will say it is "to save souls"; another will add, "to be a witness and a light to the world"; other answers include, "to fellowship"; "to worship God"; and "to grow in grace", etc.

All these answers are good, but they show a lack of understanding of the true purpose of assembling together. We need to step back to see the whole plan and work of God in and for the church. Once you see this, the works of the church, which were described in the typical answers, will be more eagerly performed by its people.

Many people seem to view the church as a holding pen that is to increase in size and numbers waiting for the return of Christ; then it is no longer useful or needed. This is a greatly limited view of the church and prevents it from fulfilling its true objective.

We need to see that the purpose and plan of God is eternal and does not end at the rapture/resurrection and return of Christ. The church is a source of spiritual birthing, growth and maturing. It is to prepare us to rule and reign with Him in His kingdom throughout all of eternity over all of His domain.

Just being saved or born-again into God's kingdom through Jesus Christ does not equip us to rule the universe of His creation with Him. We must mature into His image and likeness; having in us His character and nature so that we are fully equipped to represent Him in all of His creation. Preparing us for this eternal rule is the purpose of the church and the scriptures. The scriptures lay down clearly the principle upon which the Kingdom of God operates.

First we need to recognize what the Kingdom of God does not permit or consist of.

> Galatians 5:19-21 – *Now the works of the flesh are manifest, which are these; Adultery, fornication, uncleanness, lasciviousness, idolatry, witchcraft, hatred, variance, emulations, wrath, strife, seditions, heresies, envyings, murders, drunkenness, revellings, and such like: of the which I tell you before, as I have also told you in time past, that they which do such things shall not inherit the kingdom of God.*

Scripture also tells us what the Kingdom of God does consist of and the conformity that is required to be in it.

> Galatians 5:22-25 – *But the fruit of the Spirit is love, joy, peace, longsuffering, gentleness, goodness, faith, meekness, temperance: against such there is no law.*

It is through the church that we are to learn and develop the character traits that lead us to overcome the world and fleshly lusts. It is where we grow spiritually to be able to live and walk in the Spirit as true overcomers.

> Galatians 5:24-25 – *And they that are Christ's have crucified the flesh with the affections and lusts. If we live in the Spirit, let us also walk in the Spirit.*

Romans 8:1, 9 & 14 – *There is therefore now no condemnation to them which are in Christ Jesus, who walk not after the flesh, but after the Spirit. ... But ye are not in the flesh, but in the Spirit, if so be that the Spirit of God dwell in you. Now if any man have not the Spirit of Christ, he is none of his. ... For as many as are led by the Spirit of God, they are the sons of God.*

How is the church going to develop His character and nature, (the Fruit of the Spirit), in His believers? After Jesus ascended to the Father, and after the church was established on the Day of Pentecost, He gave specific Gift Ministries to those He called. They are to work for this very purpose in the churches.

Ephesians 4:10-13 – *He that descended is the same also that ascended up far above all heavens, that he might fill all things.) And he gave some, apostles; and some, prophets; and some, evangelists; and some, pastors and teachers; for the perfecting of the saints, for the work of the ministry, for the edifying of the body of Christ: till we all come in the unity of the faith, and of the knowledge of the Son of God, unto a perfect man, unto the measure of the stature of the fulness of Christ:*

Not only did the Lord set up certain types of ministers, but He also gave supernatural Gifts of the Spirit to aid in our spiritual growth and development in Christ.

1 Corinthians 12:28 – *And God hath set some in the church, first apostles, secondarily prophets, thirdly teachers, after that miracles, then gifts of healings, helps, governments, diversities of tongues.*

The other church generally does not function or serve the purpose of God in how it operates. The main reason is that the other church rejects the five Gift Ministries as well as rejecting the nine Gifts of the Holy Spirit. These lacking spiritual elements mean that the other church is not functioning as a true church; it lacks the God given ability to complete the followers into the full stature and image of Christ.

True believers are to take on, put on, and conform to the image of Christ. It is His Christ-likeness, godliness, holiness, and righteousness in us that will rule creation through all eternity. This character and nature is to be developed now, in this earthly life. We are not to wait until we get to heaven to begin to conform to His image; it's done here and now!

In addition to the future plans God has for His Church, there is a current function that it is to perform. The true church is being used of God to demonstrate to all of the world, and all the rest of creation, which includes God's hosts of angels, and particularly to Satan and his angles and demons, (called principalities and powers), the blessings of faithfulness and obedience. Satan and his followers then see and observe God's blessings on our spiritual growth and they take great offense at it as it is on full display by the true church.

> Ephesians 3:10-11 – *to the intent that now unto the principalities and powers in heavenly places might be known by the church the manifold wisdom of God, according to the eternal purpose which he purposed in Christ Jesus our Lord:*

Part of God's plan for the church is to show Satan and his followers the rewards God gives for faithfulness and obedience which the devil and his gang did not show to God, but rebelled against Him. The church stands as an object lesson of the sovereignty, goodness and love of Almighty God to all of creation.

> 1 Corinthians 6:2-3 – *Do ye not know that the saints shall judge the world? and if the world shall be judged by you, are ye unworthy to judge the smallest matters? Know ye not that we shall judge angels? how much more things that pertain to this life?*

Since this is part of God's purpose for the true church, it behooves us to be faithful and obedient and allow the Lord to do His work in and through us. What we, in the true church, need to be concerned about is our responsibility and fulfillment of what He desires of us as His children.

The true church is His Holy Temple, His spiritual dwelling place. In simple terms, this is what the church is. We are His Holy house, the place on earth where He abides by His Spirit; through whom He reveals Himself and manifests His character and nature, along with His ability and authority. It is also where He manifests His presence.

> Matthew 18:20 – *For where two or three are gathered together in my name, there am I in the midst of them.*

> 1 Corinthians 3:16-17 – *Know ye not that ye are the temple of God, and that the Spirit of God dwelleth in you? If any man defile the temple of God, him shall God destroy; for the temple of God is holy, which temple ye are.*

> 1 Corinthians 6:19-20 – *What? know ye not that your body is the temple of the Holy Ghost which is in you, which ye have of God, and ye are not your own? For ye are bought with a price: therefore glorify God in your body, and in your spirit, which are God's.*

How are we His dwelling place? It is by His Spirit that is welcomed into our spirit, abiding (finding a favorable environment) and living His life in the believer. This is all done by faith, believing and accepting what God has provided.

> Galatians 4:6 – *And because ye are sons, God hath sent forth the Spirit of his Son into your hearts, crying, Abba, Father.*

Then His presence begins to fill our spirit and His life is then seen in us; thus we become the image of Christ, being like Him and glorifying Him.

> Colossians 1:27 – *to whom God would make known what is the riches of the glory of this mystery among the Gentiles; which is Christ in you, the hope of glory:*

> 1 John 3:1-3 – *Behold, what manner of love the Father hath bestowed upon us, that we should be called the sons of God: therefore the world knoweth us not, because it knew him not. Beloved, now are we the sons of God, and it doth not yet appear what we shall be: but we know that, when he shall appear, we*

shall be like him; for we shall see him as he is. And every man
that hath this hope in him purifieth himself, even as he is pure.

Obviously there is a purifying process that He, by His Spirit, takes us through in order to conform us to His image as sons of God. This is the process called being made a "disciple".

Romans 12:1-2 – *I beseech you therefore, brethren, by the mercies of God, that ye present your bodies a living sacrifice, holy, acceptable unto God, which is your reasonable service. And be not conformed to this world: but be ye transformed by the renewing of your mind, that ye may prove what is that good, and acceptable, and perfect, will of God.*

Being made a disciple requires us to put off fleshly and worldly pursuits. Although salvation is a free gift, bought and paid for by Jesus on the cross, being a disciple will cost you, and not many in the church have been taught about it, and others have not been willing to go through it.

Luke 9:23 – *And he said to them all, If any man will come after me, let him deny himself, and take up his cross daily, and follow me.* (This topic will be covered in more detail in Chapter 9 – The Role of the Cross.)

Churches have not seen much of this manifestation of His presence except in a few places in recent times. Even those manifestations have been rejected by many churches because it does not conform to their religious traditions and doctrinal biases.

On this topic a warning is needed. There are, and will be false manifestations of supernatural signs and wonders that are claimed to be manifestations of His presence.

Matthew 24:24 – *For there shall arise false Christs, and false prophets, and shall shew great signs and wonders; insomuch that, if it were possible, they shall deceive the very elect.*

Such manifestations are of the enemy who wants to deceive and draw people away from the truth. Satan can imitate the supernatural gifts of the spirit; that is why Jesus told us "by their fruit ye shall know them"; that is the Fruit of the Spirit which is the character and nature of God. Please recognize that Satan loves to put on a show because people are drawn to the spectacular. God, by His presence, does not put on a show. When the presence of God manifests things change; there is genuine healing, deliverance, revelation of Christ and His Kingdom, etc. That does not happen when the devil puts on a show; no change happens to anyone.

There is a reason why we have not seen much of the manifestation of His presence in His people because much of the church has not realized its true purpose and the plan of God for it. It has not been taught or properly prepared for. In too many cases it has rejected the ministry of those who are commissioned of God to complete His work in the saints. This is about those of the full "five-fold" ministry gifts that Jesus provided as listed in Ephesians 4, (repeated again due to its importance.)

> Ephesians 4:11-13 – *And he gave some, apostles; and some, prophets; and some, evangelists; and some, pastors and teachers; for the perfecting of the saints, for the work of the ministry, for the edifying of the body of Christ: till we all come in the unity of the faith, and of the knowledge of the Son of God, unto a perfect man, unto the measure of the stature of the fulness of Christ:*

All five gift ministries are required as they labor to form Christ in the believers.

> Galatians 4:19 – *My little children, of whom I travail in birth again until Christ be formed in you,*

The typical church and its leadership actually quench the supernatural moving of the Holy Spirit through His gifts and ministries. They don't expect Him to move in their midst because they either deny Him access, or deny anyone else who would attempt to operate as inspired by the Holy Spirit; they don't allow time for Him to move as it does not fit into their order of service, or they have time constraints due to their use of TV and the media. Their service has to go by a script that does not include the Holy Spirit to operate.

Much of the other church even denies that the operation of the Holy Spirit is in effect in these days. So how can they expect to see His presence or

His purpose achieved in and through their church or through their people? Such are those who have a form of godliness but deny the power thereof.

> 2 Timothy 3:5 & 7 – *having a form of godliness, but denying the power thereof: from such turn away. … ever learning, and never able to come to the knowledge of the truth.*

This describes the "other" church which has adopted false doctrines and embraced modern day heresies. (Note Paul's instruction regarding this is simply, "*from such turn away*".

How do we become His dwelling place or temple? How does His Holy Spirit live in us? This all occurs in the spirit realm, often referred to the "fourth dimension", the realm we cannot see or understand, but accept by faith as it exists just like heaven. This is the realm in which spirit beings (angels and demons) and the Spirit of God operate.

We humans are three-part beings made after God's image consisting of spirit, soul and body. Mankind has a body, a soul and a spirit. The body is the physical package for the soul and spirit. The body is like an envelope that contains a letter, and it is the letter that has the real eternal value. The soul is the mind with its intellect, personality and emotions. The soul is what makes a person an individual, different from everybody else; even what makes identical twins different. The soul is the real you! Each person has a spirit which is the life force within that sustains us. If the spirit leaves the body, that life force is gone, and the soul goes with it, that person's body then dies. It's like opening the envelop and removing the letter and discarding the envelop.

> James 2:26 – *For as the body without the spirit is dead, so faith without works is dead also.*

Death is a separation; physical death is when the soul and spirit leave the physical body. In addition to physical death, there is a spiritual death also. Spiritual death is when the human soul and spirit is separated from God. This is the whole purpose of redemption: it is when, through faith and acceptance of Jesus work on the cross to redeem man from the penalty of sin, that man's relationship with God is fully restored – redeemed! No more separation due to unforgiven sin.

Isaiah 59:2 – *but your iniquities have separated between you and your God, and your sins have hid his face from you, that he will not hear.*

The separated soul and spirit need to be re-made alive unto God – revived. This is the experience of being "born-again" or "saved" from sin. This is not a physical process, but a spiritual one accomplished by faith and obedience.

John 3:3-8 – *Jesus answered and said unto him, Verily, verily, I say unto thee, Except a man be born again, he cannot see the kingdom of God. Nicodemus saith unto him, How can a man be born when he is old? can he enter the second time into his mother's womb, and be born? Jesus answered, Verily, verily, I say unto thee, Except a man be born of water and of the Spirit, he cannot enter into the kingdom of God. That which is born of the flesh is flesh; and that which is born of the Spirit is spirit. Marvel not that I said unto thee, Ye must be born again. The wind bloweth where it listeth, and thou hearest the sound thereof, but canst not tell whence it cometh, and whither it goeth: so is every one that is born of the Spirit.*

This spiritual rebirth is the beginning of a new life cycle, a new growth process unto full maturity when Christ is fully formed in the new believer.

Matthew 18:2-4 – *And Jesus called a little child unto him, and set him in the midst of them, and said, Verily I say unto you, Except ye be converted, and become as little children, ye shall not enter into the kingdom of heaven. Whosoever therefore shall humble himself as this little child, the same is greatest in the kingdom of heaven.*

Jesus came to bring His kind of eternal life (zoe) to mankind. This is a type of life that man did not have. This is "spirit" life; eternal life as God has it. The purpose of the true church is to grow and mature in this spiritual life, as well as to declare and represent this spiritual life to the rest the world. The other church does not do this but only reinforces itself as man's organization and tries to add to its population.

Jesus did not come to bring soulish or material abundance of life as mankind already has it and does this for himself. Unfortunately, there are preachers whose ministry focuses material wealth and prosperity; they are part of the other church.

> John 10:10 – *The thief cometh not, but for to steal, and to kill, and to destroy: I am come that they might have life* (zoe), *and that they might have it* (zoe) *more abundantly* (than bios or psuche).

The three parts of a human being are scripturally described using the Greek words: 1) *bios,* for biological or physical life form; 2) *psuche,* for soulish life, manner or style of life and social positioning; 3) *zoe,* spiritual life force and the eternal life as God has it. Natural man already possesses bios and psuche, but does not have zoe without Jesus Christ. Jesus came to bring, or more properly, to restore the zoe that was lost in the Garden due to sin. Once the zoe life is birthed in a person he is a new creation in the spirit:

> 2 Corinthians 5:17 – *Therefore if any man be in Christ, he is a new creature: old things are passed away; behold, all things are become new.*

After a natural birth the normal process is to be fed and learn to grow to maturity; to develop that bios and psuche life. It is the same after being re-born in the spirit life, we are to grow and mature in the spirit. The problem is that Christians are so busy and preoccupied with their physical needs in life that they neglect their spiritual development and maturity. Jesus gave a warning of what happens to those whose focus is on the material cares of this life in the parable of the sower of seed.

> Matthew 13:20-23 – *But he that received the seed into stony places, the same is he that heareth the word, and anon with joy receiveth it; yet hath he not root in himself, but dureth for a while: for when tribulation or persecution ariseth because of the word, by and by he is offended. He also that received seed among the thorns is he that heareth the word; and the care of this world, and the deceitfulness of riches, choke the word, and he becometh unfruitful. But he that received seed into the good*

ground is he that heareth the word, and understandeth it; which also beareth fruit, and bringeth forth, some an hundredfold, some sixty, some thirty.

The purpose of the church is feed and nurture this spiritual life, and to bring it to full maturity – *"to the stature of the fullness of the image of Christ"*. Instead, the other church indulges in almost everything else. Those who assume they are of the true church spend more effort developing the psuche, the soulish man, by ministering to intellect and imposing rules, rites and conformity rather than developing life in the Spirit. (Note: focusing on the soulish life is actually enhancing the carnal fleshly lusts of mankind.)

Romans 13:14 – *But put ye on the Lord Jesus Christ, and make not provision for the flesh, to fulfil the lusts thereof.*

Again, the purpose of the church is to build the spirit life of man by building the life of Christ (the Fruit of the Spirit) in the believers. This spirit life is based on the principles of the Kingdom of God. (Note: the foundation of the Kingdom of God is LOVE.) Again, we find that these building blocks are known as the Fruit of the Spirit and are listed in Galatians 5:

Galatians 5:22-23 – *But the fruit of the Spirit is love, joy, peace, longsuffering, gentleness, goodness, faith, meekness, temperance: against such there is no law.*

Peter listed these same principles in reverse order as building blocks starting with Faith and concluding with Love; progressive steps in building to maturity.

2 Peter 1:3-8 – *Grace and peace be multiplied unto you through the knowledge of God, and of Jesus our Lord, according as his divine power hath given unto us all things that pertain unto life and godliness, through the knowledge of him that hath called us to glory and virtue: whereby are given unto us exceeding great and precious promises: that by these ye might be partakers of the divine nature, having escaped the corruption that is in the world through lust. And beside this, giving all diligence, add to your faith virtue; and to virtue knowledge;*

*and to knowledge temperance; and to temperance patience; and
to patience godliness; and to godliness brotherly kindness; and
to brotherly kindness charity* (LOVE). *For if these things be in
you, and abound, they make you that ye shall neither be barren
nor unfruitful in the knowledge of our Lord Jesus Christ. But he
that lacketh these things is blind, and cannot see afar off, and
hath forgotten that he was purged from his old sins.*

We need to recognize the importance of what Peter is telling us in this passage. First is what is provided and multiplied through growing in knowledge of God and Jesus. We are partaking of His divine nature, becoming Christ-like, as we mature in the building blocks of the Fruit of the Spirit, (His divine nature). It is those who are mature in the Lord who are truly fruitful unto Him for His purpose. Those who fail to grow in this grace lack His divine nature and are considered to be blind, limited in their spiritual perspective, and are devoid of His divine nature.

When His character and nature are built in us; when we conform to His image; when Christ is seen in us, then the true church will have matured and the manifestation of His presence will be seen. The manifestation of His presence is His glory that will fill the assembly that is prepared to see Him! (Note: the word glory in the Greek is *doxa* and refers to one's dignity, character and nature).

> 2 Chronicles 5:14 – ... *for the glory of the* LORD *had filled the house of God.*

Scripture tells us that His Glory will be seen and the true church will be full of His Glory; it will be the glorious church He is coming for.

> Ephesians 5:27 – *that he might present it to himself a glorious church, not having spot, or wrinkle, or any such thing; but that it should be holy and without blemish.*

The early church had to be reminded of the need for spiritual maturity because it is so important. They were encouraged to get their priorities right and focus their attention on the true purpose and plan of God.

Hebrews 5:11-6;2 – *Of whom we have many things to say, and hard to be uttered, seeing ye are dull of hearing. For when for the time ye ought to be teachers, ye have need that one teach you again which be the first principles of the oracles of God; and are become such as have need of milk, and not of strong meat. For every one that useth milk is unskilful in the word of righteousness: for he is a babe. But strong meat belongeth to them that are of full age, even those who by reason of use have their senses exercised to discern both good and evil,* (able to identify what is of God and what is of the devil). *Therefore leaving the principles of the doctrine of Christ, let us go on unto perfection* (completion or finishing)*; not laying again the foundation of repentance from dead works, and of faith toward God, of the doctrine of baptisms, and of laying on of hands, and of resurrection of the dead, and of eternal judgment.*

We are to go deeper in our knowledge of God and not keep rehashing the same basic principles over and over as is done by many in church leadership. Such lack of going deeper in the Lord means believers are not growing to maturity. This is just one reason why false doctrines and demonic behavior is tolerated and even accepted in some churches. It is because they fail to *"have their senses exercised to discern both good and evil"* as stated in Hebrew 5:14 above.

CONCLUSION:

The purpose of the church is to build the spirit life in believers so that they will conform to the image and likeness of Christ. Thus we are to be prepared to rule and reign over the earth with Him when HE comes. Part of this preparation includes learning to hear and live a spirit led life here in this vile society and being overcomers of it, even in the days of calamity that precede Christ's return. Being separated from the world by His character and nature will put us at odds the most of society. That is why maturity is necessary to have God's Love so rooted in us that we stand as lights in this present darkness. We are called of the Lord to be the light in the darkness; it is His light that shines in and through those of us who are of the true church.

Philippians 2:15 – *that ye may be blameless and harmless, the sons of God, without rebuke, in the midst of a crooked and perverse nation, among whom ye shine as lights in the world;*

Ephesians 3:14-21 – *For this cause I bow my knees unto the Father of our Lord Jesus Christ, of whom the whole family in heaven and earth is named, that he would grant you, according to the riches of his glory, to be strengthened with might by his Spirit in the inner man; that Christ may dwell in your hearts by faith; that ye, being rooted and grounded in love, may be able to comprehend with all saints what is the breadth, and length, and depth, and height; and to know the love of Christ, which passeth knowledge, that ye might be filled with all the fulness of God. Now unto him that is able to do exceeding abundantly above all that we ask or think, according to the power that worketh in us, unto him be glory in the church by Christ Jesus throughout all ages, world without end. Amen.*

Chapter 6

THE WOLVES IN CHURCH LEADERSHIP

Who To Beware Of And How To Recognize The Wolves In Ministry

Both Jesus and the apostle Paul gave us warnings about those who would become false ministers, preachers and teachers; those who would have the nature of a wolf. (They used the analogy of the sheep and wolf to describe the adversarial relationship.)

Leadership in the other church is made up of very diverse personalities, characters and abilities. There is no set standard for leadership in the man-made church as each denominational organization sets their own requirements. Thus there are those who enter the ministry whose motive is not pure to start with, or is subject to change with conditions, or due to human lust and frailty. Many have, or eventually develop, the wolf nature.

The apostle Peter admonished church leadership as to the kind of motive and character they are to have in ministry.

> 1 Peter 5:1-3 – *The elders which are among you I exhort, who am also an elder, and a witness of the sufferings of Christ, and also a partaker of the glory that shall be revealed: feed the flock of God which is among you, taking the oversight thereof, not by constraint, but willingly; not for filthy lucre, but of a ready mind; neither as being lords over God's heritage, but being ensamples to the flock.*

Jesus set the standard for those who are His servants in ministry.

Mark 10:42-45 – *But Jesus called them to him, and saith unto them, Ye know that they which are accounted to rule over the Gentiles exercise lordship over them; and their great ones exercise authority upon them. But so shall it not be among you: but whosoever will be great among you, shall be your minister: and whosoever of you will be the chiefest, shall be servant of all. For even the Son of man came not to be ministered unto, but to minister, and to give his life a ransom for many.*

The wolf nature in ministry prefers recognition as "top dog" and not as a servant to all. This is one easy way to recognize a wolf personality in a minister. Jesus sounded the first warning of these false ministers identifying them as vicious wolves.

Matthew 7:15 – *Beware of false prophets, which come to you in sheep's clothing, but inwardly they are ravening wolves.*

What is a ravenous wolf? What does a wolf do? A wolf is a carnivore; a beast that feeds on flesh; or in the case of a false minister, he feeds on the fleshly nature of people. A religious carnivore is a wolf nature that seeks to feed his own carnal appetite, lusts and desires. He satisfies those carnal desires by consuming and living off of the sheep of his flock; a church.

Matthew 24:24 – *For there shall arise false Christs, and false prophets, and shall shew great signs and wonders; insomuch that, if it were possible, they shall deceive the very elect.*

The apostle Paul was even more concerned and adamant about those in church leadership. He knew human nature all too well; he knew that the zealous pursuit of position could become very harmful to the church in those whose motives were not pure and were subject to change. He was such an example when he persecuted the church before his conversion. So he gives us a very strong warning about how some in leadership can become grievous wolves.

Acts 20:28-30 – *Take heed therefore unto yourselves, and to all the flock, over the which the Holy Ghost hath made you overseers, to feed the church of God, which he hath purchased with his own blood. For I know this, that after my departing shall grievous wolves enter in among you, not sparing the flock. Also of your own selves shall men arise, speaking perverse things, to draw away disciples after them. Therefore watch, and remember, that by the space of three years I ceased not to warn every one night and day with tears.*

Those who are the wolves will draw away believers unto themselves, for their own purposes. This is how the other church of man is built. It may look like and sound like a true church, but Paul warned frequently, and in tears, that such elders would lead people astray from the truth.

These wolves could be elders, minsters, preachers, teachers and false prophets operating as leaders in churches; mostly in the other church. Wolves refer to those in leadership positions that have an un-crucified self (Luke 9:23), that they seek to satisfy at the expense of the sheep, (the church congregation). This wolf appetite may not show up until it is confronted or motivated with sufficient stimuli. This is why Paul said he knew that from among the elders who were present at his meeting with them that there would arise those who would become such wolves. Compare the "wolf" type leadership with the true shepherd type leadership.

John 10:1-5 – *Verily, verily, I say unto you, He that entereth not by the door into the sheepfold, but climbeth up some other way, the same is a thief and a robber. But he that entereth in by the door is the shepherd of the sheep. To him the porter openeth; and the sheep hear his voice: and he calleth his own sheep by name, and leadeth them out. And when he putteth forth his own sheep, he goeth before them, and the sheep follow him: for they know his voice. And a stranger will they not follow, but will flee from him: for they know not the voice of strangers.*

The shepherd will lay down his life for his sheep, while the wolf type supports his life, or takes life, from the sheep. The shepherd's concern is for feeding the sheep, sheltering them and leading them to full maturity. The wolf does not want the sheep to mature; he prefers them young and immature because they are easier prey for him to feed on. Mature sheep will recognize the wolf nature and flee.

A true shepherd will warn the sheep of a wolf's presence, and then drive the wolf away if he is in a position to do so. He will confront the wolf, even at the risk to himself, his ministry, his reputation and well-being; all in order to preserve the sheep. Not all wolves are in leadership positions; some may dwell among the flock bringing disturbance and discord which hinders the maturing process.

This writer had such an experience while pastoring a church. I sought the Lord on how to deal with this situation and He instructed me not to go after the wolf until the sheep began to stir. The reason is if I went after the wolf the rest of the flock would think that I was going after one of the sheep: they would not recognize what I was doing. Waiting until the sheep began to stir is when they sensed the presence of the wolf; then they would appreciate my effort to deal with the threat. (Note: in some situations it is a she-wolf that needs to be dealt with.)

Sheep are very dependent on leadership and need a shepherd. They are much like infants that need to be fed and cared for in their growth and development to maturity; unto which some of them could later become shepherds.

There are times that some wolves are not properly recognized as the enemy that they really are. They may hold positions of leadership in a church, and be well respected, but they have the wolf nature that has not yet shown itself. This is what Paul addressed when speaking to the elders at Ephesus in Acts 20, *"of your own selves shall men arise, speaking perverse things, to draw away disciples after them"*.

Such wolves are knowledgeable in the Word and skilled in preaching. They are also clever in manipulating people into satisfying their desires, just as a wolf is cunning in his methodical approach to obtain his objective. They may preach Christ and His Word, but he does this for his own benefit, not for the benefit of the sheep. These false ministers, preachers and teachers, may not necessarily be doing their work by evil spirits, but are likely driven by the lust of their own flesh. They are doing their own thing for personal benefit. This is what Jesus warned us about in the last days, saying many would come in His name and do wonderful things.

> Matthew 7:22-23 – *Many will say to me in that day, Lord, Lord, have we not prophesied in thy name? and in thy name have we cast out devils? and in thy name done many wonderful*

works? And then will I profess unto them, I never knew you: depart from me, ye that work iniquity.

Wolves frequently unite in with other wolves who are seeking the same objectives. They draw strength, courage, reinforcement and resourcefulness from one another. They band together in a wolf pack to uphold one another in their common objective, and even form organizations to gain notoriety.

The solution to dealing with the wolves in ministry is for the Lord to rise up His true servants, apostles, prophets, teachers, evangelists and pastors who will challenge the wolves: those who will care for His flock and tend to their protection and maturity. Even in the Old Testament God had to address wolves posing as shepherds to His people Israel:

Ezekiel 34:2-4 & 9-10 – *Son of man, prophesy against the shepherds of Israel, prophesy, and say unto them, Thus saith the Lord GOD unto the shepherds; Woe be to the shepherds of Israel that do feed themselves! should not the shepherds feed the flocks? Ye eat the fat, and ye clothe you with the wool, ye kill them that are fed: but ye feed not the flock. The diseased have ye not strengthened, neither have ye healed that which was sick, neither have ye bound up that which was broken, neither have ye brought again that which was driven away, neither have ye sought that which was lost; but with force and with cruelty have ye ruled them. ... therefore, O ye shepherds, hear the word of the LORD; Thus saith the Lord GOD; Behold, I am against the shepherds; and I will require my flock at their hand, and cause them to cease from feeding the flock; neither shall the shepherds feed themselves any more; for I will deliver my flock from their mouth, that they may not be meat for them.*

Churches need to open up to the called and anointed servants of the Lord and not to exclude His called and appointed gift ministries. Churches also need to stop seeking after personalities who tickle their ears and are more like entertainers appointed of men and their organizations, (denominations).

We need to be discerning, mature and able to judge after the Spirit and not after the eye or ear. Be a fruit inspector as Jesus instructed us to be in these last days. He said you will recognize them by their fruit, not by their gifts. Many today are judging prophets by their natural abilities: by their words, prophecies, teaching and preaching. Jesus said, *"by their fruit ye shall know them"*. This fruit is not their works, it is His character and nature in them; the Fruit of the Spirit. This fruit can only be produced as each one maintains an intimate fellowship with Christ, the vine, who is the source of spiritual life; as He is the "tree of life".

If you don't see Christ's character and nature in them, don't you dare follow them. If all you see is man, his own personality and character, then you better flee in fear of your spiritual life. Very likely he is a wolf and will satisfy his selfish desires by consuming from you. All that such a minister can reproduce in you is what is in him, and comes flowing out of him. Which would you, as a believer, prefer to be led by, the one who has the Spirit of the Christ in him, or the one who has the wolf nature?

There are some you may see have neither the true shepherd nor the wolf nature. Then get away from them too. They have nothing to offer but the dead form of church or religion. They are also part of the other church; they are like empty wells with no water. However, wolves are deceivers and the water in their wells is poison; filled with deception. How does a spiritual wolf operate? The following sub-headings deal with the operations employed by these false ministers.

THE PROSPERITY DOCTRINE

The wolves appeal to people's fleshly desires as they perform in their work in the ministry.

> Timothy 4:1 – *Now the Spirit speaketh expressly, that in the latter times some shall depart from the faith, giving heed to seducing spirits, and doctrines of devils;*

Such ministers that Paul refers to have the nature of a wolf which they use to advance themselves at the expense of the sheep. They feed off of the sheep using their ministry as the means of their own self-gratification. They encourage their people to focus on the material things of this world just as they do, following their pernicious ways.

> 2 Peter 2:1-3 – *But there were false prophets also among the people, even as there shall be false teachers among you, who*

privily shall bring in damnable heresies, even denying the Lord
that bought them, and bring upon themselves swift destruction.
And many shall follow their pernicious ways; by reason of whom
the way of truth shall be evil spoken of. And through covetousness
shall they with feigned words make merchandise of you: whose
judgment now if a long time lingereth not, and their damnation
slumbereth not.

Such preachers distort the faith of believers by getting them to focus on creation rather than the Creator. Their doctrines direct people away from what Jesus stated as was necessary to become His disciple; preferring to satisfy their own selfishly lusts. Thus they are making merchandise of the people by marketing their flesh.

Luke 9:23 – *And He said to them all, "If any man will come*
after Me, let him deny himself, and take up his cross daily, and
follow Me.

This characteristic of these false preachers has recently become most evident by those who promote the prosperity doctrine; but it is usually their own prosperity that they are actually seeking.

1Timothy 6:5 – *perverse disputings of men of corrupt minds,*
and destitute of the truth, supposing that gain is godliness: from
such withdraw thyself. But godliness with contentment is great
gain. For we brought nothing into this world, and it is certain
we can carry nothing out. And having food and raiment let
us be therewith content. But they that will be rich fall into
temptation and a snare, and into many foolish and hurtful lusts,
which drown men in destruction and perdition. For the love
of money is the root of all evil: which while some coveted after,
they have erred from the faith, and pierced themselves through
with many sorrows.

This seems to include those preachers who claim to need multi-million dollar jet planes to chauffer them around in luxury. They make demands on the sheep to pay for such extreme transportation. Such preachers also live in large palatial estates, or they have multiple fancy homes in up-scale communities. The fruit that they show is greed and lust for material things.

> Proverbs 15:27 – *He that is greedy of gain troubleth his own house; …*

The term *"troubleth his own house"* implies that he, and likely his entire family, are unsettled or discontent with what they have, and always strive, or lust, for more: bigger houses, more property, bigger and faster jet planes, more expensive cars, etc. In addition, they always want greater notoriety; a bigger following as referred to in Acts 20.

> Acts 20:30 – *Also of your own selves shall men arise, speaking perverse things, to draw away disciples after them.*

Even what they pray for is often based on their lusts.

> James 4:3 – *Ye ask, and receive not, because ye ask amiss, that ye may consume it upon your lusts.*

In evaluating what preachers, teachers or prophets you should listen to, you should not only discern what they are peaching and teaching, but consider also what they fail to speak about. They will not address the topic of sin, repentance or the work of the cross in their lives, or in their follower's lives. Yet they will claim to be doing Christ's work, as mentioned above in Matthew 7:21-23, but Christ denies them as being His ministers.

> 2 Timothy 4:3-4 – *For the time will come when they will not endure sound doctrine; but after their own lusts shall they heap to themselves teachers, having itching ears; and they shall turn away their ears from the truth, and shall be turned unto fables.*

These preachers will not tell you what true wealth and riches are. The true riches are those that you take with you when you leave this life to be with the Lord. The true wealth is the God kind of LOVE; the love we are to have for Him and others!

DECEPTION – A SIGN OF THE LAST DAYS

The whole purpose for a wolf to hide under a sheep's clothing is for deception, allowing himself to creep into the sheepfold unnoticed as a wolf. Four times in Matthew 24 Jesus warned that the last days would be filled with deception. Jesus also warned us that what we would hear, what we would see or what is reported, as news by the media, is not the whole truth or what is real. While in a time of prayer several years ago, the Holy Spirit revealed to me that "things are not what they appear to be".

This time of deception applies to every area of human experience; in politics and government; in world affairs, in peace and conflict; in science and discoveries; in economics and finance; and especially in the medical field; dealing with diseases and vaccines; as well as in religion – yes, in churches.

Deception is promoted by man because of selfish, ungodly ambitions of the carnal nature, (as influenced by the devil and his evil spirits); and, without question, such is found in many churches today. Jesus specifically warned about false prophets, teachers and preachers who would show us signs and wonders.

> Matthew 24:4-5 – *And Jesus answered and said unto them, Take heed that no man deceive you. For many shall come in my name, saying, I am Christ* (anointed); *and shall deceive many.*

> Matthew 24:24 – *For there shall arise false Christs* (anointed ones), *and false prophets, and shall shew great signs and wonders; insomuch that, if it were possible, they shall deceive the very elect.*

You must realize that just because something is supernatural, (not natural to man), does not mean it is from God, as so many presume. Satan, his angels and demons are all un-natural to man, they are supernatural. They operate in the spirit realm with results manifesting in our visible natural realm. Thus the things they do appear as miracles, signs and wonders. As the enemy tries to imitate what God does and what the Word says, many people can be deceived. This is the work of the spirit of antichrist, which is the counterfeit of the Holy Spirit.

1 John 4:3 – ... *and this is that spirit of antichrist, whereof ye have heard that it should come; and even now already is it in the world.*

Those who can be deceived have not matured enough in the knowledge of God and His Word to recognize or discern what is of God and what is not.

Hebrews 5:12-14 – *For when for the time ye ought to be teachers, ye have need that one teach you again which be the first principles of the oracles of God; and are become such as have need of milk, and not of strong meat. For every one that useth milk is unskilful in the word of righteousness: for he is a babe. But strong meat belongeth to them that are of full age, even those who by reason of use have their senses exercised to discern both good and evil.*

Yes God works signs and wonders through His servants. He does such wondrous works in response to those who seek Him and really put their trust in Him. He has to; He wouldn't be God if He didn't do supernatural things for and among people. We also need to recognize that God's Word does not have an expiration date.

Luke 21:33 – *Heaven and earth shall pass away: but my words shall not pass away.*

God hasn't changed from the things He has done for His people Israel under the Old Testament; and we now have an even better covenant – the New Testament!

Hebrews 7:22 – *by so much was Jesus made a surety of a better testament.*

Warning: not all supernatural workings are of God. This is where deception comes in. The apostle Paul instructed us to "prove all things".

1 Thessalonians 5:21 – *Prove all things; hold fast that which is good.*

Then the apostle John told us to "test the spirits"

> 1 John 4:1 – *Beloved, believe not every spirit, but try the spirits whether they are of God: because many false prophets are gone out into the world.*

So beware of those in ministry who use His name and speak of Him, but whose performance draws attention to them-selves, or to some spectacular event(s). Again, Jesus told us that ministers are to be known and recognized by their "fruit" and not by their "gifts", (Matthew 7:15-23). The fruit we are to recognize is not their works, but their character and nature, which is the Fruit of the Spirit, (the character and nature of God). (This fact is so important that it is repeated several times in this volume.)

> Galatians 5:22-23 – *But the fruit of the Spirit is love, joy, peace, longsuffering, gentleness, goodness, faith, meekness, temperance: against such there is no law.*

> John 15:5 – *I am the vine, ye are the branches: He that abideth in me, and I in him, the same bringeth forth much fruit: for without me ye can do nothing.*

God does not put on a show for people. However, these false ministers love to perform and put on a show; and Satan is the power behind it. Having people fall to the floor, or do all manner of gyrations, or laugh hysterically but have no significant change in their physical body, their soul or spirit, is merely part of a show. I have observed so-called "anointed" ministers touch people and they fall down, get up, get touched again, fall down again, repeatedly. Yet there is no change in them whatsoever as they get up just in the same condition as when they went down.

I have seen these wolf type ministers use the power of Satan to knock people to the floor; have them get up and knock them down again, and again, yet nothing changes. One such minister who has appeared frequently on television, who I am personally familiar with, is one of those who puts on such a show. He will wave his hand, blow on them and even wave his coat toward them and down they go in mass. That is a show and serves no purpose other than to amuse and entertain the audience as a spectacular event.

What most people fail to recognize that such power is demonic. I have a friend who, before he was born-again, was trained in martial arts by a real Chinese Master. This master was able to operate in supernatural powers; so much so that it sacred him. My friend said that one of the powers that they operate in is called, "the falling tree". This is when a trained person could walk by someone and touch his forehead with his finger and that person would fall to the floor totally unconscious. This is the same demonic ability that these wolf ministers use to deceive people with the spectacular. It is no more than a demonstration of occult power and a form of entertainment, and the Spirit of God is not in it!

> 2 Corinthians 11:13-15 – *For such are false apostles, deceitful workers, transforming themselves into the apostles of Christ. And no marvel; for Satan himself is transformed into an angel of light. Therefore it is no great thing if his ministers also be transformed as the ministers of righteousness; whose end shall be according to their works.*

When the Spirit of God touches a person through a truly God anointed minister, they may fall to the floor, and when they get back up, they have experienced a true change; either a physical healing, a soul cleansing from demonic oppression, or a divine revelation of the Lord and His kingdom. Human flesh cannot stand in the manifesting presence of Almighty God! For example, when the temple soldiers came to Gethsemane to arrest Jesus, He identified Himself saying, "I AM"; notice what happened when He manifested Himself to them:

> John 19:6 – *As soon then as he had said unto them, I am he, they went backward, and fell to the ground.*

In addition, when the Holy Spirit is moving in such a way on people there is a strong sense of righteousness and holiness; this verifies that it is the presence of God operating by His Spirit.

In my own experience while pastoring a church, we had a young lady who was unable to have a baby because doctors said she had a weak womb that could not hold a developing child; she would lose it at about three months, (which had already happened twice). I prayed for her, and quoted the appropriate scripture, and God touched her womb healing her. She later came for prayer while almost the full nine months pregnant because her wicked and adulterous husband had brought home multiple evil spirits due to his lifestyle as well as being verbally abusive.

As I prayed for her the Holy Spirit came upon her so fast that she was knocked to the floor with a heavy thud. Then the whole congregation jumped up in concern that she was hurt; but no, the Holy Spirit is gentle and will not allow any hurt when He is ministering to a person. As she lay there, the Lord revealed to me that she was having a vision; and when she got up I asked her what happened. She said that she saw flames of fire all over her body burning off the vileness that the enemy put on her as a result of her husband creating a wicked environment. I asked her how she felt to which she responded, "I feel light and free". She was delivered of the oppression of the devil that attacked her from the behavior of her husband. (I later was able to minister to him also, and he turned his life around.)

Please recognize that deception is at work in the church. Satan and his demons have no problem entering into many churches to bring oppression, false doctrines, causing deception and turning people away from the truth of God's Word, and their faith in Jesus Christ. The devil works through these wolves, false prophets, teachers and preachers as stated in the scriptures listed previously.

Now can you see that deception is at work in the church? Preachers who get great acclaim and attract a great deal of attention need to be looked at very closely. Are they truly God's servants or are they counterfeits, giving the convincing appearance of being "ministers of righteousness" when in fact their light, their power and anointing, (supernatural ability), comes from another source. I have observed some of these ministers begin in a good and valid way only to fall into Satan's grip through being exalted with success and pride; they end up being beguiled, yielding themselves to the power of the enemy.

> Romans 6:16 – *Know ye not, that to whom ye yield yourselves servants to obey, his servants ye are to whom ye obey; whether of sin unto death, or of obedience unto righteousness?*

Yes they use the name of Jesus, and yes, they use and quote God's Word. Satan can quote more scripture better than you can; does that mean you want to listen to him? Jesus said these wolves come in His name:

Matthew 24:5 – *For many shall come in my name, saying, I am Christ* (anointed)*; and shall deceive many.*

So how do you recognize the wolves, the false prophets, teachers and preachers? If you have no spiritual discernment to recognize what is false; if you do not have the Gift of Discernment by the Holy Spirit (1 Corinthians 12:8-10); then listen to what they say that is not in God's Word. They always add something, delete something or distort something from the Word. They mix a little un-truth with truth to make their message acceptable. Because you hear some recognizable truth, you tend to accept all the rest that they speak.

Remember, Jesus said "many", (not some or a few), would come in is name, saying that he is "Christ", (which means, anointed), thus they will deceive MANY, not a few. This means that masses of people in churches will be deceived! Don't let you be one of them!

Deception protection comes by maturing in Christ the Lord, knowing Him intimately, knowing His Word, and maintaining fellowship with Him. Then the imposters and their messages will be easily recognized. God's true servants are those whose work is to bring believers to maturity in Christ!

REVIVAL vs ENTERTAINMENT

Some wolves will employ forms of entertainment, as well as spectacular shows, in order to attract and stimulate an audience.

I have heard several claims from different sources recently saying that the church is presently experiencing a great revival. This is wonderful, however I am not seeing the results that true revival brings. When I read of historical accounts of revival such as the Welsh Revival, and those resulting from the ministry of the likes of Charles Finny, history records that whole towns were changed, all of the local society was affected in a positive way.

If the church is experiencing a great revival where is the evidence? One place where change has occurred in the past is in New York City. This was the result of the ministry of Time Square Church under the leadership of David Wilkerson. The revival has affected the immediate area of that sin-ridden city to the point that even the crime rate diminished. This is actually the result of the people of that church who have been revived and began praying fervently for their city, and as they were being a positive influence those around them.

That church had nightly prayer meetings; real prayer meetings, not social get-togethers; every night for over a year. True revival brings a change in the people who become Christ focused instead of self-focused. This is evidence that they have been revived by the Spirit of the Lord. They changed their interests, their motives and their lives. The things of the Lord and the kingdom of God became more important to them than the things of the world, and the old things they used to do. Thus these changes have affected the families and society around them as they truly show the light of God's glory shining through them to those around them. This is true revival!

I use this as an example to compare with what many are calling revival elsewhere but isn't real revival. Revive means: *to re-make alive: to stir up to active state that which is dormant.* Getting souls saved has been typically called revival in the past; but that is not revival, that is evangelism. Evangelism is the by-product of true revival, as demonstrated by the Time Square Church in New York.

Revived believers are set on spiritual fire by the Holy Spirit, and their fervency for Him attracts attention and causes the manifestation of His presence in their midst that produces true signs, wonders and the miraculous. Unbelievers are drawn; the gospel is heard and they are evangelized.

Signs and wonders are supposed to follow God's people as they speak and demonstrate God's Love and declare His Word to the world.

> Mark 16:20 – *And they went forth, and preached everywhere, the Lord working with them, and confirming the word with signs following. Amen.*

God simply acts on their faith and testimony proving His Word is real which results in miracles, signs and wonders. Man cannot manipulate God and say, "Tonight we are going to have a miracle service"; or "Come to this meeting for signs and wonders". Man does not orchestrate God, the Holy Spirit, or His power. Those who try to do such things are the false prophets, teachers and preachers; it is not God who is at work among them, but most likely the counterfeit from Satan who works to deceive.

So what is it that parts of the church are experiencing if it is not real revival? It is obvious that some churches are growing numerically and are now called "mega" churches, and they say this is revival, but is it? Is this not revival when there is a renewed interest in religion and church attendance? NO! It does show that there is a vacuum in people's lives that they are trying to fill, but church attendance and man's doctrine does not really satisfy it; thus it does not really fill the void. After a while many will get up and leave or turn to something else to fill that void unless there has been a true life changing experience in them.

Many of the churches that are growing are doing so not because of genuine revival, but due to entertainment! That's right; "entertainment", which is coupled with man's professionalism in stimulating and motivating people. This may sound rather harsh, but I personally observed this in horror as what was once a mighty move of God in real revival in a particular church became lost due to the manipulation and control of man; and the masses failed to discern the difference. Only a few others and myself recognized that those in charge dismissed the Holy Spirit as if to say, *"Thanks for the start but we'll take it from here",* as they work to control everything in the services.

The leadership began to rely on human talent and professional ability and entertainment rather than being dependent on the Holy Spirit to guide and direct. Man, personalities and performance became the center of attention rather than Jesus Christ and His Word. That church became known as *"the best show in town";* and yes it grew in numbers because it attracted a lot of attention – but it was mostly because of entertainment!

Once that happened, then all the problems of the flesh began to appear. The "weirdoes" began to arrive, or come to the surface in the congregation. Then the leadership blamed the devil for the problems when all along it was their fault for not continuing to depend on the Holy Spirit to saturate all their activities in prayer and in faithfully following the Word.

The masses still came, but now it was because of the entertainment. This attracted all the more problems. The end result was the down-fall of the leadership and their ministries. The fruit came forth and it was not of God – it was of man's carnal nature. And all along they thought they were continuing to have revival.

Many other churches that are experiencing dramatic growth today have employed entertainment as the means of attracting and keeping its people, because it works. Some church platforms and pulpits don't even look like a church anymore; many look more like a "night club" or a show stage. They depend on loud music, the hype, the comedy routines or jokes of the preachers (performers), the dramas, the dancing, and on and on it goes.

They have everything but the Holy Righteous Presence of God by His Spirit, and the awesomeness of His convicting redeeming power along with healing and deliverance that meets people's true needs. Why is this happening?

It seems to be that they are trying to appeal to the natural (carnal) man to draw people into their church. They are using the wrong techniques and calling the results revival! You do not use the world to call the world to Jesus Christ. You use the Word of God and that which is of the kingdom of God with the Holy Spirit power of God to win the world to Christ.

Please do not think that just because a church has grown tremendously in size and become very successful in the eyes of other churches that this phenomenal growth is by the Spirit of God. Man is fully capable of building what appears to be a successful church, and God may not have anything to do with it. Jesus revealed this exact same thing to the apostle John who recorded it in scripture.

> Revelation 3:14-20 – *And unto the angel of the church of the Laodiceans write; These things saith the Amen, the faithful and true witness, the beginning of the creation of God; I know thy works, that thou art neither cold nor hot: I would thou wert cold or hot. So then because thou art lukewarm, and neither cold nor hot, I will spue thee out of my mouth. Because thou sayest, I am rich, and increased with goods, and have need of nothing; and knowest not that thou art wretched, and miserable, and poor, and blind, and naked: I counsel thee to buy of me gold tried in the fire, that thou mayest be rich; and white raiment, that thou mayest be clothed, and that the shame of thy nakedness do not appear; and anoint thine eyes with eyesalve, that thou mayest see. As many as I love, I rebuke and chasten: be zealous therefore, and repent. Behold, I stand at the door, and knock: if any man hear my voice, and open the door, I will come in to him, and will sup with him, and he with me.*

The church of Laodicea was considered by men to be a great success; however, the Lord said they were spiritually impoverished and didn't know it. (Sounds like many churches in the world today.) And Jesus was left on the outside, knocking, seeking to be let in. He said that they were wretched, miserable, poor, blind and naked. Although they possessed all the material qualities man usually looks at, they were devoid of all spiritual qualities necessary to please God and to be properly equipped of Him.

There are three necessities that the Lord addressed in this so-called successful church. First - they had no real trust in God; their confidence was in their material things. This was referred to as their need to buy gold that is tried and tested in fire. This refers to faith, (trust and confidence) – tried, tested and proven as gold that has been purified by fire.

> 1 Peter 1:7 – *that the trial of your faith, being much more precious than of gold that perisheth, though it be tried with fire, might be found unto praise and honour and glory at the appearing of Jesus Christ:*

Second – since they were spiritually naked, they needed to be clothed upon with His righteousness. This refers to their carnal, fleshly behavior, motivation, passions and lusts that needed to be removed. This church, though great in the eyes of men, was full of many kinds of sin and debauchery that is found in the world. They may speak of holiness but it was far from them. They were exposed by their "soulish" ministry of how you can have this, how to get that, what is your position or title in society, etc.

The white raiment they were to be clothed with is His "righteousness". It is not to be covered or hidden deep inside so as not to be seen, but outward. Raiment is worn on the outside so it is clearly visible to all.

> Revelation 19:8 – *And to her was granted that she should be arrayed in fine linen, clean and white: for the fine linen is the righteousness of saints.*

Third – since they were spiritually blind or unable to see things of the Spirit, or able to see things as God sees them, they were in need of medication to open up their eyes. They needed eye salve to wash the world and material things out of their eyes. They were lacking discernment which allows you to see what is hidden, or what is the motivating force behind certain behavior or actions. They also needed to be able to see the Word of God in all of its truth and stop using it as a tool to obtain more worldly goods, (success, prosperity and possessions).

> Luke 12:15 – *And he said unto them, Take heed, and beware of covetousness: for a man's life consisteth not in the abundance of the things which he possesseth.*

Dependence on man's ability only reproduces more of what man is, has, and does. The church needs more of Jesus, so that in it is reproduced more of what He is, has, and does. More of Jesus is supplied by the Holy Spirit who reveals Him and guides us in all truth and teaches us all things:

> John 14:16-17 – *And I will pray the Father, and he shall give you another Comforter, that he may abide with you for ever; even the Spirit of truth; whom the world cannot receive, because it seeth him not, neither knoweth him: but ye know him; for he dwelleth with you, and shall be in you.*

> John 16:13-15 – *Howbeit when he, the Spirit of truth, is come, he will guide you into all truth: for he shall not speak of himself; but whatsoever he shall hear, that shall he speak: and he will shew you things to come. He shall glorify me: for he shall receive of mine, and shall shew it unto you. All things that the Father hath are mine: therefore said I, that he shall take of mine, and shall shew it unto you.*

The Holy Spirit is the Spirit of Truth who equips us with the Word and reveals more of Jesus as we seek the Lord first and foremost – daily. This and prayer is what produces real revival.

Another characteristic to recognize about revival is that it gives people something that not only changes them, but that they take with them wherever they go. The fruit of true revival is seen emanating out from the church as those who are revived go out into the everyday world at work, school or wherever. The signs and wonders follow the believers as they happily apply God's Word to their everyday situations and are seen by others.

In an entertainment, or man-centered revival, people have nothing of spiritual substance to take with them as they leave the meetings. All they have is enthusiasm that has been hyped up; it's mostly an emotional high. Those churches that have the wolves, the false prophets, teachers and preachers, draw people in to see the spectacular, (the counterfeit signs and wonders of the enemy); and/or the entertainment; neither of which produces real revival. This is all part of the end-time deception that Jesus warned us about.

We are not supposed to look for or follow signs and wonders; they are to follow us as we walk in obedience to Christ and His Word.

John 14:12 – *Verily, verily, I say unto you, He that believeth on me, the works that I do shall he do also; and greater works than these shall he do; because I go unto my Father.*

We are to look to God, look to His Word, speak the Word and apply our trust in God to our circumstances. Then He honors His Word and your trust in Him; then signs, wonders and miracles are the by-product of such faith. This attracts the attention of unbelievers who are then evangelized and brought to the knowledge and acceptance of Jesus Christ as Savoir and Lord.

Another characteristic about the assumed revival is that enthusiasm is generated. However, in the man-made revival, the hype and entertainment service, people get excited and begin talking about their church, or their meetings, or their pastor or preacher, or their program, or their activities, etc. In their enthusiasm and excitement, all they talk about is what man is doing, and what is going on among them.

In a true revival, where the Holy Spirit is moving and manifesting His presence, with a revelation of Jesus Christ and God's Word, people get excited about and talk about Jesus, about His Word, and about what God is doing. In a real revival, what man is doing is not even mentioned, because it is insignificant compared to what the Lord is doing by His Spirit. Even the leadership or pastor will humbly acknowledge, *"This is the Lord's doing and it is marvelous in our sight"*. The moving of God's Spirit in a true revival always humbles those charged with leadership responsibility. They too become overwhelmed at what God is doing.

Don't be satisfied with entertainment when real revival can be obtained. However, revival does not come automatically; it comes as a result of seeking Him earnestly and continually; both personally or corporately. Yes, you can have a personal revival even when others are satisfied with the status-quo, the man-made stuff, or the entertainment fads.

A sign that people have been revived and are excited about the Lord and His Word is when people arrive early for the church service, and fill the church up beginning at the front. Such people are excited about Him and that will draw others into the church for evangelism.

THE THREE "P's"

So how does a wolf feed on the sheep in a church? Since the wolf is out to satisfy his or her carnal fleshly nature, they will seek the three classic human needs of man. These three are Provision, Protection and Pleasure – the three "P's" required by the natural man.

PROVISION – resources used to satisfy the basic needs and desires of the flesh: food, water, shelter, etc. However, mankind is usually not satisfied with just his basic needs met. These wolves will rationalize and justify all manner of excesses, or needs; all at the expense of the flock. This has been the motive for some who have jumped on the success and prosperity doctrine of the past several years.

PROTECTION – the second "P" of the flesh is to form a shield of defense that would take from them what they possess or pursue. Their protection does not come from the Lord but from what they form around themselves. This is primarily obtained through their elevated position or rank which provides security and recognition. The wolves want bigger flocks, more power, influence, and control; (that is why many feel the need to be on TV). When you look past their exterior, it appears that they are building a house for themselves rather than for the Lord and His people. (Refer to Matthew 7:24-27.)

PLEASURE – the third "p" is obviously the pursuit of self-gratification, self-indulgence, and even having excess in lavishness: having great prosperity. The sequence is first having Provision; what they need to sustain themselves: then the need for Protection; to preserve themselves and their possessions: followed by Pleasure; the things they want to experience or engage in to satisfy their desires.

All three of these are natural and needed by every human being. However, these become the motivational factors in the ministry of the wolf; whether these factors are seen or concealed. The true shepherd type of minister has adopted the Lord's motives for the ministry. He has been prepared, proven and approved of God. Usually he has gone through the fiery trials that have purified his motives.

> Romans 12:1-2 – *I beseech you therefore, brethren, by the mercies of God, that ye present your bodies a living sacrifice, holy, acceptable unto God, which is your reasonable service. And be not conformed to this world: but be ye transformed by the*

renewing of your mind, that ye may prove what is that good, and acceptable, and perfect, will of God.

Those that God called and ordained for His work in the church have dealt with their carnality and desires of the flesh. Usually it is the Lord who has dealt with these areas so that they are no longer a motivational factor in the work of that one's ministry. To be a true disciple of Christ requires death to self (flesh).

> Luke 9:23-24 – *And he said to them all, If any man will come after me, let him deny himself, and take up his cross daily, and follow me. For whosoever will save his life shall lose it: but whosoever will lose his life for my sake, the same shall save it.*

Thus the result is as the apostle Paul stated.

> Galatians 2:20 – *I am crucified with Christ: nevertheless I live; yet not I, but Christ liveth in me: and the life which I now live in the flesh I live by the faith of the Son of God, who loved me, and gave himself for me.*

Those with the wolf nature reject this course of action and seek to preserve their self and, instead, enhance their flesh.

Perhaps you need to tug on some of those sheep skins to see if they come off. If you hear growls as you do this, then chances are that what you have in your hand is not a sheep, but something with a ravenous appetite.

It is your responsibility to discern godly and proper leadership. Then follow and receive what they have to impart: it will be the Life of Christ if they are the true servants of the Lord operating as one of His Gift Ministries. If they prove to be wolves, they will not impart Christ's spiritual life; their focus will be on this material and physical life. (We see a well known TV preacher with a huge church as an example of this.) They will preach to build your "self" esteem and quality of life which is just the opposite of what Jesus taught – "*deny self*" (flesh). They do this so they can gain even more off of your life; just as a parasite lives off its host by sucking the life out of it.

Your spiritual maturity is essential, not only to live as a true believer, but also to be able to recognize what is of God and what is of the evil one, be it

Satan or one of the ravenous wolves. Spiritual maturity generates the ability to discern what is of God and what is of the devil.

> Hebrews 5:12-14 – *For when for the time ye ought to be teachers, ye have need that one teach you again which be the first principles of the oracles of God; and are become such as have need of milk, and not of strong meat. For every one that useth milk is unskilful in the word of righteousness: for he is a babe. But strong meat belongeth to them that are of full age, even those who by reason of use have their senses exercised to discern both good and evil.*

Being a mature child of God you will then have His light shining in you and through you to others. This is what God wants to see in you. The wolves work to destroy this light in you. Flee the wolves!

Chapter 7

TWO KINDS OF BELIEVERS

WHICH KIND ARE YOU

During my past fifty years of ministry unto the Lord I have had to do many things to support my family as well as supporting my work in the ministry to which the Lord called me. I have functioned at times as an employer, and other times as an employee. While pastoring a church and doing evangelistic work, I was employed as a lumber jack, a heavy equipment operator, a tractor-trailer driver, a business owner and a law enforcement officer.

As an employer of my own business, I preferred to hire Christians, as they are purported to have a higher work ethic, being honest and dependable. When I served as an employee, I preferred to work for other Christians, assuming they would be more honest and fair in their business practices. I have been disappointed, both with Christians as employees as well as with Christians as employers. Their behavior may have been Christian on the surface and in name, but when it came to their character, motivation and business practices or work ethic, it was not as I expected of a born-again believer in Christ.

After several bad experiences as an employer, I felt I would rather hire non-Christians; at least I knew what to expect from them. I also determined that I don't plan to work for another Christian employer, including those who were ministers. I found that I could not trust them as they were not people of their word. Their money-making motives led them to compromise and turn away from a true biblical lifestyle in dealing with their clients; especially in using deceptive practices.

After these heartbreaking experiences I sought the Lord and asked, why do some Christians live just like non-believers of the world. (When you ask Him questions you need to be prepared for the answers.) The answer He gave showed a major problem among those who identify as Christians; thus a great need for an awakening in the church today.

The Lord showed me that there are two types of believers in the church; each is identified by category. These categories are not taken directly from scripture as a "thus sayeth the Lord": I named them for my personal means of identification. However, I did try to use a just biblical basis for these identifiers.

The first category of believers I called "Christian". These are the ones who are born again; they are "in" Christ spiritually. The second category I call the "saints". These are the ones who Christ is seen "in". There is a great difference between the two.

I found that those in the first category cannot always be trusted to exhibit the Christ-like life. This is because the "world" and the "flesh" are still visible in them, motivating, stimulating and driving them. They allow the things of the world to hold on to them more than the things of the kingdom of God and Christ.

> 1 John 2:15-16 – *Love not the world, neither the things that are in the world. If any man love the world, the love of the Father is not in him. For all that is in the world, the lust of the flesh, and the lust of the eyes, and the pride of life, is not of the Father, but is of the world.*

These believers have not yet become true disciples of the Lord Jesus Christ. (Most churches today do not teach their people to be a disciple of Christ, but to become disciples of men, a church or denomination.) A true disciple is a follower of Christ who has come to the cross and died to self-will with its fleshly lusts.

> Luke 9:23 – *And he said to them all, If any man will come after me, let him deny himself, and take up his cross daily, and follow me.*

> Luke 14:27 – *And whosoever doth not bear his cross, and come after me, cannot be my disciple.*

They know Jesus Christ, as well as what is right, but the motivational force of the un-crucified flesh is too powerful in them and hinders them from living to Christ-like standards

> Galatians 5:17 – *For the flesh lusteth against the Spirit, and the Spirit against the flesh: and these are contrary the one to the other: so that ye cannot do the things that ye would.*

They may make excuses for their actions. They say they want to do the right things but do not have the ability to do so. They still have carnality in their mind, thus they are double minded.

> Romans 8:6 – *For to be carnally minded is death; but to be spiritually minded is life and peace.*

> James 1:8 – *A double minded man is unstable in all his ways.*

Double mindedness is vacillating between the carnal and the spiritual. Too often they are led of their flesh and not of the Spirit.

> Romans 8:14 – *For as many as are led by the Spirit of God, they are the sons of God.*

> Galatians 5:16 – *This I say then, Walk in the Spirit, and ye shall not fulfil the lust of the flesh.*

The "saints", on the other hand, have not only gone through the Lord's discipleship training, having died to the selfish flesh, but they walk under the Lordship of Jesus Christ, submitting themselves to Him daily. Thus Christ is Master over them and he becomes their motivational force. This does not mean they are perfect in all their ways, but they continue to strive toward that goal.

> 2 Corinthians 4:7 – *But we have this treasure in earthen vessels, that the excellency of the power may be of God, and not of us.*

It means that their heart, their intentions and motivations are right because they have yielded up their "self-will" to be replaced with "His-will".

> Galatians 5:24-25 – *And they that are Christ's have crucified the flesh with the affections and lusts. If we live in the Spirit, let us also walk in the Spirit.*

Those that are in the saint category you can trust, even with your life. This is because their self (selfishness) has died, their motive is right, and Christ, as their true Lord, guides and monitors their walk, and they want it that way. The life of Christ is now seen in them rather than their own soulish life.

> Galatians 2:20 – *I am crucified with Christ: nevertheless I live; yet not I, but Christ liveth in me: and the life which I now live in the flesh I live by the faith of the Son of God, who loved me, and gave himself for me.*

This writer believes that the next sovereign move of the Holy Spirit in the church will be to make "saints" out of the many professing Christians. It is to take those in category one and to promote them into category two. This will be the thrust of the revival that is coming to the church. It will involve the "perfecting" of the saints unto the full stature of Christ.

> Ephesians 4:13 – *till we all come in the unity of the faith, and of the knowledge of the Son of God, unto a perfect man, unto the measure of the stature of the fulness of Christ:*

Being completely transformed from this world and conformed to His image; thus prepared for Him when He returns, a glorious church, without spot or wrinkle.

> Ephesians 5:26-27 – *that he might sanctify and cleanse it with the washing of water by the word, that he might present it to himself a glorious church, not having spot, or wrinkle, or any such thing; but that it should be holy and without blemish.*

This is God's purpose and plan that He began to fulfill through Jesus Christ and will be completed before His return.

> Romans 12:2 – *And be not conformed to this world: but be ye transformed by the renewing of your mind, that ye may prove what is that good, and acceptable, and perfect, will of God.*

> Romans 8:29 – *For whom he did foreknow, he also did predestinate to be conformed to the image of his Son, that he might be the firstborn among many brethren.*

The next move of God in the church will focus on the Fruit of the Spirit, which is the character and nature of God, and was fully revealed to us in the person of His Son, Jesus Christ.

> Galatians 5:22-23 – *But the fruit of the Spirit is love, joy, peace, longsuffering, gentleness, goodness, faith, meekness, temperance: against such there is no law.*

This divine fruit is produced in His saints as the life of Christ is allowed to flow through the believers who are referred as the branches that are attached to the vine – Jesus.

> John 15:1, 4-5 – *I am the true vine, and my Father is the husbandman. ... ... Abide in me, and I in you. As the branch cannot bear fruit of itself, except it abide in the vine; no more can ye, except ye abide in me. I am the vine, ye are the branches: He that abideth in me, and I in him, the same bringeth forth much fruit: for without me ye can do nothing.*

Christ's divine nature is to be fully revealed to the world in and through His Saints.

> 2 Peter 1:3-4 – *according as his divine power hath given unto us all things that pertain unto life and godliness, through the knowledge of him that hath called us to glory and virtue: whereby are given unto us exceeding great and precious promises: that by*

these ye might be partakers of the divine nature, having escaped the corruption that is in the world through lust.

In this passage, Peter goes on to give a similar listing of the Fruit of the Spirit, (but in reverse order as the one in Galatians 5), stating that the qualities of this divine nature shall make your life fruitful unto Him.

2 Peter 1:5-8 – *And beside this, giving all diligence, add to your faith virtue; and to virtue knowledge; and to knowledge temperance; and to temperance patience; and to patience godliness; and to godliness brotherly kindness; and to brotherly kindness charity. For if these things be in you, and abound, they make you that ye shall neither be barren nor unfruitful in the knowledge of our Lord Jesus Christ.*

Notice the effort that God will put forth to produce this divine fruit. He will cut and prune the branches – those who claim Christ.

John 15:2 – *Every branch in me that beareth not fruit he taketh away: and every branch that beareth fruit, he purgeth it, that it may bring forth more fruit.*

The last great move of God in the church was called the Charismatic Renewal. That move of God focused on the supernatural power of God through His Holy Spirit. This was done with the restoration of the "Gifts of the Spirit" and accompanying signs and wonders as listed in 1 Corinthians 12.

1 Corinthians 12:8 – *For to one is given by the Spirit the word of wisdom; to another the word of knowledge by the same Spirit; to another faith by the same Spirit; to another the gifts of healing by the same Spirit; to another the working of miracles; to another prophecy; to another discerning of spirits; to another divers kinds of tongues; to another the interpretation of tongues:*

The supernatural gifts, healings, signs and wonders, were used to get people's attention to draw them to the Jesus. This is how Jesus ministered; it is also how He told His twelve disciples to minister when He sent them out; then the same with seventy additional followers.

Matthew 10:1, 7-8 – *And when he had called unto him his twelve disciples, he gave them power against unclean spirits, to cast them out, and to heal all manner of sickness and all manner of disease. ... And as ye go, preach, saying, The kingdom of heaven is at hand. Heal the sick, cleanse the lepers, raise the dead, cast out devils: freely ye have received, freely give.*

Luke 10:1, 9, 17 – *After these things the Lord appointed other seventy also, and sent them two and two before his face into every city and place, whither he himself would come. ... ... and heal the sick that are therein, and say unto them, The kingdom of God is come nigh unto you. And the seventy returned again with joy, saying, Lord, even the devils are subject unto us through thy name.*

After Jesus ascended back to the Father He gave even more ability to believers to minister by the authority of His name with the same power.

John 14:12 – *Verily, verily, I say unto you, He that believeth on me, the works that I do shall he do also; and greater works than these shall he do; because I go unto my Father.*

Mark 16:17-18 – *And these signs shall follow them that believe; In my name shall they cast out devils; they shall speak with new tongues; they shall take up serpents; and if they drink any deadly thing, it shall not hurt them; they shall lay hands on the sick, and they shall recover.*

Thus these spiritual gifts began to be restored to the church in the late 1960's and 70's. However, since most churches refuse to believe, they were denied such supernatural ability, and some churches even preached against it. They are denying the divine power, (just as Paul stated in 2 Timothy 3:5). They claim that the marvelous works of the Holy Spirit are not for today, but they ignore what Paul clearly stated that these Gifts will be in operation right up to the time of Christ's return.

1 Corinthians 1:7 – *so that ye come behind in no gift; waiting for the coming of our Lord Jesus Christ:*

Jesus knew that everyone is concerned about their physical well-being more than their soul and spiritual well-being: so this is where He began with His ministry. When people saw that He had the power of God to heal, they came; and they sat down to listen to His teaching and declaring the kingdom of God: that He was His way to do it. So it has been in the Charismatic Renewal. The power of God got people's attention; then they came to learn more of Him and His Word.

However, signs, wonders and the Gifts of the Holy Spirit do not build and mature the church. Some churches and ministries were built on the gifts, signs and wonders. This is wrong; it is evidence of the flesh trying to capitalize or make merchandise of the things of God. Saints do not do such things, but Christians of category one do. That is why the need for revival, which is to get us back on God's track and His way of doing things.

It may come as a surprise to some, but the Charismatic Renewal is over; in fact, it ended by 1980. Many have been trying to keep it alive because they built their ministries on it.

The sovereign moves of God can be described as waves of the sea crashing onto the shore. The Charismatic movement was one of those waves. If you have ever been to the seashore and watched the waves come in, you would see a cycle of events that describes these moves of God.

When a wave breaks, it comes up on the shoreline. As it advances it covers the sand with inches of water. The sand is no longer visible, only the water. As you stand on the beach watching these events, you noticed that you did not have to go to the water, it came to you, reached you, and wetted you.

Then the wave recedes back into the deep. When this happens the sand of the shore becomes visible again. Not only is the sand now visible, but a rapid drying of it occurs as the moisture in it decreases. This drying continues until suddenly the next wave moves in to cover the sand again with water.

Those standing on the shore and who are aware, looking out over the sea, can see and hear the next wave approaching. Those who are not looking and not aware or paying attention are often taken by surprise as the wave hits. They have mixed reactions to the water brought in by the wave: so it is with the moves of God.

Some reactions are: get away from the wave, they don't want to get wet; anger, because the wave and its water disturbed their comfortable position; they are startled because it caught them by surprise. However, some enjoyed it; excited, as a child may express, and go running gleefully into the water for more.

The church has been drying out since the last wave of the move of God in the Charismatic Renewal. Many have felt that dryness since the early 1990's. However, those who are watching the waters see and hear the approach of the next wave, the next wonderful move of God.

This next wave of the move of God will deal with the appearance of the church. Compared to a bride waiting and preparing for the marriage ceremony, the true church of Christ in these remaining days will be primping; cleansing itself, getting ready, putting on Christ's righteousness as a spotless garment in preparation for joining Him at His coming.

It is the Holy Spirit that leads and motivates in this final day of preparation. Christ is coming for a "glorious" church, not the defiled and divided mess we have now. The task at hand is for the Christians to become Saints, and that the church will be filled with His glory. This means that there is a lot of work to do because those in the Christian category are greatly spotted and blemished, and their age old traditions of men and demons are the wrinkles that must be removed and straightened out. This requires the removal of false doctrines and a return to the truth of the Word of God in its entirety.

> Ephesians 5:26-27 – *that he might sanctify and cleanse it with the washing of water by the word, that he might present it to himself a glorious church, not having spot, or wrinkle, or any such thing; but that it should be holy and without blemish.*

This also requires the restoration of all five of the gift ministries that Christ ordained, including those that the "other" church has rejected. Why their restoration is needed is because without them the church is lacking the necessary forms of ministry to accomplish what He ordained.

> Ephesians 4:11-16 – *And he gave some, apostles; and some, prophets; and some, evangelists; and some, pastors and teachers; for the perfecting of the saints, for the work of the ministry, for the edifying of the body of Christ: till we all come in the unity of the faith, and of the knowledge of the Son of God, unto a perfect man, unto the measure of the stature of the fulness of Christ: that we henceforth be no more children, tossed to and fro, and carried about with every wind of doctrine, by the sleight of men, and cunning craftiness, whereby they lie in wait to deceive; but speaking the truth in love, may grow up into him*

in all things, which is the head, even Christ: from whom the whole body fitly joined together and compacted by that which every joint supplieth, according to the effectual working in the measure of every part, maketh increase of the body unto the edifying of itself in love.

The gloriousness seen in the church will be His glory; it comes by His character and nature seen in His people – the Saints. It is the Fruit of the Spirit, the quality of His life that can only come from Him abiding in, and evident in each saint.

John 15:8 – *Herein is my Father glorified, that ye bear much fruit; so shall ye be my disciples.*

What many fail to realize is that this divine fruit is not the works, or the results of man's efforts, as is commonly believed. Man has nothing to do with producing this fruit on his own. Man can do many things apart from Christ, but he cannot produce spiritual fruit apart from Christ. Man can even build a church that appears to be great and successful, yet without having Christ in it. Such was the case with the man-made church of Laodicea in which Jesus was left standing on the outside wanting to come in.

Revelation 3:14-20 – *And unto the angel of the church of the Laodiceans write; These things saith the Amen, the faithful and true witness, the beginning of the creation of God; I know thy works, that thou art neither cold nor hot: I would thou wert cold or hot. So then because thou art lukewarm, and neither cold nor hot, I will spue thee out of my mouth. Because thou sayest, I am rich, and increased with goods, and have need of nothing; and knowest not that thou art wretched, and miserable, and poor, and blind, and naked: I counsel thee to buy of me gold tried in the fire, that thou mayest be rich; and white raiment, that thou mayest be clothed, and that the shame of thy nakedness do not appear; and anoint thine eyes with eyesalve, that thou mayest see. As many as I love, I rebuke and chasten: be zealous therefore, and repent. Behold, I stand at the door, and kn**ock**: if any man hear my voice, and open the door, I will come in to him, and will sup with him, and he with me.*

This was a church that had the form of godliness but no power due to the lack of His presence. Jesus identifies what they lack, telling them to open up to Him, (and His Holy Spirit) and calling them to repentance. They were obviously lacking the Fruit of the Spirit, but thought that they had it all being "*rich, and increased with goods, and have need of nothing*".

This Fruit of the Spirit is His life seen in you, as a branch of Him: it is not your works, it is His Life, his nature, the new man that is fashioned after Him. This makes the saint a living testimony and witness of Jesus; thus the saints are manifesting as the sons of God.

> Romans 8:19 – *For the earnest expectation of the creature waiteth for the manifestation of the sons of God.*

How will this next move of God, bringing with it the Fruit of the Spirit, come about in the church? It will come through a new order of leadership to the church. This will be, as is already beginning, the appearance of tested and proven ministers, true servants, who have been through the fire and are properly motivated. Called of God and ordained for this purpose of end-time ministry to perfect, (complete) what is lacking in the church. They are meek, humble, not wanting fame for themselves, but only seeking recognition for their Lord Jesus Christ.

These end-time servants will be full of power and authority; they will have a new anointing, like a double portion of what Elisha received from Elijah. There will be power in the words they speak because it will come from pure vessels who are properly motivated and equipped of God by His Spirit.

These will be different and unknown ministers compared to what we now see in churches. They will be opposed by many of the current order of prominent church leadership and those steeped in tradition. They are God's called servants who have been in preparation for ten, fifteen, twenty or more years. Some were called of God more than fifty years ago; who have seen and experienced some of the many extremes and errors in churches, and longed for purity to be restored in them as it was in the beginning.

These will not be traditional ministers having traditional ministerial training and certifications. They have gone through the fiery trials of purging and purification of God. They have spent time in the wilderness where the excess baggage falls of and they learn to depend on the Lord far greater than many just in order to survive. They learn much from the Lord in these experiences and are thus better equipped to serve the church of Christ; similar to what the apostle Paul experienced.

These called ones, God has prepared His way, and they shall be similar to John the Baptist who prepared the way for the coming of the Lord. They are also preparing the church for the coming of the Lord.

> Malachi 3:2-3 – *Behold, I will send my messenger, and he shall prepare the way before me: … But who may abide the day of his coming? and who shall stand when he appeareth? for he is like a refiner's fire, and like fullers' soap: and he shall sit as a refiner and purifier of silver: and he shall purify the sons of Levi,* (His ministers), *and purge them as gold and silver, that they may offer unto the* LORD *an offering in righteousness.* (A purified church, without spot, wrinkle or blemish).

This preparation of God has made these end-time servants humble, lowly, faithful, truly serving in any way. They have climbed down the ladder of servitude while others have been climbing up the ladder of worldly success. When they minister it will be as if it is the Lord, Himself, who is ministering. They are not building their name or ministry, but His. They lead by example.

> Philippians 3:17-19 – *Brethren, be followers together of me, and mark them which walk so as ye have us for an ensample. (For many walk, of whom I have told you often, and now tell you even weeping, that they are the enemies of the cross of Christ: whose end is destruction, whose God is their belly, and whose glory is in their shame, who mind earthly things.)*

These servants, who walk circumspectly, can figuratively be compared to Christ the King's eunuchs; the ones who tend to the King's bride and help prepare her for His pleasure. They do not touch, molest, abuse, live off of, or rape the bride of the king; (as many other ministers and ministries have done throughout history). They have "made themselves eunuchs" for His purpose.

> Mathew 19:12 – *For there are some eunuchs, which were so born from their mother's womb: and there are some eunuchs, which were made eunuchs of men: and there be eunuchs, which have made themselves eunuchs for the kingdom of heaven's sake.*

He that is able to receive it, let him receive it. (Meaning this is a difficult preparation process to go through).

These end-time ministers will perfect the saints. To *perfect* means to thoroughly equip, to complete, to finish the work that begins with salvation and discipleship.

> Hebrews 6:1 – *Therefore leaving the principles of the doctrine of Christ, let us go on unto perfection; not laying again the foundation of ... .*

Let's look again at what new order of ministers the Lord will use to bring us to full maturity and able to bear the Fruit of the Spirit.

> Ephesians 4:11-13 – *And he gave some, apostles; and some, prophets; and some, evangelists; and some, pastors and teachers; for the perfecting of the saints, for the work of the ministry, for the edifying of the body of Christ: till we all come in the unity of the faith, and of the knowledge of the Son of God, unto a perfect man, unto the measure of the stature of the fulness of Christ:*

It was teachers and some pastors who brought the church the knowledge of the Gifts of the Spirit, and then instructed in the use of them during the Charismatic Renewal. During this next move of God it will be His true apostles and prophets who will bring us into the Fruit of the Spirit. Their work is to "form Christ in you"; as was the work of the apostle Paul. (Beware of the false prophets and apostles what the Lord warned us about.)

> Galatians 4:19 – *My little children, of whom I travail in birth again until Christ be formed in you,*

> Colossians 1:26-27 – *even the mystery which hath been hid from ages and from generations, but now is made manifest to his saints: to whom God would make known what is the riches of the glory of this mystery among the Gentiles; which is Christ in you, the hope of glory:*

Thus, Christ is formed in us by His character and nature, the fruit that is the result of abiding intimately in Him so we can experience the "fullness of God" as being His children.

> Ephesians 3:17-19 – *that Christ may dwell in your hearts by faith; that ye, being rooted and grounded in love, may be able to comprehend with all saints what is the breadth, and length, and depth, and height; and to know the love of Christ, which passeth knowledge, that ye might be filled with all the fulness of God.*

Christians aren't perfected yet! Why? Because of the lack of the two remaining gift ministries functioning in churches until now; the apostle and prophet.

> 1 Corinthians 12:28-31 – *And God hath set some in the church, first apostles, secondarily prophets, thirdly teachers, after that miracles, then gifts of healings, helps, governments, diversities of tongues. Are all apostles? are all prophets? are all teachers? are all workers of miracles? have all the gifts of healing? do all speak with tongues? do all interpret? But covet earnestly the best gifts: and yet shew I unto you a more excellent way.*

It is obvious that the other church has rejected or denied the best gifts; not only those gifted ministers ordained of God necessary for the perfecting of the believers, but also the power gifts demonstrating His love for us. Note that the *"more excellent way"* is love – referred to as "charity" (as revealed in 1 Corinthians 12).

There will be opposition to this next move of God. It will even include persecution coming from those who are part of the other church. Why, because the leadership of the other church will not accept it since they will not be able to control it. This rejection will likely add to the apostasy, the falling away, as prophesied. They prefer to hold on to their traditions, which is where their comfort and security is.

> Mark 7:6-8 – ... ... *This people honoureth me with their lips, but their heart is far from me. Howbeit in vain do they worship me, teaching for doctrines the commandments of men. For laying aside the commandment of God, ye hold the tradition of men, ...*

In upholding their traditions, they will think that they are doing God a favor, "defending their faith", and upholding what they think are His ways, not realizing it is their own ideas and security that they are defending.

> John 16:2 – *They shall* (excommunicate you) *put you out of the synagogues* (places of worship)*: yea, the time cometh, that whosoever killeth you will think that he doeth God service,* (amplified by author).

Note that persecution precedes the return of Christ.

> Matthew 24:8-14 – *All these are the beginning of sorrows. Then shall they deliver you up to be afflicted, and shall kill you: and ye shall be hated of all nations for my name's sake. And then shall many be offended, and shall betray one another, and shall hate one another. And many false prophets shall rise, and shall deceive many. And because iniquity shall abound, the love of many shall wax cold. But he that shall endure unto the end, the same shall be saved. And this gospel of the kingdom shall be preached in all the world for a witness unto all nations; and then shall the end come.*

Christ will be seen in those He is coming for; they will be like Him.

> 1 John 3:2 – *Beloved, now are we the sons of God, and it doth not yet appear what we shall be: but we know that, when he shall appear, we shall be like him; for we shall see him as he is.*

His character is the "righteousness" that we are to seek first with Him in this life.

> Matthew 6:33 – *But seek ye first the kingdom of God, and his righteousness; and all these things shall be added unto you.*

God then provides all that you need and puts into you what He desires. The problem is that man puts his own character and nature into all that he does, builds and organizes; even in church organizations and structures. Such a church then reflects the character of the builder; either man, or Christ, whoever the builder is. Thus we end up with two churches in the world, man's church, (the other church), and Christ's true church.

The true church is supposed to reflect Christ's character and nature. Do you see Him in your church? If not, seek Him and His anointed servants to bring this next move of God into you and your church.

> Matthew 16:18 – *and upon this rock* (Peter's statement that Jesus is the Son of God) *I will build my church; and the gates of hell shall not prevail against it.*

Jesus said He would build His church; thus it will reflect Him because He puts His qualities into it. It will be full of godliness and righteousness. These are the very things that are missing in many churches today: but, He is sending His unique builders to finish (perfect) that which He began, and the finished product will reflect Him; it will be holy, set apart and sanctified.

In this next move of God the two categories of believers, previously listed, are to be transformed into one classification, saints – sanctified, holy, set apart, godly. To be in any other category is to be disqualified to enter into the kingdom of God.

A question for you: how can you be identified now; as a Christian, one who is in Christ; or as a Saint, one who Christ is seen in? When His life is seen in the church, and in His people, then we will experience the manifestation of His Presence, which is His glory. This is what happened in Moses' tabernacle, and also in Solomon's temple.

> Exodus 40:34-35 – *Then a cloud covered the tent of the congregation, and the glory of the LORD filled the tabernacle. And Moses was not able to enter into the tent of the congregation, because the cloud abode thereon, and the glory of the LORD filled the tabernacle.*
>
> 1 Kings 8:10-11 – *And it came to pass, when the priests were come out of the holy place, that the cloud filled the house of the LORD, so that the priests could not stand to minister because of the cloud: for the glory of the LORD had filled the house of the LORD.*

As mentioned previously, the saints are the temple of God, the house of the Lord; we are His dwelling place. When we become what we are supposed to be, and conformed to His image, then His Glory will fill His temple, the dwelling place which we, the true church, are. Then the world, and the other church, will see the manifestation of his presence which should draw them in.

His Glory is seen when He manifests or reveals Himself to or through one of His servants who has an intimate fellowship with Him, as was the case with Moses. His Glory has been seen, can be seen and will be seen in those who are filled with Him. Just as Moses had a close intimate fellowship with the Lord on the mountain, so can we.

> Exodus 34:29-30 – *And it came to pass, when Moses came down from mount Sinai with the two tables of testimony in Moses' hand, when he came down from the mount, that Moses wist not that the skin of his face shone* (glowed with His glory) *while he talked with him. And when Aaron and all the children of Israel saw Moses, behold, the skin of his face shone (glowed with His glory); and they were afraid to come nigh him.*

The next move of God will lead to the manifestation of His presence in, upon and with His people. This happens just prior to Christ's return to set up His Kingdom. The saints, those of the true church that He built, will be glorious, glowing with the radiance of Him. They made themselves ready for Him.

However, there is a third group that does not fit in with either category discussed in this chapter because they are not believers. They may know who Jesus is, but they have no personal relationship with Him. They may go to church and, as a result, call themselves Christians, but there is no evidence that they are in Christ, or that Christ is in them. Thus you get the behavior that the apostle Paul identified that would be prevalent in these last days.

> 2 Timothy 3:1-5 – *This know also, that in the last days perilous times shall come. For men shall be lovers of their own selves, covetous, boasters, proud, blasphemers, disobedient to parents, unthankful, unholy, without natural* affection, *trucebreakers, false accusers, incontinent, fierce, despisers of those that are good, traitors, heady, highminded, lovers of pleasures more than lovers of God; having a form of godliness, but denying the power thereof: from such turn away.*

This third group composes part of the other church. They may have "*a form of godliness*", but they deny the life changing power of Christ and the gospel. Thus, Paul says. "*from such turn away*", or to stay away from such a group or church. This is because the knowledge that they have, and seek to enhance, is of the world and carnal flesh. Such people are actually walking in idolatry, worshipping what they do not know. Thus we see the results as Paul stated.

> 2 Timothy 3:6-7 – *For of this sort are they which creep into houses, and lead captive silly women laden with sins, led away with divers lusts, ever learning, and never able to come to the knowledge of the truth.*

The danger of being in this group is what they are going to experience if they don't turn to the truth, and repent. They are being led away from Christ, instead of to Him, by their wicked and corrupt leadership. Their problem is that they love the world, with its unrighteousness, and not the truth; thus they are subject to great deception and will be among the followers of the antichrist.

> 2 Thessalonians 2:10-12 – *and with all deceivableness of unrighteousness in them that perish; because they received not the love of the truth, that they might be saved. And for this cause God shall send them strong delusion, that they should believe a lie: that they all might be damned who believed not the truth, but had pleasure in unrighteousness.*

What category do you identify with; or are you even in one of these categories. Have you received what Almighty God has provided for you? It's a free gift!

> John 3:16-18 – *For God so loved the world, that he gave his only begotten Son, that whosoever believeth in him should not perish, but have everlasting life. For God sent not his Son into the world to condemn the world; but that the world through him might be saved. He that believeth on him is not condemned: but he that believeth not is condemned already, because he hath not believed in the name of the only begotten Son of God.*

Chapter 8

DECEPTION OF THE ENEMY

The Choice Between Life And Death

From the time that God began to deal with the nation of Israel, to make them a people for Himself, Satan has been standing in opposition. Satan, the thief and destroyer, has used the base carnality of man to resist God and to try to prevent His will from being fulfilled in His people.

Today the evidence of this struggle is overwhelming, even in churches and among God's people, those who claim to be Christians. How has our enemy been able to accomplish this in the church? The answer is simple: Christ warned us about it, and the scriptures give us a record of exactly how it happens.

The key that opens the door of the church to the deception of the enemy and his infiltration into the flock of the Lord is in the hands of the leadership of the church. This is caused by those who become Satan's servants, the "wolves in sheep's clothing"; the false prophets, preachers and teachers.

First we must understand that there are two terms that we all must deal with; "life" and "death". The life that God provides that we all need, is the life that Jesus Christ came to bring. This is life that man does not have apart from Christ, the *zoe* form of life; the eternal Spirit life as God has it. Without this life we are in spiritual death, separated from God. Death means separation: physical death is when the soul and spirit are separated from the body; spiritual death is when the soul and spirit are separated from God. Sin separates us from God; thus we need to be born-again in order to gain spiritual life (zoe).

> Isaiah 59:2 – *but your iniquities have separated between you and your God, and your sins have hid his face from you, that he will not hear.*

We may think we have life, but we only have it materially and physically, but not spiritually as God ordained for mankind when He formed man in His own image and likeness. That spiritual form of eternal life died as a result of sin. Satan offers the soulish and selfish substitute form of life which is filled with lusts for possessions and positions.

> Luke 12:15 – *And he said unto them, Take heed, and beware of covetousness: for a man's life consisteth not in the abundance of the things which he possesseth.*

We can see this clearly as we look at ancient Israel and see the options given them along with the results of their choices. Some preachers in the church today refer back to this time in Israel's history as object lessons. Unfortunately, there are ministers that are "wolves" in sheep's clothing, who preach a soulish and materialistic doctrine of the devil that does not bring spiritual life, but results in death. All the while their congregations think they are advancing in "life"; but it is material life, not true spiritual life.

It all comes down to one simple fact: it is all about the "choices" that we make in how we live. A blessing and a curse, (life and death), was a choice presented to God's people of ancient Israel. Their choices were presented to them after they entered the Promised Land.

> Deuteronomy 30:15, 19 – *See, I have set before thee this day life and good, and death and evil; … I call heaven and earth to record this day against you, that I have set before you life and death, blessing and cursing: therefore choose life, that both thou and thy seed may live:*

The Lord emphasized the importance of the choices that Israel was to make by naming two mountains in Samaria; one as a mount of blessing, the other as a mount of the curse.

> Deuteronomy 11:26-29 – *Behold, I set before you this day a blessing and a curse; a blessing, if ye obey the commandments of the LORD your God, which I command you this day: and a curse, if ye will not obey the commandments of the LORD your God, but turn aside out of the way which I command you this day, to go after other gods, which ye have not known. And it shall*

come to pass, when the LORD thy God hath brought thee in unto the land whither thou goest to possess it, that thou shalt put the blessing upon mount Gerizim, and the curse upon mount Ebal.

These two mountains still remain in the Promised Land and continue to serve as an illustration about choices. They are, Mt. Gerizm, for the blessing (life), and Mt. Ebal for the curse (death). Both mountains are also figuratively in the church as a matter of choice for each of us to make. Only now we identify these two mountains and "truth", (God's Word), and "deception", (the lies of the enemy).

A study of the character of these two mountains reveals what they represent. Mt. Ebal, the mount of cursing, stands approximately 3000 feet high and is the highest peak in the land. This mountain is steep, barren and rocky. The name Ebal means "bald" or bare, which implies its actual condition of being empty, a waste place. Mt. Ebal also represents the mountain of the Law, or the "curse of the Law". Joshua was instructed by the Lord to build an altar and record the Law etched in stone on this mountain to be a permanent record.

Joshua 8:30, 32, 34 – *Then Joshua built an altar unto the LORD God of Israel in mount Ebal, … And he wrote there upon the stones a copy of the law of Moses, which he wrote in the presence of the children of Israel. … And afterward he read all the words of the law, the blessings and cursings, according to all that is written in the book of the law.*

Mt. Ebal, stands for the curse of the law; the law which no human could fulfill but Jesus Christ. Those who look to this mountain will only find barrenness, emptiness, waste, spiritual bankruptcy and death. However, Mt. Gerizm represents the Mount of Blessing, (spiritual life). This mountain is across the valley to the south of Mt. Ebal. It stands 2849 feet high, lower than Mt. Ebal.

Ancient Hebrew traditions say that Mt. Gerizim was the site of the altars built to the Lord by Adam, Seth, Jacob and Noah. They also believe that this is where Abraham offered up his son Isaac to be sacrificed; (but that belief appears to be an error of ancient Hebrew tradition as Isaac was offered as a sacrifice on Mt. Moriah, the same place that Solomon built the Temple).

Jacob's well is located at Mt. Gerizim; it is also where Jesus spoke with the Samaritan woman, and revealed Himself as the Messiah to her.

> John 4:4-6 & 19-20 – *And he* (Jesus) *must needs go through Samaria* (to bring the gospel there). *Then cometh he to a city of Samaria, which is called Sychar, near to the parcel of ground that Jacob gave to his son Joseph. Now Jacob's well was there. … The woman saith unto him, Sir, I perceive that thou art a prophet. Our fathers worshipped in this mountain; and ye say, that in Jerusalem is the place where men ought to worship.*

> Amos 6:1 – *Woe to them that are at ease in Zion, and trust in the mountain of Samaeria, …*

Between these two mountains, at the eastern end, lies the city of Shechem. This is where Abram (Abraham) dwelt when he was first called by God to leave his family and go to a land that God wanted him to dwell in. Joseph's bones were also buried there.

The name Shechem means "neck"; "between the shoulders"; or "forms the shoulders". It represents a place of turning, a pivot point for the head to be able to turn and look at either mountain: it is as a place to look from and to choose which mountain to gaze upon.

Standing in this location of Shechem, what do people see when they look westward toward these two mountains? To the north, they see Mt. Ebal, which represents the world and its material wealth. From this highest mountain, one can view the world with its riches that appeals to the pursuit of selfish and lustful flesh, but the end result is the curse – death.

> 1 John 2:15-16 – *Love not the world, neither the things that are in the world. If any man love the world, the love of the Father is not in him. For all that is in the world, the lust of the flesh, and the lust of the eyes, and the pride of life, is not of the Father, but is of the world.*

This is a means of the deception that the enemy uses; making death look like life: as some may say, "This is really living, having all this wealth and possessions". Satan wants people to think that Mt. Ebal is the place of life when they look at it. Most people look to satisfy their carnal fleshly desires; represented by this mountain, but the end result is death. The enemy misrepresents this mountain to us, just like he misrepresented the tree of the Knowledge of Good and Evil to Eve in the garden. He gets people to desire this mountain, and the view of the world from there is impressive.

Most likely Mt. Ebal is the high mountain that the devil took Jesus up to in order to tempt Him with the possession of all the kingdoms of the world.

> Luke 4:5-7 – *And the devil, taking him up into an <u>high mountain</u>, shewed unto him all the kingdoms of the world in a moment of time. And the devil said unto him, All this power will I give thee, and the glory of them: for that is delivered unto me; and to whomsoever I will I give it. If thou therefore wilt worship me, all shall be thine.*

Satan still gets his false prophets and preachers to declare that this mountain is the place of life and blessing. They preach such because they have the "wolf" nature which is satisfied by the lustful things this mountain represents – the wealth of the world and its material possession. In reality, such ministers are preaching the curse - death. Unfortunately, they get many people to follow them up this mountain; they are part of the other church. (Recall the vision of Chapter One.)

This is part of the deception that Jesus warned about in these last days. Such preachers are not preaching the *zoe* life, but their focus is on the *psuche* or soulish life of the carnal mind. This is the materialistic doctrine of "success and prosperity" that gets people's attention off of God, The Creator, and onto the world and creation. To pursue this kind of material life is death. We all get to make a choice between life (zoe) and death.

> Romans 8:5-8 – *For they that are after the flesh do mind the things of the flesh; but they that are after the Spirit the things of the Spirit. For to be carnally minded is death; but to be spiritually minded is life and peace. Because the carnal mind is enmity against God: for it is not subject to the law of God, neither indeed can be. So then they that are in the flesh cannot please God.*

Satan likes us to look at Mt. Ebal because it is his domain; the kingdoms of the world, which are under his control; *for that is delivered unto me; and to whomsoever I will I give it.*

The devil uses the temptations of the riches of this world along with positions of power and influence that man can have if they yield to him. All these material worldly things are in his hands.

The result of selfish, soulish, fleshly pursuits is the curse of death; the curse that is the result of disobedience and cannot be broken by rebuking it, as many have been trying to do. Such a curse can only be broken by confession and true repentance. True repentance means that you have made a choice, turned around making a change in desires and direction. You now desire to focus upon Mt. Gerizm, seeking first the kingdom of God instead of the kingdoms of this world.

This world is Satan's kingdom represented by Mt. Ebal; it is his domain, the god of this world, and prince of the air, whom Jesus will eliminate upon His return to take possession of the earth and to establish His Kingdom.

From Shechem, looking south toward Mt. Gerizim, we gaze upon God's provision that gives true life and prosperity, which is eternal, not temporal. This blessing is obtained through faith and obedience, and spiritually represents the Kingdom of God – His blessings.

> Matthew 6:33 – *But seek ye first the kingdom of God, and his righteousness; and all these things shall be added unto you.*
>
> 2 Corinthians 4:18 – *while we look not at the things which are seen, but at the things which are not seen: for the things which are seen are temporal; but the things which are not seen are eternal.*
>
> 1Timothy 6:6-10 – *But godliness with contentment is great gain. For we brought nothing into this world, and it is certain we can carry nothing out. And having food and raiment let us be therewith content. But they that will be rich fall into temptation and a snare, and into many foolish and hurtful lusts, which drown men in destruction and perdition. For the love of money is the root of all evil: which while some coveted after,*

they have erred from the faith, and pierced themselves through with many sorrows.

Real and eternal prosperity is represented by Mt. Gerizim. People do not like to look at this mountain because they see an altar on it. This is an altar of sacrifice. Sacrifice is a form of death; it represents death to the self, the flesh, the soulish and selfish carnal sin nature of unredeemed man with all of its lusts. It is the Old Testament representation of the cross of Jesus Christ.

> Luke 9:23-25 – *And he said to them all, If any man will come after me, let him deny himself, and take up his cross daily, and follow me. For whosoever will save his life shall lose it: but whosoever will lose his life for my sake, the same shall save it. For what is a man advantaged, if he gain the whole world, and lose himself, or be cast away?*

People don't want their selfish desires to die or be denied; that is unless they have had a genuine encounter with Jesus Christ as Savior and Lord. That is why so many prefer to remain focused on Mt. Ebal; this includes much of the other church. But a true follower of Jesus becomes His disciple and is willing to die to "self" with it's soulish lusts.

> Galatians 2:20 – *I am crucified with Christ: nevertheless I live; yet not I, but Christ liveth in me: and the life which I now live in the flesh I live by the faith of the Son of God, who loved me, and gave himself for me.*

Mt. Gerizim is also likely to be the "mount of transfiguration" where Jesus met with Moses and Elijah. This mountain was along the route as He journeyed from Galilee back south to Jerusalem.

> Luke 9:28-31 – *And it came to pass about an eight days after these sayings, he took Peter and John and James, and went up into a mountain to pray. And as he prayed, the fashion of his countenance was altered, and his raiment was white and glistering. And, behold, there talked with him two men, which were Moses and Elias: who appeared in glory, and spake of his decease which he should accomplish at Jerusalem.*

As Jesus was returning from Galilee He passed through Samaria on the normal route which goes by Shechem. He lingered there for a time, and leaving most of His disciples in the city while He took Peter, John and James with Him up into the mountain. This special mountain is where the patriarchs built altars of sacrifice to God. It was an obvious place to meet with the transformed and glorified Moses and Elijah who spoke with Him about His soon offering of Himself as the sacrifice for all mankind's sins. (Note: Jesus was transfigured to appear just like Moses and Elijah who were now in their eternal resurrected and glorified bodies).

> Luke 9:37 – *And it came to pass, that on the next day, when they were come down from the hill, much people met him.*

Jesus then ministered in this Samaritan city where He cast out a demon from a child that His disciples, whom He left behind in town, but they could not cast out. After the amazing things the people of that city saw, they sent word to the surrounding area that Jesus was coming; but that was not in His plan because Jesus determined that it was time for Him to resume His journey with His disciples to Jerusalem without spending any more time ministering in other Samaritan cities, because He had an appointment to keep.

> Luke 9:51-53 – *And it came to pass, when the time was come that he should be received up, he stedfastly set his face to go to Jerusalem, and sent messengers before his face: and they went, and entered into a village of the Samaritans, to make ready for him. And they did not receive him, because his face was as though he would go to Jerusalem.*

It is only fitting that the place where Abraham offered up his son as a sacrifice to God, that it would be the place where God responded to Abraham's covenant act of faith by offering His own Son, the Lamb of God, as sin's sacrifice on Mt. Moriah in Jerusalem.

Special attention needs to be paid on the topic of discussion with Moses and Elijah on top of Mt. Gerizim at the time of His transfiguration. They both spoke of His crucifixion in Jerusalem, and how it will be the total fulfillment of the prophesied promised Lamb of God, and what it will accomplish. What an ideal location for that conversation to occur, on the mountain of blessing; the mountain that truly represents LIFE for God's faithful people.

All believers are to place themselves on a symbolic altar of sacrifice, the cross, to die to self, so that we might live unto Him, allowing His life to flow through us. This is the redeeming life, the zoe of God; the blessing represented by Mt. Gerizim.

> Galatians 5:24 – *And they that are Christ's have crucified the flesh with the affections and lusts.*

> Romans 12:1 – *I beseech you therefore, brethren, by the mercies of God, that ye present your bodies a living sacrifice, holy, acceptable unto God, which is your reasonable service.*

This is what God's servants and ministers are to do; it is also what the wolves refuse to do.

> John 12:24-25 – *Verily, verily, I say unto you, Except a corn of wheat fall into the ground and die, it abideth alone: but if it die, it bringeth forth much fruit. He that loveth his life shall lose it; and he that hateth his life in this world shall keep it unto life eternal.*

The name Gerizim means: cut, cut up, or cut off, as to remove the old, to eliminate the fleshly carnal nature, as in being circumcised.

> Colossians 2:11 – *in whom also ye are circumcised with the circumcision made without hands, in putting off the body of the sins of the flesh by the circumcision of Christ:*

Mt. Gerizim is the mount of Blessing, it can also be called the mount of Grace, because God's Grace is provided and represented by this mountain; and it was to be significant to Israel. Both mountains were prophetic for Israel: Mt. Ebal is the mount of the Law with its results; Mt. Gerizim is the mount of Grace and its results.

Contrary to many teachings on the blessing of Deuteronomy chapter 27 which have been touted in the 1970's and 80's; you do not, and cannot, "claim" these blessing, as many ministers in the Word of Faith organization teach. You cannot rebuke the curse of disobedience to God. You walk in these blessings by a life of faithfulness and obedience to Him. This was the lesson that Israel failed to learn.

> Deuteronomy 28:15 – *But it shall come to pass, if thou wilt not hearken unto the voice of the LORD thy God, to observe to do all his commandments and his statutes which I command thee this day; that all these curses shall come upon thee, and overtake thee:*

The endless grace of God still beckons from Mt. Gerizim. It calls for His people to turn, repent and walk in obedience to Him, so they can still be blessed.

> Deuteronomy 30:1-5, 15-16 – *And it shall come to pass, when all these things are come upon thee, the blessing and the curse, which I have set before thee, and thou shalt call them to mind among all the nations, whither the LORD thy God hath driven thee, and shalt return unto the LORD thy God, and shalt obey his voice according to all that I command thee this day, thou and thy children, with all thine heart, and with all thy soul; that then the LORD thy God will turn thy captivity, and have compassion upon thee, and will return and gather thee from all the nations, whither the LORD thy God hath scattered thee. If any of thine be driven out unto the outmost parts of heaven, from thence will the LORD thy God gather thee, and from thence will he fetch thee: and the LORD thy God will bring thee into the land which thy fathers possessed, and thou shalt possess it; and he will do thee good, and multiply thee above thy fathers. See, I have set before thee this day life and good, and death and evil; in that I command thee this day to love the LORD thy God, to walk in his ways, and to keep his commandments and his statutes and his judgments, that thou mayest live and multiply: and the LORD thy God shall bless thee in the land whither thou goest to possess it.*

The zoe life that Jesus came to bring is Life in the Spirit; Life as God has it; the life that God placed in Adam when He formed him from the dust of the earth: the same life that was lost through sin. It is currently the life that man does not have apart from Christ and abiding with Him. This is the life we are to walk in so we can experience the blessing of Mt. Gerizim, and His presence.

True success and prosperity are in Mt. Gerizim, even though all you can see is the altar of sacrifice on it. That is because this is eternal success and spiritual prosperity; however it will cost you your life; your carnal, soulish, lustful, selfish life that seeks self-gratification. The life you are to live now on this earth is His life seen in you: His manners, His ways, His truth, His morals, His character and nature. This is a life of faith, being faithful and walking in fellowship with Him as the sons of God.

Jesus warned that the deception in these last days is designed to turn the heads of God's people, looking from Shechem toward these mountains, but focusing on Mt. Ebal. Thus it will require faith and endurance to resist the lure of the world and remain faithful to the Lord in order to enjoy the blessing of Mt. Gerizim.

> Matthew 24:11-12 – *And many false prophets shall rise, and shall deceive many. And because iniquity shall abound, the love of many shall wax cold. But he that shall endure unto the end, the same shall be saved.*

The false doctrines of men and demons are the product of Mt. Ebal, even though they are preached in His name.

> Ephesians 4:14 – *that we henceforth be no more children, tossed to and fro, and carried about with every wind of doctrine, by the sleight of men, and cunning craftiness, whereby they lie in wait to deceive;*

> Matthew 24:4-5 – *And Jesus answered and said unto them, Take heed that no man deceive you. For many shall come in my name, saying, I am Christ; and shall deceive many.*

Such are the false prophets, preachers and teachers whose lives are focused on Mt. Ebal and have never died to self as required to be a true servant of Christ.

> Matthew 7:22-23 – *Many will say to me in that day, Lord, Lord, have we not prophesied in thy name? and in thy name*

have cast out devils? and in thy name done many wonderful works? And then will I profess unto them, I never knew you: depart from me, ye that work iniquity.

Notice that Jesus said, "I never knew you", to these false ministers. This may not mean that they were not born-again, but it does mean that they never had an intimate fellowship with Christ. The word "knew" is the same word used when describing a man's most intimate relationship with his wife. Jesus said He never had the experience of close and intimate fellowship with them. They were too busy doing their own thing, or their ministry, to know what He wanted of them.

They did not take time to be close to Him, so He never "knew" them as He wanted; they were not abiding in the vine so that His life and His will could flow through them. Such ministers did not work as Jesus would have them do as they did not know or follow His directions in performing their ministry. Thus they offer the counterfeit life represented by Mt. Ebal.

The key to understanding this passage is in the word "obedience" in how to build the Lord's house – His church.

Matthew 7:24-27 – *Therefore whosoever heareth these sayings of mine, and doeth them, I will liken him unto a wise man, which built his house upon a rock: and the rain descended, and the floods came, and the winds blew, and beat upon that house; and it fell not: for it was founded upon a rock. And every one that heareth these sayings of mine, and doeth them not, shall be likened unto a foolish man, which built his house upon the sand: and the rain descended, and the floods came, and the winds blew, and beat upon that house; and it fell: and great was the fall of it.*

Building in obedience to Christ is to build on the rock – Mt. Gerizim. When preachers do not build in obedience to Christ, but build their own way instead of building His way, then they are building on sand – on Mt. Ebal. When the storms of life hit the church (believers), only those built on the rock – Mt. Gerizim, will stand. Those lives built on the sand, or on Mt. Ebal, will not endure when the trials and tribulations of this life; they will collapse.

Do not be deceived; no matter how appealing preachers make the things of this vile world look, as things seen from Mt. Ebal, the deception of the enemy leads to death. It may have been disguised as life when looked at from this world's point of view, or from the other church's point of view, but it is all deception.

God's command to His people is to choose life, the right kind of life; the zoe, eternal kind of life, that God gives through Jesus Christ.

> Deuteronomy 30:19-20 – *I call heaven and earth to record this day against you, that I have set before you life and death, blessing and cursing: therefore choose life, that both thou and thy seed may live: that thou mayest love the LORD thy God, and that thou mayest obey his voice, and that thou mayest cleave unto him: for he is thy life, and the length of thy days: that thou mayest dwell in the land which the LORD sware unto thy fathers, to Abraham, to Isaac, and to Jacob, to give them.*

Note: since the Word and promises of God are eternal, that which God, and Jesus, spoke is still valid today.

> Luke 21:33 – *Heaven and earth shall pass away: but my words shall not pass away.*

Therefore: -------------**CHOOSE LIFE !**--------------

Chapter 9

REDEMPTION –
TOTAL OR PARTIAL

Which Will You Believe

Redemption: as used in a variety of situations means being set free from an adverse condition; the process of being redeemed; being completely restored to original condition or ownership; having all outstanding liable conditions and obligations satisfied. The idea of redemption being total or partial sounds extreme, but this topic needs a closer look.

In the Bible, redemption is recognized as God having restored His people, be they ancient Israel of the Old Testament, or the church of the New Testament. God brings them back into being His children; restored from their being separated from Him by their corrupt and sinful state, which is spiritual darkness.

God provided redemption for Israel from their slavery in Egypt. Their redemption was initiated by means of the Passover sacrifice of a lamb.

> Exodus 15:13 – *Thou in thy mercy hast led forth the people which thou hast redeemed: thou hast guided them in thy strength unto thy holy habitation.*

> 1 Chronicles 17:21 – *And what one nation in the earth is like thy people Israel, whom God went to redeem to be his own people, to make thee a name of greatness and terribleness, by driving out nations from before thy people, whom thou hast redeemed out of Egypt?*

Israel's redemption from slavery in Egypt was a shadow of their redemption from sin and iniquity that followed nearly fifteen hundred years later when Jesus became the Passover Lamb at His crucifixion.

> Psalm 130:7-8 – *Let Israel hope in the Lord; for with the Lord there is mercy, and with him is plenteous redemption. And he shall redeem Israel from all his iniquities.*

The old covenant of God was replaced with a new and better covenant that provided redemption for all the rest of mankind, not just Israel. Thus Jesus provided for all of mankind's redemption when He became our Passover Lamb.

> 1 Corinthians 5:7b – ... *For even Christ our passover is sacrificed for us:*

> Romans 3:23-24 – *for all have sinned, and come short of the glory of God; being justified freely by his grace through the redemption that is in Christ Jesus:*

> Ephesians 1:7 – *in whom we have redemption through his blood, the forgiveness of sins, according to the riches of his grace;*

> Colossians 1:13-14 – *who hath delivered us from the power of darkness, and hath translated us into the kingdom of his dear Son: in whom we have redemption through his blood, even the forgiveness of sins: who hath delivered us from the power of darkness, and hath translated us into the kingdom of his dear Son:*

To better understand what God provided in the Passover we need to go back and look at the original Passover that delivered Israel from the bondage of Egypt. The story of Israel's redemption and deliverance from Egypt is summarized as follows:

> Psalm 105:26-37 – *He sent Moses his servant; and Aaron whom he had chosen. They shewed his signs among them, and wonders in the land of Ham. He sent darkness, and made it*

dark; and they rebelled not against his word. He turned their waters into blood, and slew their fish. Their land brought forth frogs in abundance, in the chambers of their kings. He spake, and there came divers sorts of flies, and lice in all their coasts. He gave them hail for rain, and flaming fire in their land. He smote their vines also and their fig trees; and brake the trees of their coasts. He spake, and the locusts came, and caterpillers, and that without number, and did eat up all the herbs in their land, and devoured the fruit of their ground. He smote also all the firstborn in their land, the chief of all their strength. He brought them forth also with silver and gold: and there was not one feeble person among their tribes.

Note: the ten plagues that God sent upon the Egyptians were not to convince Pharaoh of God's sovereignty, but to convince the Israelites that Moses was the one that they should follow. Otherwise, without the demonstration of God's power being with the word that came from Moses, they would not have obeyed him and placed the lamb's blood on their doorposts.

Israel's bondage in Egypt symbolizes mankind's bondage to the evils of sin in this vile world. Just as God's people Israel were set free as a result of the blood sacrifice that delivered them, so it is with the blood sacrifice of Jesus on the cross at the time of Passover about fifteen hundred years later that sets people free from the curse and penalty of sin.

Consider the result of that first Passover: the oppression that the Israelites were under completely ended; they were now a free people. Not only were they free of physical torment, but also from the mental and emotional oppression that their captors placed on them in their depressed condition. Then recognize that God had healed every single one of the Israelites, including the aged ones; as it is written: *"and there was not one feeble person among their tribes"*. (Feeble means weak or infirmed.) Thus God healed all that had a physical infirmity so that they could make the journey to the Promised Land. On top of this, their enemy gave them of their own riches: *"He brought them forth also with silver and gold"*. (This sounds like a promise from God's Word to us.)

Proverbs 13:22b – ... *and the wealth of the sinner is laid up for the just.*

An exact parallel to the first Passover was fulfilled when Jesus became the Passover Lamb, being made the sacrifice for the bondage of sin to free all of mankind who believe on His blood atonement on the cross – (as in 1 Corinthians 5:7b sbove).

By faith in what Jesus did on the cross frees all that accept His atonement from the bondage of sin which results in spiritual death, separation from God. As a result of being freed from the curse of sin's enslavement, we are also delivered from the mental and emotional torment that the enemy oppresses us with. On top of this is the fact that, in His atonement Jesus provided physical healing to all – if they will accept it by faith in the complete deliverance in His sacrifice.

> Isaiah 55:4-5 – *Surely he hath borne our griefs, and carried our sorrows: yet we did esteem him stricken, smitten of God, and afflicted. But he was wounded for our transgressions, he was bruised for our iniquities: the chastisement of our peace was upon him; and with his stripes we are healed.*

What Jesus did for those of us who believe in Him is for us to be fully restored to the blessings and life in the kingdom of God, even now in this life. Thus we have total redemption provided for mankind by almighty God through His Son, Jesus Christ, and His atoning work on the cross. The total redemption means God provided for man's spirit, soul and body. This may sound strange, but the topic of redemption has divided churches since the time of the "reformation" back in the sixteenth century.

The Reformation began when Martin Luther proclaimed that it is by faith that we receive the redemptive work of Christ, and not by the works the Roman Catholic Church, or the other churches: this includes infant baptism, catechism, and communion. Following Luther's revelations, various theologians began to dispute the "how and what" of that which is provided in Christ's atonement.

This introduces the topic of REDEMPTION – TOTAL or PARTIAL. There are variations of church denominations based on their particular beliefs and doctrines. Some churches accept Christ's total redemption for spirit, soul and body, while other churches only accept partial redemption, that of only the soul and spirit; they deny that physical healing is in the atonement. But, as already noted as in the original Passover, deliverance from feebleness and infirmity (physical healing) was, and still is provided.

A major conflict between total redemption and partial redemption comes from those who hold to Calvinist doctrines. It appears that the Calvinists accept partial redemption for the soul and spirit but they cannot accept the supernatural works of God that He has provided for in total redemption. They don't believe in healing; they don't believe the works of demons, (the afflictions and oppressions of the devil); they don't believe in the Baptism of the Holy Spirit or in the supernatural Gifts of the Spirit. Thus they come up short in all that God has given; and as a result, they cannot live in the overcoming victories that God provides.

Partial redemption will get them "saved", but many are still in physical and emotional bondages of the enemy that oppresses them. They deny the supernatural power, and therefore they are lacking in what is available in total redemption. It is a matter of fully trusting and believing all of God's Word in order to walk in total redemption.

If you don't believe, you don't receive it! That is why many only accept partial redemption. Yet there are still other churches that preach a soulish or social gospel that offers nothing but the religion of "humanism"; man as god and who rules his own destiny. Such churches are living according to the dictates of the flesh and this vile world. They reject what God has done and provided, therefore they have no redemption at all.

So which redemption do you accept, total or partial, or none at all? You will have what you believe for!

Chapter 10

KEY ITEMS OF MINISTRY

- THE CROSS IN YOUR LIFE
- WHOSE MINISTRY ARE YOU DOING
- OPERATING IN THE FEAR OF GOD
- OBEDIENCE IN MINISTRY
- BEING QUALIFIED TO RULE

THE CROSS IN YOUR LIFE

The very first requirement to be a true servant or minister of the Lord Jesus Christ is to be His disciple. The word "disciple" means being under the discipline of the master who you follow. Furthermore the first requirement to being a disciple of Jesus is the value of the cross in your life as one of His ministers.

> Luke 9:23 – *And he said to them all, If any man will come after me, let him deny himself, and take up his cross daily, and follow me.*

The cross is the symbol of death. Jesus declared that in order to be His disciple you must deny self, the fleshly desires of the base human nature; take up the cross, the symbol of death to selfishness, then go on to follow Him.

> Luke 14:27 – *And whosoever doth not bear his cross, and come after me, cannot be my disciple.*

This passage has been used multiple times in this volume because it is so important. Even Jesus repeated this need for the cross in the life of His disciples. There are a few questions that each person in the service of the Lord's ministry that need to be addressed.

- Have you come to your cross and accepted it?
- What have you done with your cross?
- What hinders your fellowship and walk with Christ?
- What do you need to place on the cross, to die to and deny?
- Do you deal with it daily so as to not allow the selfish carnal nature to rule over you?

Jesus said that the cross needs to be embraced daily in order to prevent the flesh from engaging in its selfish lusts, (which we all have).

Please be aware that what you place on the cross will likely be painful in some way, because it will be a loss of something that you have long held onto as part of your life. It may be something that actually does not belong, because it may hinder your obedience and walk with the Lord. It turns out that self is the issue, a daily issue that needs to be under His discipline and eliminated.

Unfortunately, there are those in the ministry of some churches that have not been under the discipleship of Christ, and have not taken up their cross. Instead they may have been made man's disciples of their denomination, organization, or the Institutionalized Religious System, (the I.R.S.). Thus there has been no cross in their lives. These are the ministers that are not truly servants of Christ. There is too much "self" in their lives and ministry. These are the kind of ministers that are doing things their own way in building a church.

> Matthew 7:22-23 – *Many will say to me in that day, Lord, Lord, have we not prophesied in thy name? and in thy name have cast out devils? and in thy name done many wonderful works? And then will I profess unto them, I never knew you: depart from me, ye that work iniquity.*

> Matthew 10:38 – *And he that taketh not his cross, and followeth after me, is not worthy of me.*

There is another issue that some who are called to the ministry must endure, and it is similar to the cross experience: it is called the "wilderness" experience. This is like what the apostle Paul went through after his conversion.

Galatians 1:15-17 – But when it pleased God, who separated me from my mother's womb, and called me by his grace, to reveal his Son in me, that I might preach him among the heathen; immediately I conferred not with flesh and blood: neither went I up to Jerusalem to them which were apostles before me; but I went into Arabia, and returned again unto Damascus.

This time that Paul spent in the wilderness of Arabia was equivalent to the cross experience. In the wilderness, which is a lonely place, is where the excess religious baggage falls off and is left behind. This is where the erroneous doctrines and traditions that were previously learned are exposed, eliminated or amended with the truth as revealed by the Holy Spirit. It is where the apostle Paul received his understanding of how the Old Testament scriptures were fulfilled in Jesus Christ, enabling him to declare and write much of the New Testament.

The wilderness experience is a process by which those who have been in a form of traditional ministry within the Institutionalized Religious System, but have been awakened and renewed by the Holy Spirit to move deeper into their relationship with the Lord, can be used by Him and building the church His way.

WHOSE MINISTRY ARE YOU DOING – YOURS OR HIS?

Is a minister serving out of a sense of duty, or as a result of a divine call and direction? There is a big difference, as will be seen in the results. While serving as a seminary professor, I spoke at a commencement ceremony to a large group of ministers who were receiving their advanced degrees. I told them that if they are feeling overwhelmed, or burned out in their ministry, then they need to consider the possibility that they have taken upon themselves tasks that the Lord has not assigned to them. Then I gave them the "Word of the Lord".

Matthew 11:28-30 – Come unto me, all ye that labour and are heavy laden, and I will give you rest. Take my yoke upon you, and learn of me; for I am meek and lowly in heart: and ye shall find rest unto your souls. For my yoke is easy, and my burden is light.

Those truly ordained of the Lord to do His ministry have been given His direction and ability to do what He has assigned. Those who feel overwhelmed, or burned out by their work in the ministry, are doing things that Christ has not directed them to do. This means that they are doing their own thing, or things that man has mandated them to do; they are not being led by the Holy Spirit.

Jesus gave us an example of those who labor in ministry out of a sense of duty. He mentions that it can become a troubling burden of undue care. It seems that, many in ministry have fallen into this category of serving, which is simply – functioning in ministry according to human assumption, a sense of duty.

> Luke 10:38-42 – *Now it came to pass, as they went, that he entered into a certain village: and a certain woman named Martha received him into her house. And she had a sister called Mary, which also sat at Jesus' feet, and heard his word. But Martha was cumbered about much serving, and came to him, and said, Lord, dost thou not care that my sister hath left me to serve alone? bid her therefore that she help me. And Jesus answered and said unto her, Martha, Martha, thou art careful and troubled about many things: but one thing is needful: and Mary hath chosen that good part, which shall not be taken away from her.*

Martha represents a minister, busy, concerned, consumed and troubled with an excessive sense of duty and responsibility. There were many things that occupied her time and attention that she thought was her duty. (Note: serving and ministry means the same thing.)

Scripture says that she was "cumbered" with serving. Being cumbered means to be distracted; drawn away; drawn in different directions and burdened down with the care of serving. It was not a joy to her, but a burden that she did out of that sense of duty.

She was actually trying to earn recognition for her labor in ministry. However, Jesus only recognized her troubled heart which was revealed in a jealousy over her sister who was not serving. Instead, Mary was enjoying the benefits of a relationship and fellowship with her Lord.

It seems that many ministers today are striving to attain recognition through achievement in our goal oriented society. They feel they have to build bigger churches, have more programs, get more people into their buildings, have their services on television or social media in order to have greater public exposure. They make all kinds of efforts that eventually lead to "burn-out".

"Burn-out" is the result of the Martha complex, being cumbered about much serving that one has assumed is necessary. Jesus said that His "yoke was easy and His burden was light". If this is not the case in your ministry then you need to consider stopping your vain activities and sit down at Jesus feet for a personal re-evaluation from Him about what He called you to do. You need to choose the one thing that is necessary for any and all ministry.

Those who are consumed with a sense of duty, may indeed achieve many wonderful works; but instead of a reward for their labors, they may receive a rebuke as did the church at Ephesus. This church suffered from the "Martha complex" which distracted it and drew it away from its "first love".

> Revelation 2:1-5 – *Unto the angel of the church of Ephesus write; These things saith he that holdeth the seven stars in his right hand, who walketh in the midst of the seven golden candlesticks; I know thy works, and thy labour, and thy patience, and how thou canst not bear them which are evil: and thou hast tried them which say they are apostles, and are not, and hast found them liars: and hast borne, and hast patience, and for my name's sake hast laboured, and hast not fainted. Nevertheless I have somewhat against thee, because thou hast left thy first love. Remember therefore from whence thou art fallen from* (your intimate relationship and fellowship with Me), *and repent,* (of your distancing yourself from close fellowship with Me, and come back and sit at my feet); *and do the first works; or else I will come unto thee quickly, and will remove thy candlestick* (your status as an assembly of mine) *out of his place, except thou repent.* (Amplification added by author).

This church expressed its zeal for the Lord in the wrong way. They did it in works for Him rather than expressing their zeal toward Him and allowing Him to direct their works. He does not need us to work for Him; He wants to work through us. It is not to be our works, but His works that He does through us. The only way this can be achieved is when we become like Mary, stop our ministry and sit at His feet and learn from Him.

Mary laid down her ministry for the sake of drawing close to Jesus and hearing what He had to say – (Luke 10:39). Jesus said that Mary chose that which was obviously better at that particular time rather than being busy with ministry. She did what was necessary for preparation of the true, pure and powerful ministry unto the Lord. She chose to draw closer to Him, to be in His presence, to observe Him and to hear Him.

This we all need to do at any time we are to serve Him in ministry. Just as God spoke from the cloud to Peter while on the Mount of Transfiguration, "Hear Him"!

> Matthew 17:5 – *While he yet spake, behold, a bright cloud overshadowed them: and behold a voice out of the cloud, which said, This is my beloved Son, in whom I am well pleased; hear ye him.*

Peter wanted to embark on a task of his own, (well-meaning though it may be, erecting monuments to Moses and Elijah); but it would have been a major distraction from what God wanted of him. So Peter was sovereignly corrected and prevented from doing his own works. Thus it is very important to hear Him, just as Mary chose to do.

The many Martha's in ministry are those who are busy laboring for the Lord, but they are "doing their own thing". They are doing what Peter tried to do; they are building tabernacles of their own ministries, by their own efforts. The results are not God's plans being accomplished but their own presumed ideas of what God's will is. They are too busy in ministry to take time to sit at Jesus feet, as Mary did, to hear Him, to find out what He is doing, and wants them to do.

Mary gave us the example of preparation and maintenance of ministry. By sitting at Jesus feet, she was able to learn how to minister the way He wanted her to. By focusing on Him, rather than on her serving in ministry, she was equipped and prepared of Him; shown by Him what to speak, what to do, and how to do it. She learned from Him how to minister to others.

Who else is better qualified to equip us for ministry than He is? Instead, nearly all those in the ministry today are taught by men in organized educational institutions. Such education is necessary, but for the Lord's work, He needs to be involved in our preparation. Man's training and preparation rarely requires us to sit at His feet for periods of time to behold Him. Man cannot control this activity; nor can he put a passing grade on it for completing a course. Most educators cannot even comprehend the idea of doing such a thing, thinking it is a waste of time; this is the Martha way of thinking.

Therefore, ministers trained in seminaries by man's way go off in their own efforts to do the work of God with limited ability, led by their own human spirit, driven by a need to work out of a sense of duty to show himself as a faithful servant. However, the truly faithful servant can only function when he has heard from his Lord and Master, and goes in obedience to the Master's directions.

Sitting at His feet to hear Him is done by prayer and fasting, spending quality time in His presence. Ministry can then be directed by Him. As we see Him spiritually, we hear Him speak; then we can go and do what He directs us to do, because it is He and the Father by His Spirit that works in and through us.

> John 14:12 – *Verily, verily, I say unto you, He that believeth on me, the works that I do shall he do also; and greater works than these shall he do; because I go unto my Father.*

As a result of being led by His Holy Spirit we will see supernatural manifestations that natural man cannot accomplish. This is because it is His work that He does through His obedient servants.

This is the same principle of work that Jesus used in fulfilling His ministry. He spent time in His Father's presence and got direction from the Father on what to say, and what to do. This example from Jesus is given for us to follow so that all ministry is ultimately of and from God, our Heavenly Father. Consider what Jesus said concerning the works He did and wants us to do also.

> John 14:10-11 – *Believest thou not that I am in the Father, and the Father in me? the words that I speak unto you I speak not of myself: but the Father that dwelleth in me, he doeth the works. Believe me that I am in the Father, and the Father in me: or else believe me for the very works' sake.*

> John 5:19 – *Then answered Jesus and said unto them, Verily, verily, I say unto you, The Son can do nothing of himself, but what he seeth the Father do: for what things soever he doeth, these also doeth the Son likewise.*

John 7:16 – *Jesus answered them, and said, My doctrine is not mine, but his that sent me.*

John 8:26-28 – *I have many things to say and to judge of you: but he that sent me is true; and I speak to the world those things which I have heard of him. They understood not that he spake to them of the Father. Then said Jesus unto them, When ye have lifted up the Son of man, then shall ye know that I am he, and that I do nothing of myself; but as my Father hath taught me, I speak these things.*

As Jesus spent time in prayer with the Father, He received divine direction and instruction of what to say, where to go, and what to do. Nothing in Jesus' ministry was hap-hazard but deliberate.

So it is as we sit at Jesus feet as Mary did. We are to receive His instruction of what to say, where to go, and what to do. This is actually being led of the Holy Spirit which we are commanded to do, just as Paul learned it.

Romans 8:14 – *For as many as are led by the Spirit of God, they are the sons of God.*

To do His work, the Spirit of God had to be upon Jesus, and He did what the Father told Him, and showed Him. He did all things in the Father's timing and at the Father's direction.

Please be aware that it is possible to do the right thing in the wrong place or at the wrong time; in doing so we may make a mess of things. This is why we must hear from Him so that we obey and do, or say the right thing at the right time in the right place. It is a sad presumption for us to continue to just go and do out of a sense of duty without divine directives which insures the greatest productivity with the least amount of effort.

This makes His yoke easy and His burden light. There is no being "cumbered", troubled, burdened or burned-out in ministry when we follow His leading.

Here is another issue to consider: you may be embarking on a work that God has assigned to another minister, and by you attempting to move in where you were not directed will interfere with what God ordained through the other. Thus you could actually mess things up.

Now a note of caution: do not engage in presumption. Only go as far as the Lord directs, no further; even if it looks like wonderful doors of opportunity are open. To go beyond his direction is to be disobedient and unfaithful. Doing so can cause you to take upon yourself more than He has given you the ability to handle. Then the extra measure you have engaged in will have to be carried on by your own strength, and you will also have to support with your own means and finances. This has been a common mistake of many well-known ministries.

Likewise, say only what you hear the Holy Spirit say, no more. Do only what you see He wants you to do, nothing else. Then your ministry will be just like His; it will be Him working and not you. This requires patience in ministry; particularly when we feel that we must be doing something and not waiting. We need to learn to wait on the Lord; sit at His feet and not move until we are instructed when and where to go, what say, and what to do.

> Isaiah 40:31 – *but they that wait upon the Lord shall renew their strength; they shall mount up with wings as eagles; they shall run and be weary; they shall walk and not faint.*

This kind of faithfulness and obedience will produce a great deal more results than what we can achieve by putting forth our own efforts, programs and ideas. Then when you complete each task that He assigns to you, do as Jesus' disciples did; return to Him to sit at His feet to hear Him, to receive more of Him. There is always more He wants to teach you and show you; more to receive. How will you receive of Him if you don't stop your serving, as Martha, and wait on Him as Mary did. Sit at His feet for more words to speak, places to go, and things to do; let Him direct your ministry. Then you will see great and mighty things happen because your ministry will actually be as though He is doing it.

The question for those in ministry is: whose ministry are you engaged in; yours, the church's, the organization's, or His? Whose servant are you: your church and its organizational denomination; or His? Who are you going to obey in building His church: man, as taught in schools and seminaries, or Christ, as taught by the Holy Spirit?

OPERATING IN THE FEAR OF GOD

In ministry, and in many churches, there is no fear of God! This fear is the reverential respect that one has for absolute authority; just as a child has for his father. It is in knowing that you are under the one who has authority over you; the one who can mete out blessings or punishments in accordance with your devotion and obedience. It is in knowing that His power is absolute and cannot be escaped or avoided except through repentance and asking forgiveness, or obedience. It is also in knowing that His power can cover you and be with you in all that you submit to Him to do.

The lack of the fear of God is evidenced by how some ministers perform in their ministry; how churches operate, and by what the results are. This evidence became so pronounced back in the 1960's, that Time magazine featured an article stating "God Is Dead"; and so it seemed in far too many churches. The main reason for this is the lack of the life, and light of Christ, that the world is supposed to see, was not evident in most of the churches. Jesus said that His believers are to be the salt of the earth; salt is a preservative that stops fleshly corruption; and we are also to be the light that illuminates the way to truth and righteousness.

> Matthew 5:13-16 – *Ye are the salt of the earth: but if the salt have lost his savour, wherewith shall it be salted? it is thenceforth good for nothing, but to be cast out, and to be trodden under foot of men. Ye are the light of the world. A city that is set on an hill cannot be hid. Neither do men light a candle, and put it under a bushel, but on a candlestick; and it giveth light unto all that are in the house. Let your light so shine before men, that they may see your good works, and glorify your Father which is in heaven.*

It appears that the salt of most churches is no longer of any use; and the light went out as many churches have nothing of spiritual quality of life to offer. This is mostly because of the lack of the fear of God in the believers. It was not, and still is not, being taught to most believers! Thus there is no true reverence of the Lord and His Word in much of the church today, especially in the other church.

In 1 Chronicles 13 we read the story of how King David wanted to return the Ark of the Covenant back to Jerusalem. His intentions were very noble, as are most of those in ministry today. However, things did not work out as he thought because he did it "his" way and not according to God's established way. When things went wrong, David got upset at God.

> 1 Chronicles 13:3-4 – *and let us bring again the ark of our God to us: for we enquired not at it in the days of Saul. And all the congregation said that they would do so: for the thing was right in the eyes of all the people.*

God had originally given directions in how the Ark was to be transported, but those directions were not followed resulting in dire consequences, even death.

> 1 Chronicles 13:9-10 – *And when they came unto the threshing floor of Chidon, Uzza put forth his hand to hold the ark; for the oxen stumbled. And the anger of the LORD was kindled against Uzza, and he smote him, because he put his hand to the ark: and there he died before God.*

David got upset at God for this, which is normal behavior for man when he does not get his own way.

> 1 Chronicles 13:11 – *And David was displeased, because the LORD had made a breach upon Uzza:*

But this situation brought the fear of God upon David, so he stopped his effort until he received directions from God on how to properly transport the Ark.

> 1 Chronicles 13:12 – *And David was afraid of God that day, saying, How shall I bring the ark of God home to me?*

From this experience David learned to not make a move until he inquired of God for directions; and God did give specific directions. When His directions are followed the task becomes easier and successful.

> 1 Chronicles 14:10, 13-15 – *And David enquired of God, saying, Shall I go up against the Philistines? and wilt thou*

deliver them into mine hand? And the LORD said unto him, Go up; for I will deliver them into thine hand. ... And the Philistines yet again spread themselves abroad in the valley. Therefore David enquired again of God; and God said unto him, Go not up after them; turn away from them, and come upon them over against the mulberry trees. And it shall be, when thou shalt hear a sound of going in the tops of the mulberry trees, that then thou shalt go out to battle: for God is gone forth before thee to smite the host of the Philistines.

To not inquire of God for directions in your ministry shows that you have no fear of Him, or no trust in Him; your trust is in your own efforts; thus your results are less than what they could have been if you sought Him first. The fear of God is having respect for His sovereignty over every situation. This means we are to seek Him before embarking on a task; before making a change, lest our actions go contrary to the predetermined plan and direction that God already has in mind in that situation. God does not prevent man from being rebellious, thus they may end up interfering with the lives and ministries of others because they are performing outside of the will of God.

King David learned this lesson after it cost the life of another; then he proceeded to carry out the plan to transport the Ark following God's directions to do things the right way.

1 Chronicles 15:2, 12-13 – *Then David said, None ought to carry the ark of God but the Levites: for them hath the LORD chosen to carry the ark of God, and to minister unto him for ever. ... and said unto them, Ye are the chief of the fathers of the Levites: sanctify yourselves, both ye and your brethren, that ye may bring up the ark of the LORD God of Israel unto the place that I have prepared for it. For because ye did it not at the first, the LORD our God made a breach upon us, for that we sought him not after the due order.*

Many minsters (and churches) presume to know the will of God and how to fulfill it. They make up their own plans and programs without consulting Him for His opinion or direction. Then they ask Him to bless their efforts. It doesn't work that way!

The following is a personal example of this from a church that I was part of in the 1970's that had experienced a great increase in attendance. The senior pastor asked us to be in prayer about plans to increase the size of the church building which would be discussed at a church business meeting the following Wednesday night. I went home and began praying about it, and Lord showed me what He had planned for the church; so I listed it down and prepared for the business meeting.

At the business meeting the senior pastor presented the architectural plans for a new church building that had already been prepared months ago. There was no input from the members as to what we prayed and asked the Lord about. To the leadership the plans were all predetermined; the only purpose for the business meeting was for the congregation to approve those plans; that was what their prayer request was for – to rubber stamp the pre-consieved plans.

I interjected: "Does it seat fifteen hundred people"? "No", came the response; "it will seat thirteen hundred and seventy-seven people". I told them that I prayed as you asked, and the Lord showed me it needs to seat fifteen hundred. To which they objected saying thirteen hundred was sufficient. Then I asked, "Is the building expandable to allow more seating to be added in the future"? "No", was the response again, that won't be necessary. This means that they did not inquire of God as to what to do in this matter as they made their own determination. Then when I made known what the Lord showed me, it was rejected.

They went ahead with "their" building plans and erected a totally new building. While they were in the building process over the next year and half I had embarked on the road in the ministry that God called me to. I was pastoring a newly formed church in Minnesota when I heard that my home church just had their first service in the new building. They had fifteen hundred in attendance and had people sitting on the stairs going up to the balconies, along with extra folding chairs set up in the aisles. Attendance was this and more each week to the point that before long they were having two services each Sunday morning because they could not expand the building.

They called it God's house, so why did they not ask God how He wanted His house built. They could have gotten the answer just as I did. The lesson is, don't embark on any new endeavor until you have inquired and heard from the Lord! They left God out of their considerations and suffered problems as a result. A few years later they had to build another bigger building. To fear God is to always consider Him and His will in your plans.

> Proverbs 3:5-6 – *Trust in the Lord with all your heart; and lean not unto thine own understanding. In all thy ways acknowledge him, and he shall direct thy paths.*

Acknowledging Him is having the reverential respect, the fear of God, that He deserves; and allowing Him to direct your affairs for His "will" to be done. Note that His "general" will as it applies to all people is in His Word, the Holy Bible. His "specific" will must be sought individually. How to fulfill His general will may need to be sought for specifics before going forth to perform it.

> 1 Chronicles 15:13 – *For because ye did it not* (seek Him) *at the first, the LORD our God made a breach upon us, for that we sought him not after the due order.* (*due order* means "how to …".)

When man does not fear God, he simply does things on his own. Man "doing his own thing" is rebellion (iniquity). He does so because he has no sense of accountability. He does not realize that he will have to answer to God for everything he does, whether good or bad.

> 2 Corinthians 5:10 – *For we must all appear before the judgment seat of Christ; that every one may receive the things done in his body, according to that he hath done, whether it be good or bad.*

Having a proper fear of God will prevent this kind of human endeavor in the Lord's work. Consider some scriptures about the Fear of the Lord God.

> Proverbs 3:7 – *Be not wise in thine own eyes; fear the Lord, and depart from evil.*

> Proverbs 14:26-27 – *In the fear of the LORD is strong confidence: and his children shall have a place of refuge. The fear of the LORD is a fountain of life, to depart from the snares of death.*

> Proverbs 16:6 – *By mercy and truth iniquity is purged: and by the fear of the Lord men depart from evil.*

Proverbs 19:23 – *The fear of the LORD tendeth to life: and he that hath it shall abide satisfied; he shall not be visited with evil.*

Proverbs 22:4 – *By humility and the fear of the Lord are riches, and honor, and life.*

Isaiah 33:6 – *And wisdom and knowledge shall be the stability of thy times, and strength of salvation: the fear of the Lord is his treasure.*

Those who fear God are submissive to Him. They will not be arrogant or prideful, but will possess Christ-like meekness and obedience.

Proverbs 8:13 – *The fear of the Lord is to hate evil; pride, and arrogancy, and the evil way, and the forward mouth, do I hate.*

They do not presume or assume things; they humbly wait on the Lord, then move at His specific commands and do things His way as King David finally did.

Proverbs 1:29-31 – *for that they hated knowledge, and did not choose the feat of the Lord: they would none of my counsel: they despised all my reroof. Therefore shall they eat of the fruit of their own way, and be filled with their own devices.*

Jesus spoke about those in ministry who "do their own thing", supposedly in service to Him, but without His direction. Obviously they do not have the fear of the Lord and submit themselves to Him; thus they acted presumptively in "their" ministry.

Matthew 7:21-23 – *Not every one that saith unto me, Lord, Lord, shall enter into the kingdom of heaven; but he that doeth the will of my Father which is in heaven. Many will say to me in that day, Lord, Lord, have we not prophesied in thy name? and in thy name have cast out devils? and in thy name done many wonderful works? And then will I profess unto them, I never knew you: depart from me, ye that work iniquity,* (doing your own thing).

Note who makes the claim of doing the works: – "we"; (more on this topic in the next chapter on Obedience.)

When such ministries just go and do presumptively, without the Lord's directives, they may actually get in the way of what God is doing with and through others. A true servant of the Lord, with a humble spirit and having the Fear of God, is not going to do the Lord's work his own way. He follows the example set by John the Baptist when he said:

John 3:30 – *He must increase, but I must decrease.*

This humbleness was acknowledged by Jesus by what He said about John:

Matthew 11:11 – *Verily I say unto you, Among them that are born of women there hath not risen a greater than John the Baptist:*

God can only use these "self-determined" ministers and churches to a small degree; that is, only to the degree that they use His Word. Where His Word is proclaimed results are achieved regardless of who declares it. God honors His Word; God confirms His Word, and God fulfills His Word. Thus it is God's Word that produces the results.

Mark 16:20 – *And they went forth, and preached every where, the Lord working with them, and confirming the word with signs following.*

Thus there are those who preach His Word and think that "their" achievements are God's confirmation of "their" ministry; and so they assume that they are God's anointed. They are deceiving themselves and their followers. Yes, they have followers (or disciples), but those followers should be focused on Christ and not on a man's ministry. Such followers also have no fear of God either; instead they are enamored with man which is a dangerous foundation to build on. They will follow him and his doctrines. Please recognize that such followers will always quote from those whom they follow.

God works through those who seek Him for His will, for His guidance, for His directions, for His assignments, for His ability to work through them. These are the kind of ministers who fear "missing" God, or missing His sovereign Will and Plan. They also fear God not receiving the glory that is due Him. They seek Him first, and then they proceed in obedience to Him. This is the faithfulness that is rewarded.

> Hebrews 11:6 – *But without faith it is impossible to please him: for he that cometh to God must believe that he is, and that he is a rewarder of them that diligently seek him.*

They diligently seek Him for directives and for His will to be made known specifically. They do not presume to know His exact will, nor do they assume tasks to fulfill as their perception of what He wants. They fear "missing the mark", being disobedient, or less than fully obedient. They place God first in their life rather than their ministry, their church, or their work.

Jesus had the Fear of God in Him by the Spirit of the Lord resting upon Him.

> Isaiah 11:2 – *and the spirit of the Lord shall rest upon him, the spirit of wisdom and understanding, the spirit of counsel and might, the spirit of knowledge and of the fear of the Lord;*

For this reason, Jesus did no ministry of His own. His ministry consisted of only what He saw His Father do, and speak only what He heard His Father speak.

> John 8:28 – *Then said Jesus unto them, When ye have lifted up the Son of man, then shall ye know that I am he, and that I do nothing of myself; but as my Father hath taught me, I speak these things.*

> John 5:17, 19 – *But Jesus answered them, My Father worketh hitherto, and I work. … Then answered Jesus and said unto them, Verily, verily, I say unto you, The Son can do nothing of himself, but what he seeth the Father do: for what things soever he doeth, these also doeth the Son likewise. … … I can of mine own self do nothing: as I hear, I judge: and my judgment is just; because I seek not mine own will, but the will of the Father which hath sent me.*

Can you imagine the wonderful results we would see if all those in ministry did as Jesus did, and not do anything until we heard from God about what to do, what to say and where to go.

Where and when did Jesus hear and see His Father to get His instructions? It was in His frequent times of prayer and getting alone with the Father to receive His instructions. For example, Jesus sought God for who would be His apostles:

> Luke 6:12-13 – *And it came to pass in those days, that he went out into a mountain to pray, and continued all night in prayer to God. And when it was day, he called unto him his disciples: and of them he chose twelve, whom also he named apostles;*

Jesus could select only those to be His apostles whom the Father wanted. Jesus may have struggled with these choices in the natural because He already knew that one would betray Him; nevertheless, He got His directives from the Father while in prayer enabling Him to make the choices that God ordained.

The result was that Jesus had pure and perfect ministry as directed by God the Father; and it culminated with His own crucifixion and resurrection initiated by the one who betrayed Him. All those in ministry today should follow Christ's example of giving our lives for the benefit of the sheep.

> Acts 6:4 – *But we will give ourselves continually to prayer, and to the ministry of the word.*

Since Jesus ascended back to heaven to be seated with the Father, He sent the Holy Spirit to assist us, not only in living, but assisting and directing in ministry.

> John 16:7-14 – *Nevertheless I tell you the truth; It is expedient for you that I go away: for if I go not away, the Comforter will not come unto you; but if I depart, I will send him unto you. And when he is come, he will reprove the world of sin, and of righteousness, and of judgment: of sin, because they believe not on me; of righteousness, because I go to my Father, and ye see me no more; of judgment, because the prince of this world is judged. I have yet many things to say unto you, but ye cannot bear them now. Howbeit when he, the Spirit of truth, is come,*

he will guide you into all truth: for he shall not speak of himself;
but whatsoever he shall hear, that shall he speak: and he will
shew you things to come. He shall glorify me: for he shall receive
of mine, and shall shew it unto you.

As we seek Him in fellowship and prayer, He responds by the Holy Spirit who directs, instructs, and provides divine knowledge and all the assistance that we need to do His will. We are to be led of the Spirit which means we are under the direction and control of the Lord, proving that we are His ministers.

Romans 8:14 – *For as many as are led by the Spirit of God,*
they are the sons of God.

Through the fear of God and our submission to Him, the work of the ministry becomes His work and not man's. It is God's work that is done by Him working through those who seek Him, yield to Him, and obey Him as His humble servants.

The word "minister" means "servant", but to most in ministry today that word is merely a title that requires reverence and respect, thus the title "Reverend". True ministers, those with a humble servants attitude and motive, carry out their ministry with the fear of God, irrespective of popularity, prestige or celebrity status.

What a difference between His true ministers and the man-made ministers. The difference is the fear of God that is in His servants. The man-made ministers serve those who govern them or pay them: they also fear those who gave them their "credentials" and authority to minister. Their fear is in the wrong place. They fear losing popularity, position, influence, recognition, money, their credentials, their pulpit, their ministry and their personal security.

The apostles, especially Paul, feared none of those things becaus they feared the Lord who called them, and whom they represent. Likewise, we should fear God with that same reverential fear to serve Him. It is He who gives the Gifts of Ministry; and it is He who gives us His Holy Spirit with the ability to carry out His assignments with the Gifts of the Holy Spirit. After all, it is His work, not ours! We are merely vehicles through whom He operates. King David learned this when he was struck with the respectful fear of God.

Therefore, let us seek Him, Fear Him, whereby we are made able to serve Him. The end result to those who are obedient and faithful is, "they shall reign with Him in His kingdom.

> Ecclesiastes 12:13 – Let us hear the conclusion of the whole matter: Fear God, and keep his commandments: for this *is* the whole *duty* of man.

THE IMPORTANCE OF OBEDIENCE IN MINISTRY

This is a study of Matthew 7, and 1 Corinthians 3, regarding the work of the ministry. Several references to Matthew 7 have already been previously made, but the importance of its contents is so significant that a closer examination is needed. What you are about to read will take you far from what has been traditionally understood; but we must look more carefully at these scriptures. We will find that much of the seventh chapter of Matthew deals with false ministers and ministries; almost all of the third chapter of 1 Corinthians deals with wrongly motivated ministers and ministries.

The term "ministry" is used in regard to doing the "Lord's" work of service to Him, and His people. This work is building the Holy Habitation, the temple of God, His dwelling place which is not built with human hands. This dwelling place, during this age, is in the believer; it is also the assembly of believers, the Body of Christ referred to as "church". We begin with Jesus' warning:

> Matthew 7:15 – *Beware of false prophets, which come to you in sheep's clothing, but inwardly they are ravening wolves.*

Jesus told us there would be false ministers infiltrating the churches; they had the appearance of one in the disguise of one that belonged. The term "prophets" is used because the people that Jesus was addressing knew that prophets were representatives and spokesmen for God; both foretelling, but mostly forth-telling, (inspired preaching). We are given a warning, "to beware"! Such a warning means that to not be aware is to experience deception and its grave consequences.

Jesus said they may appear gentle enough as they tend to look like they belong among the sheep fold. However, their inward motivation is selfish.

The term "ravening wolves" describes those who feed on the sheep, live off the sheep, or use the sheep to satisfy their carnal (fleshly) wolf nature.

> Matthew 10:16-17 – *Ye shall know them by their fruits. Do men gather grapes of thorns, or figs of thistles? Even so every good tree bringeth forth good fruit; but a corrupt tree bringeth forth evil fruit.*

Jesus tells us of the rottenness of their ministry. We are chided in a sense, because we can usually identify good fruit from bad fruit while it is still on the tree; but most Christians are unable to distinguish good ministers from bad or rotten ones because they only see the sheep disguise.

What happens when you consume bad or rotten fruit? There are variations of reactions depending on the deteriorated condition of the fruit. These reactions could be mild as having a bad taste that you repel immediately, to the toxicity of the rot which will make you sick.

Bad fruit trees are to be cut down and burned; they are eliminated so no one will run the risk of eating rotten fruit. So the fruit is the identifier of the false minister. Where you see believers spiritually starving, or dwarfed from lack of spiritual nourishment; or where you see them sick and dying; it is the result of eating the fruit of the doctrines and tradition of men and demons. Such is the result of false ministers.

The Lord's true ministers will be revealed by their fruit; it will be seen! Their fruit is the character and nature of God in them, which is the Fruit of the Spirit.

> Galatians 5:22-23 – *But the fruit of the Spirit is love, joy, peace, longsuffering, gentleness, goodness, faith, meekness, temperance: against such there is no law.*

This is the fruit that can only be produced by the life of Christ, (the vine), flowing through the life of the minister, (and each believer), as they continue in intimate fellowship with Christ. This is also the fruit that God the Father is looking for in us.

> John 15:1-5 – *I am the true vine, and my Father is the husbandman. Every branch in me that beareth not fruit he taketh away: and every branch that beareth fruit, he purgeth*

it, that it may bring forth more fruit. Now ye are clean through the word which I have spoken unto you. Abide in me, and I in you. As the branch cannot bear fruit of itself, except it abide in the vine; no more can ye, except ye abide in me. I am the vine, ye are the branches: He that abideth in me, and I in him, the same bringeth forth much fruit: for without me ye can do nothing.

It is important to note that the next verse says that if they don't have this fruit that they are to be cast off and burned.

John 15:6 – *If a man abide not in me, he is cast forth as a branch, and is withered; and men gather them, and cast them into the fire, and they are burned.*

Matthew 7:19 – *Every tree that bringeth not forth good fruit is hewn down, and cast into the fire.*

The life of Christ is to be seen in the ministers before you start partaking of their fruit: the false ministers will make claims about their ministry but such claims are rejected by the Lord, because they were not His true servants.

Matthew 7:20-23 – *Wherefore by their fruits ye shall know them. Not every one that saith unto me, Lord, Lord, shall enter into the kingdom of heaven; but he that doeth the will of my Father which is in heaven. Many will say to me in that day, Lord, Lord, have we not prophesied in thy name? and in thy name have cast out devils? and in thy name done many wonderful works? And then will I profess unto them, I never knew you: depart from me, ye that work iniquity.*

These ministers are not lying about what "they" have done or how they served in the church. They will even ask Jesus to confirm "their" works. However, Jesus does not respond to their questions about "their" works. Instead, He charges them with rebellion (iniquity). He cites their disobedience in performing their ministry. They were "doing their own thing", which is what rebellion or iniquity is. They are disqualified from His kingdom reign because of their disobedience; thus they could not be trusted to rule with

Christ in His kingdom. They were not numbered among those that *doeth the will of my Father which is in heaven.*

When Jesus said, "I never knew you", He identified their lack of intimate fellowship with Him, (the vine). The word "knew" as used here is the same word used as when a husband "knew" his wife in the most intimate way. This kind of relationship with Him is necessary so as to be aware of how to perform His ministry to His people: what to say, where to go and how to do it. Such intimacy allows you to know His thoughts, His ways, His desires: all done in obedience to Him, which is the will of the Father in heaven.

Those who are doing their own thing may have had intentions that were very good, and they go forth with a zeal for God, but actually they are selfishly motivated; and because they do not fear God, they go forth acting on their own presumption; doing things man's way.

The result is "their" works "fall short of the glory of God". God's glory is not revealed, nor does God receive the glory and recognition of what is done; man usually gets that recognition because that is what he was striving for.

God reveals Himself through "His" works; and man is seen through the works that "man" performs, even while claiming to be doing God's work. Let God do is own work by letting Him work through man. He can only work through man as man obeys His directive.

How discouraging it will be for those in ministry who are expecting a great reward for their diligent service and wonderful works, when they find out at the Judgment Seat of Christ that they were only getting in the way; that they were actually working contrary to the specific will of God. At that time they will cry out; *Lord, Lord, have we not prophesied in thy name? and in thy name have cast out devils? and in thy name done many wonderful works?*

They have no reward and no position of ruling with Him in His coming Kingdom: this is because they didn't prove to be faithful and obedient unto Him. These are those who are identified as whose works are *wood, hay and stubble* which will be burned up leaving them with no reward.

> 1 Corinthians 3:12-15 – *Now if any man build upon this foundation gold, silver, precious stones, wood, hay, stubble; every man's work shall be made manifest: for the day shall declare it, because it shall be revealed by fire; and the fire shall try every man's work of what sort it is. If any man's work abide which he hath built thereupon, he shall receive a reward. If any*

*man's work shall be burned, he shall suffer loss: but he himself
shall be saved; yet so as by fire.*

They have been building on the foundation of sand, and not on Christ
the Rock. They may be preaching Christ, but their motives are man centered.
They are most likely more concerned about numbers, position, recognition and
building a name or reputation for their own ministry. How many ministries
do you see today that are promoted by a man's name or have man's pictures all
over them. That tells much about their ministry and who they really represent!

What is the purpose of those that God called to the ministry? It is to build
His house; which is His temple where HE can abide and fellowship in. Thus
HE will direct in the building of His house – the believers who compose the
church. It can only be built in a lasting way when we obey Him!

> Matthew 7:24-27 – *Therefore whosoever heareth these sayings
> of mine, and doeth them, I will liken him unto a wise man,
> which built his house upon a rock: and the rain descended, and
> the floods came, and the winds blew, and beat upon that house;
> and it fell not: for it was founded upon a rock. And every one
> that heareth these sayings of mine, and doeth them not, shall
> be likened unto a foolish man, which built his house upon the
> sand: and the rain descended, and the floods came, and the
> winds blew, and beat upon that house; and it fell: and great
> was the fall of it.*

Whose house are we building? Who is in charge of the building process?

> Psalm 127:1 – *Except the* LORD *build the house, they labour
> in vain that build it:*

It appears that those who are "doing their own thing" refers to those
ministers who are not led by the Holy Spirit of the Lord. They are doing
"their" thing, or man's religious thing. These are the ones that are instructed
by man's ideas and ways which they learn in Bible college, Seminary, or from
denominational teaching and training, but not taught how to hear what the
Spirit is saying.

Luke 8:8 – *And other fell on good ground, and sprang up, and bare fruit an hundredfold. And when he had said these things, he cried, He that hath ears to hear, let him hear.*

The same command to hear what the Spirit is saying is repeated to each of the seven churches in Revelation 2 and 3.

This is a similar thing that happened to the Pharisees who confronted Jesus. Their religious training and education relied on their own limited human understanding, void of the Spirit of God, which prohibited them from seeing, hearing, discerning or recognizing the truth by God's Spirit. As a result, the Pharisees opposed what they saw and heard of Jesus because it did not match their religious mindset.

Likewise, these false ministers depend on their own understanding and training, as well as any personal accomplishments, or their works. However, the works of natural man have no merit in the kingdom of God, but only in the kingdom of man. Jesus is the standard by which all things are compared and is why we must learn to depend on Him, seek Him, hear Him, obey Him and be led by His Holy Spirit.

When Christ returns to set up His Kingdom, His domain where He has total dominion on the earth, His plan is to have His faithful and obedient followers participate in ruling with Him. This is why He is called the KING of Kings, and LORD of Lords; both are expressions for rulers under His ultimate dominion.

Revelation 19:16 – *And he hath on his vesture and on his thigh a name written, KING OF KINGS, AND LORD OF LORDS.*

When He returns to earth to set up His Kingdom, He brings these rewards with Him.

Revelation 22:12 – *And, behold, I come quickly; and my reward is with me, to give every man according as his work shall be.*

One of the keys to Godly and fruitful ministry is obedience to Him, as emphasized in verse 21: *but he that doeth the will of my Father which is in heaven.* This is not the presumed will of the Father as natural man tries to operate in; it is direct, divine guidance; not relying on your intellect or understanding of what God's Word says. We need to acknowledge Him and His plan.

> Proverbs 3:5-6 – *Trust in the Lord with all tine heart,* (not just your head)*; and lean not unto your own understanding. In all your ways acknowledge Him* (in obedience)*, and He shall direct your paths.* (Emphasized by author.)

The Lord rewards us for being faithful and obedient; being led of God by His Holy Spirit.

> Romans 8:14 – *For as many as are led by the Spirit of God, they are the sons of God.*

As stated previously, the Fruit of the Spirit is to be the key identifier of those who serve in the ministry. The apostle Paul gave a contrast between those who are obedient compared to those who are disobedient, self-willed, and motivated by the flesh.

> Galatians 5:24-26 – *And they that are Christ's have crucified the flesh with the affections and lusts. If we live in the Spirit, let us also walk in the Spirit. Let us not be desirous of vain glory, provoking one another, envying one another.*

A question to ponder: when did the requirements change for entering into the kingdom of God, (the domain of our Lord)? Are not the words of Jesus' "sermon on the mount" still in effect?

> Matthew 5:3-12 – *and he opened his mouth, and taught them, saying, Blessed are the poor in spirit: for theirs is the kingdom of heaven. Blessed are they that mourn: for they shall be comforted. Blessed are the meek: for they shall inherit the earth. Blessed are they which do hunger and thirst after righteousness: for they shall be filled. Blessed are the merciful: for they shall obtain mercy. Blessed are the pure in heart: for they shall see God. Blessed are the peacemakers: for they shall be called the children of God. Blessed are they which are persecuted for righteousness'*

sake: for theirs is the kingdom of heaven. Blessed are ye, when men shall revile you, and persecute you, and shall say all manner of evil against you falsely, for my sake. Rejoice, and be exceeding glad: for great is your reward in heaven: for so persecuted they the prophets which were before you.

The work of the ministry is to carry on and finish the work that Jesus began; to build a Holy Temple, a habitation for God's Spirit, a divine dwelling place not built with human hands. Jesus commissioned the work, and the Holy Spirit is His agent on earth directing it. What is now being built we call the church; but the church is much more than what man perceives it to be. It is His Holy Habitation!

Jesus is like the financier; He is also the architect and prime contractor, building a dwelling for His Father; He paid the price, made the plans and laid the foundation, or corner stone. He has enlisted His chosen Gift Ministers to perform specific functions in this building process.

Ephesians 4:11-12 – *And he gave some, apostles; and some, prophets; and some, evangelists; and some, pastors and teachers; for the perfecting of the saints, for the work of the ministry, for the edifying of the body of Christ:*

By His Holy Spirit He trains those He chooses, equips them and then places them.

1 Corinthians 12:27-28 – *Now ye are the body of Christ, and members in particular. And God hath set some in the church, first apostles, secondarily prophets, thirdly teachers, after that miracles, then gifts of healings, helps, governments, diversities of tongues.*

The Lord can even direct His servant to a specific person at a specific location. He can also supernaturally transport that servant to a different location; as shown when Philip was directed to reveal the gospel to the Ethiopian eunuch who he also baptized.

Acts 8:26, 39-40 – *And the angel of the Lord spake unto Philip, saying, Arise, and go toward the south unto the way that goeth down from Jerusalem unto Gaza, which is desert. … And when they were come up out of the water, the Spirit of the Lord caught away Philip, that the eunuch saw him no more: and he went on his way rejoicing. But Philip was found at Azotus: and passing through he preached in all the cities, till he came to Cæsarea.*

Unfortunately, man thinks he can do the job on his own; so man's organization will train, commissions and places people in this building program. The problem is that Christ may not have called them, trained them or placed them. They are building in vain creating the other church. Thus they lack the Lord's supernatural ability to work building His dwelling.

Psalm 127:1 – *Except the LORD build the house, they labour in vain that build it:*

There appears to be many who consider that they are working for the Lord, doing His work, but in fact, they are doing their own thing by not hearing from Him to follow His directions. As they presume to build the building their way they may actually be getting in the way of the true building process. They may interfere, hinder and even cause damage to what the Lord directs: then they ask God to bless their efforts.

Such ministers tend to oppose the supernatural workings through Christ's ordained ministers because they do not accept or understand the supernatural gifts that are employed. Thus they may ridicule, reject, slander and oppose those who are truly placed by the Lord. They do this in ignorance because they do not understand the ways that the Lord uses. They do not have ears to hear in the Spirit, so they are not led of the Spirit. They are trying to work on His task without being under His direction or supervision. They may accomplish something, but it falls short of what Christ has purposed. This produces the other church.

Jesus set different positions, talents and levels of authority for His workers.

1 Corinthians 3:8-9 – *Now he that planteth and he that watereth are one: and every man shall receive his own reward according to his own labour. For we are labourers together with God: ye are God's husbandry, ye are God's building.*

The Lord has ordained gifts for His work in this building process. These gifts vary widely, but all work in the same unit called the "Body", which also refers to the church or the corporate dwelling place of God.

> Romans 12:4-8 – *For as we have many members in one body, and all members have not the same office: so we, being many, are one body in Christ, and every one members one of another. Having then gifts differing according to the grace that is given to us, whether prophecy, let us prophesy according to the proportion of faith; or ministry, let us wait on our ministering: or he that teacheth, on teaching; or he that exhorteth, on exhortation: he that giveth, let him do it with simplicity; he that ruleth, with diligence; he that sheweth mercy, with cheerfulness.*

> 1 Corinthians 12:27-30 – *Now ye are the body of Christ, and members in particular. And God hath set some in the church, first apostles, secondarily prophets, thirdly teachers, after that miracles, then gifts of healings, helps, governments, diversities of tongues. Are all apostles? are all prophets? are all teachers? are all workers of miracles? have all the gifts of healing? do all speak with tongues? do all interpret?*

Consider the specifics of the five Gift Ministries of apostle, prophet, evangelist, pastor and teacher, as they pertain to this unique building process:

> Ephesians 4:10-12 – *He that descended is the same also that ascended up far above all heavens, that he might fill all things.) And he gave some, apostles; and some, prophets; and some, evangelists; and some, pastors and teachers; for the perfecting of the saints, for the work of the ministry, for the edifying of the body of Christ:*

Jesus established His master builders, the apostles, who have the blueprints to this spiritual building.

> 1 Corinthians 3:10-11 – *According to the grace of God which is given unto me, as a wise masterbuilder, I have laid the foundation, and another buildeth thereon. But let every man*

*take heed how he buildeth thereupon. For other foundation can
no man lay than that is laid, which is Jesus Christ.*

The apostles work very closely with the prophets who function like
building inspectors.

> Ephesians 2:19-22 – *the household of God; and are built upon
> the foundation of the apostles and prophets, Jesus Christ himself
> being the chief corner stone; in whom all the building fitly
> framed together groweth unto an holy temple in the Lord: in
> whom ye also are builded together for an habitation of God
> through the Spirit.*

Jesus is the rock upon which the church is built; He is also the chief
cornerstone, or the starting place; the foundation upon which the apostle and
prophet do their work. The prophet is to continually check on the building
process just like a building inspector. If something is out of place or missing,
he addresses the issue for correction or re-direction.

The evangelists are the ones who go out to preach the gospel to the nations,
adding and bringing in sheep to the fold. The pastors tend to the sheep to
maintain a proper spiritual environment for maturity and development. The
pastor may not actually feed the sheep, but leads them to green pastures and
still waters, as in Psalm 23. They see that the sheep are fed by bringing in the
teachers if they are not fully equipped as teachers. Pastors are referred to as
shepherds because they are responsible for the nurture, feeding, healing and
protection. (Note: much of this function is not being done by many pastors).

The teachers are like the brick layers who actually erect the building by
making up the walls; line upon line, precept upon precept; doctrine upon
doctrine.

> Isaiah 28:9-10, 13 – *Whom shall he teach knowledge? And
> whom shall he make to understand doctrine? Them that are
> weaned from the milk, and drawn from the breasts. For precept
> must be upon precept, precept upon precept; line upon line, line
> upon line; here a little and there a little:*

In too many situations the pastors think they are to do it all by themselves;
thus they reject or ignore the Lord's qualified gift ministers that He has given

to provide these functions. This produces a deficit among the sheep since they are not receiving the benefit of all of the gift ministries that Christ established to build His church.

> Hebrews 5: 11-14 – *Of whom we have many things to say, and hard to be uttered, seeing ye are dull of hearing. For when for the time ye ought to be teachers, ye have need that one teach you again which be the first principles of the oracles of God; and are become such as have need of milk, and not of strong meat. For every one that useth milk is unskilful in the word of righteousness: for he is a babe. But strong meat belongeth to them that are of full age, even those who by reason of use have their senses exercised to discern both good and evil.*

The result of spiritual immaturity is that there is a lack of discernment as to what is of God and what is evil, or of the devil. This applies to false doctrines and traditions that men and demons have snuck into churches.

> Ephesians 4:14 – *that we henceforth be no more children, tossed to and fro, and carried about with every wind of doctrine, by the sleight of men, and cunning craftiness, whereby they lie in wait to deceive;*

Today there is obviously a great lack of spiritual discernment; especially in the other church. This is seen by these other churches embracing overt sinful behavior, even among their leadership.

The other church, by following man's doctrines and traditions, say that apostles and prophets are not for today. They reject these two key foundation builders. No wonder the church is so split, divided, fractured and falling apart. This is the result of man's ministry, doing things his own way; actually working in rebellion to God – doing iniquity. (Note: it may not be a deliberate rebellion but one caused by ignorance of the Word and Will of God. It is no less rebellion.)

The disobedient will be quite surprised at the Judgment Seat of Christ. They think they will receive great rewards for their wonderful works. Actually, their works will be considered as *wood, hay and stubble* that will be burned up. They will lose the reward they were expecting because they stubbornly labored their own way and actually hindered the building process.

1 Corinthians 3:12-15 – *Now if any man build upon this foundation gold, silver, precious stones, wood, hay, stubble; every man's work shall be made manifest: for the day shall declare it, because it shall be revealed by fire; and the fire shall try every man's work of what sort it is. If any man's work abide which he hath built thereupon, he shall receive a reward. If any man's work shall be burned, he shall suffer loss: but he himself shall be saved; yet so as by fire.*

Consider the building process as Paul describes it when he wrote 1 Corinthians 3. He identifies the immature church as being carnal, following after human nature's fleshly lusts.

1 Corinthians 3:1-4 – *And I, brethren, could not speak unto you as unto spiritual, but as unto carnal, even as unto babes in Christ. I have fed you with milk, and not with meat: for hitherto ye were not able to bear it, neither yet now are ye able. For ye are yet carnal: for whereas there is among you envying, and strife, and divisions, are ye not carnal, and walk as men? For while one saith, I am of Paul; and another, I am of Apollos; are ye not carnal?*

The other church has continued in this manner ever since, this is because of reliance on the natural mind and human will; not being a laborer with God. Verses 5 to 9 refer to the various crafts and skills employed in building the church that are to be directed by the Holy Spirit.

1 Corinthians 3:5-9 – *Who then is Paul, and who is Apollos, but ministers by whom ye believed, even as the Lord gave to every man? I have planted, Apollos watered; but God gave the increase. So then neither is he that planteth any thing, neither he that watereth; but God that giveth the increase. Now he that planteth and he that watereth are one: and every man shall receive his own reward according to his own labour. For we are labourers together with God: ye are God's husbandry, ye are God's building.*

Each of His ministers has a specific area of responsibility, and must recognize each other's God ordained function, then allow them to operate as shown in verse 10 and 11. Don't allow jealousy or the effort to be in total control to disenfranchise the work of the other gift ministries in the church. Such was the case reported by the apostle John.

> 3 John 1:9-10 – *I wrote unto the church: but Diotrephes, who loveth to have the preeminence among them, receiveth us not. Wherefore, if I come, I will remember his deeds which he doeth, prating against us with malicious words: and not content therewith, neither doth he himself receive the brethren, and forbiddeth them that would, and casteth them out of the church.*

The unity of the faith that God wants is to have all five gift ministries to have the freedom to operate in the church. The other church rejects this because it wants to be in control. (The same reason it rejects the Gifts of the Holy Spirit is because they want control, rather than allowing the Lord to lead by His Spirit.) Each Gift Ministry has a specific function that is needed in the church.

> 1 Corinthians 3:10-11 – *According to the grace of God which is given unto me, as a wise master builder, I have laid the foundation, and another buildeth thereon. But let every man take heed how he buildeth thereupon. For other foundation can no man lay than that is laid, which is Jesus Christ.*

One should not embark on a task that he is not skilled in, trained for, and called to do. Remember what happened to King Saul when he assumed the priestly duties that belonged to the prophet Samuel?

> 1 Samuel 13:8-14 – *And he tarried seven days, according to the set time that Samuel had appointed: but Samuel came not to Gilgal; and the people were scattered from him. And Saul said, Bring hither a burnt offering to me, and peace offerings. And he offered the burnt offering. And it came to pass, that as soon as he had made an end of offering the burnt offering, behold, Samuel came; and Saul went out to meet him, that he might salute him. And Samuel said, What hast thou done? And Saul*

said, Because I saw that the people were scattered from me, and that thou camest not within the days appointed, and that the Philistines gathered themselves together at Michmash; therefore said I, The Philistines will come down now upon me to Gilgal, and I have not made supplication unto the LORD: I forced myself therefore, and offered a burnt offering.

The consequences of ministerial disobedience can be costly because God despises rebellion; "doing your own thing"! This is when one minister must yield to and submit to the function of another ministry. It is not the man, but the gift of God, that we must recognize and work in conjunction with.

1 Samuel 13:13-14 – And Samuel said to Saul, Thou hast done foolishly: thou hast not kept the commandment of the LORD thy God, which he commanded thee: for now would the LORD have established thy kingdom upon Israel for ever. But now thy kingdom shall not continue: the LORD hath sought him a man after his own heart, and the LORD hath commanded him to be captain over his people, because thou hast not kept that which the LORD commanded thee.

There are rewards for proper use of the gifts, and proper flowing with other gifting as mentioned in 1 Corinthians 12:12-15 above. The end product will testify of the quality of worker and workmanship that was used. Likewise, there will be a loss of rewards for those who labored outside of the will of the Lord. Presumption in ministry is eternally dangerous; eternal rewards are at stake!

When man's ways are used in building His church the result is usually a form of defilement of the Holy dwelling, as described. The things of God and His kingdom do not mix with the carnal things of man.

1 Corinthians 3:18-21 – Let no man deceive himself. If any man among you seemeth to be wise in this world, let him become a fool, that he may be wise. For the wisdom of this world is foolishness with God. For it is written, He taketh the wise in their own craftiness. And again, The Lord knoweth the thoughts of the wise, that they are vain. Therefore let no man glory in men.

A mixture of flesh and Spirit is defilement of the church, individually and corporately!

> 1 Corinthians 3:17 – *If any man defile the temple of God, him shall God destroy; for the temple of God is holy, which temple ye are.*

Man's ideas, intellect, methods, and doctrines are pollutants in the Kingdom of God, and the church.

> 1 Corinthians 2:4-5, 13-14 – *And my speech and my preaching was not with enticing words of man's wisdom, but in demonstration of the Spirit and of power: that your faith should not stand in the wisdom of men, but in the power of God. … Which things also we speak, not in the words which man's wisdom teacheth, but which the Holy Ghost teacheth; comparing spiritual things with spiritual. But the natural man receiveth not the things of the Spirit of God: for they are foolishness unto him: neither can he know them, because they are spiritually discerned.*

During this church age the church, and each believer, has the kingdom of God within. The true church is where He abides and rules; but does He abide in the other church? Do we need some sort of major re-building, utilizing His gifted builders?

> 1 Corinthians 3:20-23 – *And again, The Lord knoweth the thoughts of the wise, that they are vain. Therefore let no man glory in men. For all things are yours; whether Paul, or Apollos, or Cephas, or the world, or life, or death, or things present, or things to come; all are yours; and ye are Christ's; and Christ is God's.*

In summing up the building process, we are told that the whole thing is in His hands. Each believer is also in His hands. So how and where are you as a minister supposed to function? Be careful, attentive and obedient. Otherwise you may have found that all your efforts were in vain when you have to stand before Him whose house you are either properly building, or you are meddling with.

Finally, we see that all of us are accountable to the Lord for the ministry we have done. Faithfulness and obedience as His servant is required in order for is to be entrusted with the things of the kingdom that are soon coming. There are those that will lose their reward; let it not be you!

Now let us return to Matthew 7 for our conclusion of the matter of obedience in ministry.

> Matthew 7:24-27 – *Therefore whosoever heareth these sayings of mine, and doeth them, I will liken him unto a wise man, which built his house upon a rock: and the rain descended, and the floods came, and the winds blew, and beat upon that house; and it fell not: for it was founded upon a rock. And every one that heareth these sayings of mine, and doeth them not, shall be likened unto a foolish man, which built his house upon the sand: and the rain descended, and the floods came, and the winds blew, and beat upon that house; and it fell: and great was the fall of it.*

Here we see the difference between obedience to God and disobedience in rebellion, "doing your own thing". These have been popular verses for some great illustrative preaching. Please consider: whose house are you building? Who is it for? Whose glory is to be there? Who is the architect? Who is the inspector? Who is the contractor? Don't take on responsibility that isn't yours or that has not been assigned to you by the Lord!

Recognize that you are a servant who is to obey the Master's command. Don't listen to man, even if he is religious and holds titles or credentials if what he says is contrary to the Word of God, or the Spirit of God. He could be a false prophet or a wolf in sheep's clothing. Your task is to be faithful and obedient to the Lord; to move at His command; to do what He directs you to do and no more.

There are some in ministry who declare that you must be under their "covering", or under some other man's covering. This is a doctrine of the devil that they use to control and manipulate you; even to make money off of you. (Years ago it was called the "shepherding" or "covering" doctrine.)

When your labors are done, and you have finished building your part, will your building stand when the storms of life, or the shaking comes?

Hebrews 12:25-29 – *See that ye refuse not him that speaketh. For if they escaped not who refused him that spake on earth, much more shall not we escape, if we turn away from him that speaketh from heaven: whose voice then shook the earth: but now he hath promised, saying, Yet once more I shake not the earth only, but also heaven. And this word, Yet once more, signifieth the removing of those things that are shaken, as of things that are made, that those things which cannot be shaken may remain. Wherefore we receiving a kingdom which cannot be moved, let us have grace, whereby we may serve God acceptably with reverence and godly fear: for our God is a consuming fire.*

Will the house that you helped build endure when the fire is put to it in order to test of what sort of construction materials you used?

1 Corinthians 3:12-13 – *Now if any man build upon this foundation gold, silver, precious stones, wood, hay, stubble; every man's work shall be made manifest: for the day shall declare it, because it shall be revealed by fire; and the fire shall try every man's work of what sort it is.*

Are you hearing and obeying the Lord in your ministry, or are you walking according to what man expects of you. Again, consider whose house or temple you are building, and why. Not all who operate in signs and wonders will be qualified to rule with Him in His kingdom. Why? They did what "they" thought, or were taught. Not what the Lord directed.

Jesus said, "You shall know them by their Fruit", not by their gifts. Why is this important to understand? Because Satan can counterfeit the supernatural gifts; but he can't counterfeit the Fruit of the Spirit which is totally opposite of his nature. Miracles, or even self-sacrifice, are not the keys to building the Lord's house. There are many that are employing one or the other or both to build the house; but, it is obedience and faithfulness, being led of the Spirit, that is the key to the spiritual building of the House of the Lord.

This author's desire is for you to receive your full reward from the Lord along with His voice saying, "well done good and faithful servant", being obedient to Him.

ARE YOU QUALIFIED TO RULE WITH HIM

> Revelation 20:4, 6 – *And I saw thrones, and they sat upon them, and judgment was given unto them: and I saw the souls of them that were beheaded for the witness of Jesus, and for the word of God, and which had not worshipped the beast, neither his image, neither had received his mark upon their foreheads, or in their hands; and they lived and reigned with Christ a thousand years. ... ... Blessed and holy is he that hath part in the first resurrection: on such the second death hath no power, but they shall be priests of God and of Christ, and shall reign with him a thousand years.*

We are all looking forward to the time when Jesus returns to take possession of the earth and to set up His kingdom. We, as His believers, have a blessed hope and promise of participating in governing with Him in His kingdom. Although we are all eager for this time, we are not yet ready for it.

There are qualifications that we must meet in order to be ready to rule and reign with Him. Unfortunately, most Christians do not meet these requirements because we fail to understand the principles required to reign with Him.

> Matthew 20:25-28 – *But Jesus called them unto him, and said, Ye know that the princes of the Gentiles exercise dominion over them, and they that are great exercise authority upon them. But it shall not be so among you: but whosoever will be great among you, let him be your minister; and whosoever will be chief among you, let him be your servant: even as the Son of man came not to be ministered unto, but to minister, and to give his life a ransom for many.*

Jesus identified natural man's role as having dominion over others as being the "top dog" in the order of things. This is the opposite of the role of reigning in His kingdom as He gives Himself as the example: to serve others rather than being served. Jesus said it is those that are meek that will inherit and rule the earth.

Matthew 5:5 – *Blessed are the meek: for they shall inherit the earth.*

It is the meek, the humble, not the haughty and arrogant, or the "top dogs".

James 4:10 – *Humble yourselves in the sight of the Lord, and he shall lift you up.*

As far as qualifications go, being born-again just gets you onto His kingdom; but in order to be kings and priests with Him ruling over His inheritance, we must prove ourselves worthy by being faithful to what He commands. Positions of rule with Him are the rewards that He will give to those who were obedient in this life.

Revelation 22:12 – *And, behold, I come quickly; and my reward is with me, to give every man according as his work shall be.*

Fortunately we still have time to learn and obey to qualify for eternal positions with Him in His kingdom. One of the purposes of the church is to prepare and equip us to be what He wants us to be – like Him.

Romans 8:29 – *For whom he did foreknow, he also did predestinate to be conformed to the image of his Son, that he might be the firstborn among many brethren.*

1 John 3:2 – *Beloved, now are we the sons of God, and it doth not yet appear what we shall be: but we know that, when he shall appear, we shall be like him; for we shall see him as he is.*

This final equipping of the saints, referred to as perfecting or completing, is the task of all five of the gift ministries that Jesus designated for the maturing of the saints.

Ephesians 4:11-13 – *And he gave some, apostles; and some, prophets; and some, evangelists; and some, pastors and teachers; for the perfecting of the saints, for the work of the ministry, for the edifying of the body of Christ: till we all come in the unity of the faith, and of the knowledge of the Son of God, unto a perfect man, unto the measure of the stature of the fulness of Christ:*

This final equipping consists of forming Christ, His character and nature, in His people so that Jesus is seen in the saints; the church He is coming back for. It is quite obvious that we do not see much of Christ in churches now!

These ministries are being restored in these last days because the task is not done. Christ wants what consists of the other church to be transformed into the true church. Thus we need to beware of the self-appointed, or man appointed apostles, prophets, etc. As previously stated, you shall know them by their fruit, the Fruit of the Spirit which is the character and nature of God. They need to be recognized as His servants so they are allowed to do their work. Not allowing them to work means such churches will fall short of the plan and the will of God; they will suffer loss.

The ministry of the last day apostles and prophets will focus on the kingdom principle by which we shall live throughout eternity, as well as developing the character and nature of our Lord which we are to emulate. Such character and nature are not being accurately or truly presented to the church. Instead, we are getting man's ideas, doctrines, dogma, programs and character pushed in churches.

Are you qualified to rule and reign with Him? Check yourself against the scriptures and see if there is any more "perfecting" needed in your life.

Leadership in the kingdom of God, during the millennial reign of Christ, will be by God's standards, not man's standards. Those who qualify, or who will be rewarded with leadership positions, are those who meet God's requirements of obedience and faithfulness. Jesus gave us an illustration of this as a parable.

Matthew 25:14-23 — *For the kingdom of heaven is as a man travelling into a far country, who called his own servants, and delivered unto them his goods. And unto one he gave five talents, to another two, and to another one; to every man according to his several ability; and straightway took his journey. Then he that had received the five talents went and traded with the same, and made them other five talents. And likewise he that had received two, he also gained other two. But he that had received one went and digged in the earth, and hid his lord's money. After a long time the lord of those servants cometh, and reckoneth with them. And so he that had received five talents came and brought other five talents, saying, Lord, thou deliveredst unto me five talents: behold, I have gained beside them five talents more. His lord said unto him, Well done, thou good and faithful servant: thou hast been faithful over a few things, I will make thee ruler over many things: enter thou into the joy of thy lord. He also that had received two talents came and said, Lord, thou deliveredst unto me two talents: behold, I have gained two other talents beside them. His lord said unto him, Well done, good and faithful servant; thou hast been faithful over a few things, I will make thee ruler over many things: enter thou into the joy of thy lord.*

Note that the rewards were being made a ruler with and under the master. The remainder of this parable shows the consequences of being disobedient and unfaithful resulting in, not only the loss of reward but utter destruction. The destruction is because of having personally known the master, he should have done according to what was expected of him, but didn't.

Matthew 24:24-30 — *Then he which had received the one talent came and said, Lord, I knew thee that thou art an hard man, reaping where thou hast not sown, and gathering where thou hast not strawed: and I was afraid, and went and hid thy talent in the earth: lo, there thou hast that is thine. His lord answered and said unto him, Thou wicked and slothful servant, thou knewest that I reap where I sowed not, and gather where I have not strawed: thou oughtest therefore to have put my money to the exchangers, and then at my coming I should have received mine own with usury. Take therefore the talent from him, and give it unto him which hath ten talents. For unto every one that hath shall be given, and he shall have abundance: but from him that hath not shall be taken away even that which he hath. And cast ye the unprofitable servant into outer darkness: there shall be weeping and gnashing of teeth.*

There are many working as ministers today, but they are doing it according to man's ways and not His. They will be disappointed because their works may be consumed when the examining fire of that special day touches them.

> 1 Corinthians 3:12-13, 15 – *Now if any man build upon this foundation gold, silver, precious stones, wood, hay, stubble; every man's work shall be made manifest: for the day shall declare it, because it shall be revealed by fire; and the fire shall try every man's work of what sort it is. ... If any man's work shall be burned, he shall suffer loss: but he himself shall be saved; yet so as by fire.*

These likely will be those that have been referred to previously.

> Matthew 7:22-23 – *Many will say to me in that day, Lord, Lord, have we not prophesied in thy name? and in thy name have we cast out devils? and in thy name done many wonderful works? And then will I profess unto them, I never knew you: depart from me, ye that work iniquity.*

To find out how and what we are to do in order to qualify for godly leadership we need to look at Jesus – God's type of leadership. Jesus not only taught kingdom principles in leadership qualities, and He also demonstrated them.

> Mark 10:44-45 – *and whosoever of you will be the chiefest, shall be servant of all. For even the Son of man came not to be ministered unto, but to minister, and to give his life a ransom for many.*

The greatest leadership quality in the kingdom seems to be the least taught, least demonstrated and least seen in the church; these are meekness and lowliness.

> Matthew 11:29 – *Take my yoke upon you, and learn of me; for I am meek and lowly in heart: and ye shall find rest unto your souls.*

From Jesus we are to see and learn of these qualities. Meekness is not weakness, it is a strength of spiritual character; it has nothing to prove to others to demand recognition. To be meek means to be: gentle; humble; mild mannered; having an easy going disposition; not pushy; not promoting self; willing to serve and help without acknowledgement; being secure in your position and attitude.

To be lowly similarly means to be possessing a low estate or degree; not rising up but deferring to others in assisting them to achieve; not self-assuming; and not offensive. It is for this reason that Jesus Christ is called "The Lamb of God" in multiple places in scripture. A lamb illustrates the gentle and meek nature we know of. Jesus was as a lamb under the Great Shepherd, God the Father. As we understand the divine order of authority, stated in 1 Corinthians 11, then we see that we are to be as lambs under Christ's shepherding.

> 1 Corinthians 11:3 – *But I would have you know, that the head of every man is Christ; and the head of the woman is the man; and the head of Christ is God.*

This gentle lamb is also the King of Glory, the fierce warrior coming to claim His inheritance, as the "Lion of Judah". Jesus humbled Himself and became lowly, the opposite of being exalted, knowing that God will exalt Him and give Him a position and name above all other.

> Philippians 2:7-11 – *but made himself of no reputation, and took upon him the form of a servant, and was made in the likeness of men: and being found in fashion as a man, he humbled himself, and became obedient unto death, even the death of the cross. Wherefore God also hath highly exalted him, and given him a name which is above every name: that at the name of Jesus every knee should bow, of things in heaven, and things in earth, and things under the earth; and that every tongue should confess that Jesus Christ is Lord, to the glory of God the Father.*

Thus we see the kingdom principles of obedience and faithfulness being rewarded. These principles need to be recognized and understood because they apply to us as believers.

Luke 1:52 – *He hath put down the mighty from their seats, and exalted them of low degree.*

1 Peter 5:6 – *Humble yourselves therefore under the mighty hand of God, that he may exalt you in due time:*

Surprisingly, the qualities of meekness and lowliness have recently been taught against in some churches. Instead they have been taught to be self-assertive; to make your own way; to set goals for ourselves and use God's Word as a divine leverage to pursue our self-seeking and to raise our self-esteem. These are man's ideas, not God's! When man sets his own course then he is not submitted to the will of God.

Jeremiah 10:23 – *LORD, I know that people's lives are not their own; it is not for them to direct their steps.* (NIV version)

Proverbs 3:5-6 – *Trust in the Lord with all thine heart; and lean not to thine own understanding. In all thy ways acknowledge Him, and He shall direct thy paths.*

Leadership in His kingdom will be meek, loving, kind, gentle, patient, and temperate; basically, all filled with and manifesting the Fruit of the Spirit, as listed in Galatians 5:22-23. It is just the opposite of man's type of leadership exercised in this world.

Un-redeemed man rules the same way Satan does. He uses fear, force, intimidation, threats, violence, power-plays, manipulation by money or other means, along with various other forms of control. Such are the standards and qualifications for leadership to rule in the kingdoms of this world under the present system. It is all to have control over the populations.

Luke 4:5-6 – *And the devil, taking him up into a high mountain, shewed unto him all the kingdoms of the world in a moment of time. And the devil said unto him, All this power will I give thee, and the glory of them: for that is delivered unto me; and to whomsoever I will I give it.*

Note that the worldly system has been under Satan's control until Jesus came and defeated him. However, we need to understand that even though

Jesus defeated Satan on the cross and with His resurrection, that Jesus has not eliminated Satan. That day is awaiting the return of Jesus.

> Revelation 20:2-3 – *And he laid hold on the dragon, that old serpent, which is the Devil, and Satan, and bound him a thousand years, and cast him into the bottomless pit, and shut him up, and set a seal upon him, that he should deceive the nations no more, ...*

Our Lord does not use man's means of governing and control; He uses love and its related virtues. God does not fear, so He does not use terror or fright to rule. However, man does fear; he knows and understands the power of it, as does Satan. Therefore the use of fear, force and intimidation is commonly used by man and Satan in order to dominate people.

> 2 Timothy 1:7 – *For God hath not given us the spirit of fear; but of power, and of love, and of a sound mind.*

God the Father, Jesus, His Son and His true servants rule by using authority of His name and His Word to raise up, hold up and lift up others to the place He would have them. Their motive is love, desiring the best for others, even if it is at their own expense: Jesus being our example.

> John 15:13 – *Greater love hath no man than this, that a man lay down his life for his friends.*

> 1 John 4:16-18 – *And we have known and believed the love that God hath to us. God is love; and he that dwelleth in love dwelleth in God, and God in him. Herein is our love made perfect, that we may have boldness in the day of judgment: because as he is, so are we in this world. There is no fear in love; but perfect love casteth out fear: because fear hath torment. He that feareth is not made perfect in love.*

God's method of government in His kingdom is far greater than, and more powerful, more desirable than man's methods. The world's principles or rule, as used by man, will not work in the kingdom of God. This is because they are actually Satan's principles that are understood and employed by carnal man. The sin nature of man does not receive the things of God, so the Satanic, worldly methods are in use here on earth for now. However, when Jesus comes to set up His kingdom, only His methods and principles will be seen.

> 1 Corinthians 2:14 – *But the natural man receiveth not the things of the Spirit of God: for they are foolishness unto him: neither can he know them, because they are spiritually discerned.*

We are to progress beyond the things of this current world order into the kingdom of God's divine order. This is the purpose of the church and the five gift ministries, preparing us for His kingdom rule. We must learn of Him; be conformed to His image and likeness, which is His character and nature, and live by His standards in preparation for His return.

We won't qualify for leadership in His kingdom unless we learn of it and start to walk in obedience in it now! Meekness and lowliness, as shown by Him is the place He wants us to start. He said we are to learn from Him as our example, as previously stated.

> Matthew 11:29 – *Take my yoke upon you, and learn of me; for I am meek and lowly in heart: and ye shall find rest unto your souls.*

Jesus demonstrates the meekness and lowliness of heart by not presuming to do things on His own. Instead, Jesus showed His dependence on His Father. This lack of self-effort, and the display of submission to the will of the Father, is the meekness and lowliness He spoke of.

From Christ's example, we learn that we are to submit to Him and depend on Him for all direction in ministry, as well as in our personal life. This way we will be doing His ministry His way. Failure to submit and depend on Him for direction means we are doing things on our own. Doing things on our own, especially in ministry, no matter how honorable or well-meaning the attempt, it is rebellion against God; refusing to submit to Him. They are building His house on sand, and it will not stand.

> Psalm 127:1 – *except the Lord build the house, they labor in vain that build it.*

What a sad awakening it will be for many well-meaning, hard-working ministers to realize that their labors have been in vain and not producing what God wants. They have studied and labored to build churches according to what they were taught in seminary only to find out in the end that their efforts were all for naught. They were out there trying to build the Lord's house without checking with Him on what to do; where to do it, who to do it, or even when to do it. Based on scripture, it appears that all their works are considered to be *wood, hay and stubble* that will be burned up leaving them no reward for their efforts.

Would to God that they had done things His way! Like those leaders of the church of Laodicea, they built what appeared to be successful to man. But in the Lord's eyes it made Him so sick to His stomach that He said He would symbolically vomit them out of His mouth. He said they were in spiritual poverty; and He was left standing outside, knocking to gain access to set things right.

> Revelation 3:16-17, 20 – *So then because thou art lukewarm, and neither cold nor hot, I will spue thee out of my mouth. Because thou sayest, I am rich, and increased with goods, and have need of nothing; and knowest not that thou art wretched, and miserable, and poor, and blind, and naked: ... Behold, I stand at the door, and knock: if any man hear my voice, and open the door, I will come in to him, and will sup with him, and he with me.*

He is still knocking on the spiritual doors of many churches, ministers and individuals. He wants to come in so that He can have an intimate fellowship and to reveal more of Himself, His plans, His desires, His character and nature. There is still time, so please make sure the door of intimacy with Christ is open in order to receive of Him. (This is not referring to salvation but to life being led by His Spirit.)

Jesus can only work through and use leadership that follows His example: those who are meek and lowly in heart; those who have nothing of themselves to prove; those who are not building a name or ministry for themselves.

Those who submit to Him and truly depend on Him are the ones He will call His *"good and faithful servants"*. They will be qualified to rule and reign with Him because they are obedient and can be trusted to do things His way, as He directs. He is truly Lord of their lives and ministries. Such submission and obedience pleases the Father and the Son.

Note that ruling and reigning with Him is not just for the thousand years of the seventh millennium, (the real Sabbath), but for all of eternity following.

> Revelation 22:3-5 — *And there shall be no more curse: but the throne of God and of the Lamb shall be in it; and his servants shall serve him: and they shall see his face; and his name shall be in their foreheads. And there shall be no night there; and they need no candle, neither light of the sun; for the Lord God giveth them light: and they shall reign for ever and ever.*

Chapter 11

THE MANIFESTATION OF HIS PRESENCE AND THE CLOUD OF HIS GLORY

THE GLORY OF GOD SHALL FILL HIS TEMPLE HIS TRUE CHURCH

As the life of Christ, (the *zoe*, life as God has it), is formed in His people, and as they conform to His image, then we will begin to see the manifestation of His presence when we assemble together as His church. This means that God will make Himself known in and through His people. His glory will be seen; His glory will be in and on His people as they mature and overflow with the fullness of God's Holy Spirit.

> Ephesians 3:14-19 – *For this cause I bow my knees unto the Father of our Lord Jesus Christ, of whom the whole family in heaven and earth is named, that he would grant you, according to the riches of his glory, to be strengthened with might by his Spirit in the inner man; that Christ may dwell in your hearts by faith; that ye, being rooted and grounded in love, may be able to comprehend with all saints what is the breadth, and length, and depth, and height; and to know the love of Christ, which passeth knowledge, that ye might be filled with all the fulness of God.*

This manifestation is initially the revelation of Christ in and through His people as they abide in Him and reveal the Fruit of the Spirit in their lives, (as discussed in previous chapters).

The key to seeing and experiencing the manifestation of His presence is for those in leadership to truly function as servants to others, as Jesus instructed, and thus set the example for the rest of the Body of Christ.

> Matthew 20:25-28 – *But Jesus called them unto him, and said, Ye know that the princes of the Gentiles exercise dominion over them, and they that are great exercise authority upon them. But it shall not be so among you: but whosoever will be great among you, let him be your minister; and whosoever will be chief among you, let him be your servant: even as the Son of man came not to be ministered unto, but to minister, and to give his life a ransom for many.*

Jesus is our example of how to minister to others; so what is it that He did? He gave of Himself for the people – even His own life. This is an act of love.

> John 15:13, 17 – *Greater love hath no man than this, that a man lay down his life for his friends. ... ... These things I command you, that ye love one another.*

The power of love activates the supernatural Gifts of the Spirit which is a manifestation of His Presence.

> 1 Corinthians 12:31 – *But covet earnestly the best gifts: and yet shew I unto you a more excellent way.*

That "*more excellent way*" is ministering to others with love, caring for them, as in the 13th chapter which details love as "charity" which is giving and caring.

> 1 Corinthians 13:1-3 – *Though I speak with the tongues of men and of angels, and have not charity, I am become as sounding brass, or a tinkling cymbal. And though I have the gift of prophecy, and understand all mysteries, and all knowledge; and though I have all faith, so that I could remove mountains, and have not charity, I am nothing. And though I bestow all my goods to feed the poor, and though I give my body to be burned, and have not charity, it profiteth me nothing.*

Ministry without love for those being ministered to is not the Jesus kind of ministry! It will be devoid of His presence manifesting. However, when the Jesus kind of leaders begin to function in love as His servants, then they will begin to see the manifestation of His Presence in their ministry. Miracles will even become common, because it will be as though Jesus Himself was performing the ministry. This is the Manifestation of His Presence; when His glory fills His people, the church, which is the assembled as the corporate temple of God.

> John 14:12 – *Verily, verily, I say unto you, He that believeth on me, the works that I do shall he do also; and greater works than these shall he do; because I go unto my Father.*

Then many will see that it was Christ, by His Spirit, that did the miraculous. No thought will be on the minister who the Spirit of the Lord worked through. A servant receives no glory or recognition for doing what his Lord commands.

> Luke 17:10 – *So likewise ye, when ye shall have done all those things which are commanded you, say, We are unprofitable servants: we have done that which was our duty to do.*

This way Christ will receive all the glory and recognition. Natural man does not operate this way in leadership positions as he seeks recognitions for his efforts. Man's form of leadership exercises authority rather than servitude; and generally has more love for him-self than for those he is supposed to serve.

The church and its leadership may be subject to circumstances that will cause it to re-align its ways of thinking, acting and performing leadership. There is coming a time of severe conditions and circumstances occurring nationwide, and even worldwide, that will bring turmoil and persecution to true believers; even martyrdom. This will probably occur as the open miracles will be seen in true and pure ministry.

God will allow this time of difficulty; it is not to afflict the church, but to purify it. Persecution never hurt the church, but material affluence has always hurt it! This time of turmoil is what will help believers to seek Christ more and more, which will help them to conform to His image, forsaking the works of the flesh, the world and its immoral values.

Such severe conditions, tribulations and persecution will bring the Lord's presence closer to His people so that they can see His helping, sheltering and loving provision and protective hand at work in their midst. This will encourage each believer to draw closer and become more intimate with Him.

As we draw closer and demonstrate our total dependence upon Him, He will become more precious to us as we receive His loving care for His flock. This special care for the "sheep of His pasture" can be paralleled to Israel's experience upon leaving Egypt. They were pursued by the Egyptian army who were bent on slaughtering the Israelites. But Israel had a divine protection and provision that went with them. It was the cloud of His glory which contained His Presence and through which God performed miracles for His people. (Note: God's cloud appears to be His mode of transportation and the means of revealing Himself to His people when needed.)

Consider what the manifestation of His presence by this cloud did for Israel.

> Exodus 13:21-22 — *And the LORD went before them by day in a pillar of a cloud, to lead them the way; and by night in a pillar of fire, to give them light; to go by day and night: he took not away the pillar of the cloud by day, nor the pillar of fire by night, from before the people.*

> Exodus 14:19-20 — *And the angel of God, which went before the camp of Israel, removed and went behind them; and the pillar of the cloud went from before their face, and stood behind them: and it came between the camp of the Egyptians and the camp of Israel; and it was a cloud and darkness to them, but it gave light by night to these: so that the one came not near the other all the night.*

This cloud and fire was the manifestation of His divine presence on behalf of His people. So it will be in the days ahead. It may not be a literal cloud, but it will be a similar covering, protecting, providing and guiding by the Presence of the Lord for His people. A study of this cloud in Exodus reveals:

- It was, or is a means of transportation that God employs without being seen, yet revealing His presence.

- All God's people came under the cloud: the good, the young, the old, the leaders and the followers; even those who would be disobedient.
- As they went on with this cloud, the evil non-conformers were weeded out. Their carnal nature was revealed by the circumstances that the cloud led them through.
- The cloud gave them coolness during the day in the hot dessert, and heat in the night when it got cool; as well as providing light for the camp.
- The cloud provided food (manna) and water (from the rock), all in supernatural and miraculous ways.
- The cloud provided direction: when to move; when to stop and camp; and where to go. (Note: they never knew in advance when and where, so they had to learn to obey and be completely dependent upon His leading through His cloud.

Consider the multiple references in scripture about His Glory seem to refer to the manifestation of this cloud, particularly in regard to the Tabernacle and Temple. In addition, God made a declaration to Peter as He spoke from His cloud on the mount of Transfiguration.

> Matthew 17:5 – *While he yet spake, behold, a bright cloud overshadowed them: and behold a voice out of the cloud, which said, This is my beloved Son, in whom I am well pleased; hear ye him.*

In a parallel way, the future manifestation of His presence will act much like the cloud did for the Israelites. His Presence, if we obey and follow Him, will provide for us in the same way; and probably even more glorious and miraculous.

> Isaiah 4:5-6 – *And the LORD will create upon every dwelling place of mount Zion, and upon her assemblies, a cloud and smoke by day, and the shining of a flaming fire by night: for upon all the glory shall be a defence. And there shall be a tabernacle for a shadow in the daytime from the heat, and for a place of refuge, and for a covert from storm and from rain.*

God provides a defense for His people that look to Him. Most believers understand that Zion refers to God's people, which includes the church at this present time. Zion, or the church, will go through a difficult time of judgment as foretold.

> 1 Peter 4:17 – *For the time is come that judgment must begin at the house of God: and if it first begin at us, what shall the end be of them that obey not the gospel of God?*

This will be its purging of the filth within along with its spots wrinkles and blemishes. It will require the "washing of the water of the Word" for a renewal.

> Ephesians 5:26-27 – *that he might sanctify and cleanse it with the washing of water by the word, that he might present it to himself a glorious church, not having spot, or wrinkle, or any such thing; but that it should be holy and without blemish.*

It is time to awaken the church from its spiritual slumber and to put off the carnal things of the flesh and material pursuits of the world and be totally committed to Him as His children.

> Romans 13:11-14 – *And that, knowing the time, that now it is high time to awake out of sleep: for now is our salvation nearer than when we believed. The night is far spent, the day is at hand: let us therefore cast off the works of darkness, and let us put on the armour of light. Let us walk honestly, as in the day; not in rioting and drunkenness, not in chambering and wantonness, not in strife and envying. But put ye on the Lord Jesus Christ, and make not provision for the flesh, to fulfil the lusts thereof.* (Note: this passage was written to the Church, the Body of Christ that was in Rome.)

Every believer and every church assembly is referred to as the dwelling place (temple) of God. It's time to eliminate those things that defile the temple of God and make sure it is Holy for Him.

> 1 Corinthians 3:16-17 – *Know ye not that ye are the temple of God, and that the Spirit of God dwelleth in you? If any man defile the temple of God, him shall God destroy; for the temple of God is holy, which temple ye are.*

> 1 Corinthians 6:19-20 – *What? know ye not that your body is the temple of the Holy Ghost which is in you, which ye have of God, and ye are not your own? For ye are bought with a price: therefore glorify God in your body, and in your spirit, which are God's.*

Obviously the cloud as seen in Israel's Exodus from Egypt will not function the same as it will for the Body of Christ; but it will function exactly as God wants it to for us in these last days. We don't depend on the cloud or worship it; we depend on the one who uses the cloud and speaks from it if He chooses to do so. It is the manifestation of His Presence that we seek as a divine covering for us, not the cloud.

We need not fear what the days ahead shall bring because Jesus promised that He would never leave His people.

> Matthew 28:19-20 – *Go ye therefore, and teach all nations, baptizing them in the name of the Father, and of the Son, and of the Holy Ghost: teaching them to observe all things whatsoever I have commanded you: and, lo, I am with you alway, even unto the end of the world. Amen.*

> Hebrews 13:5b-6 – *for he hath said, I will never leave thee, nor forsake thee. So that we may boldly say, The Lord is my helper, and I will not fear what man shall do unto me.*

In the above passage He tells us of His protective and providing covering that is to be with us during a time of purging and chastening. This may be what the church will experience as challenging events that Jesus foretold would precede His return.

> Luke 21:25-28 – *And there shall be signs in the sun, and in the moon, and in the stars; and upon the earth distress of nations, with perplexity; the sea and the waves roaring; men's hearts*

failing them for fear, and for looking after those things which are coming on the earth: for the powers of heaven shall be shaken. And then shall they see <u>the Son of man coming in a cloud</u> with power and great glory. And when these things begin to come to pass, then look up, and lift up your heads; for your redemption draweth nigh.

The apostle Paul tells us that the experiences that Israel had were written for our example:

1 Corinthians 10:1-5 – *Moreover, brethren, I would not that ye should be ignorant, how that all our fathers were under the cloud, and all passed through the sea; and were all baptized unto Moses in the cloud and in the sea; and did all eat the same spiritual meat; and did all drink the same spiritual drink: for they drank of that spiritual Rock that followed them: and that Rock was Christ. But with_many of them God was not well pleased: for they were overthrown in the wilderness.*

Consider why these things are written for our example: it's about the purge that is needed to cleanse the temple of its fleshly impurities.

What happened to Israel is an object lesson for the church, specifically in these last days. Thus we each need to do a serious "self-examination" so that we are qualified to experience His presence.

1 Corinthians 10:6-10 – *Now these things were our examples, to the intent we should not lust after evil things, as they also lusted. Neither be ye idolaters, as were some of them; as it is written, The people sat down to eat and drink, and rose up to play. Neither let us commit fornication, as some of them committed, and fell in one day three and twenty thousand. Neither let us tempt Christ, as some of them also tempted, and were destroyed of serpents. Neither murmur ye, as some of them also murmured, and were destroyed of the destroyer.*

1 Corinthians 10:11-12 – *Now <u>all these things happened unto them for ensamples</u>: and they are written for our admonition,*

upon whom the ends of the world are come. Wherefore let him that thinketh he standeth take heed lest he fall.

These verses from 1 Corinthians 10 tell us how to behave and react when we experience a similar thing as Israel did. It tells us that we will experience persecution and severe opposition from the enemy at the end of this age; and we are entering that time now! This can be called "spiritual warfare" because it will be Satan and his evil forces that will oppose us right up to the time of the antichrist.

> Daniel 7:21-22 – *I beheld, and the same horn made war with the saints, and prevailed against them; until the Ancient of days came, and judgment was given to the saints of the most High; and the time came that the saints possessed the kingdom.*

> Revelation 13:7-8 – *And it was given unto him to make war with the saints, and to overcome them: and power was given him over all kindreds, and tongues, and nations. And all that dwell upon the earth shall worship him, whose names are not written in the book of life of the Lamb slain from the foundation of the world.*

Most Christians have come to believe that we will be raptured out of here before the manifestation of the antichrist; however this is being taught in error and is contrary to the Word of God. Consider what the apostle Paul wrote to the church at Thessalonica.

> 2 Thessalonians 2:1-4 – *Now we beseech you, brethren, by the coming of our Lord Jesus Christ, and by our gathering together unto him, that ye be not soon shaken in mind, or be troubled, neither by spirit, nor by word, nor by letter as from us, as that the day of Christ is at hand. Let no man deceive you by any means: for that day shall not come, except there come a falling away first, and that man of sin be revealed, the son of perdition; who opposeth and exalteth himself above all that is called God, or that is worshipped; so that he as God sitteth in the temple of God, shewing himself that he is God.*

Note: "the son of perdition" is a direct reference to the antichrist. This means that the church will see and experience him before *the coming of our Lord Jesus Christ, and by our gathering together unto him*!

Therefore we must prepare our hearts and minds for what is coming. We need to purify our desires and motives so we are not found murmuring, rebelling and complaining about the things we are likely to experience in the days ahead. If we truly look to the Lord, learn to trust Him, rest in Him, obey Him and follow His directions; then His cloud will overshadow us like it did with Israel.

The hand of the Lord will lead, guide, protect, provide, then we will see and experience His glory. God's true servants as His leadership, will be those like Moses through whom His glory is seen, will provide the Lord's direction for His people, just as Moses did.

The record of the cloud's effect and provision for Israel is given for us to see that God will again take care of His true people when the modern Egypt, (which represents the world with its wicked and corrupt religious system), moves against His church.

The cloud of His presence has always been with His church, much like it was with Israel when it filled the Tabernacle of Moses and the Temple of Solomon.

> Exodus 40:34-38 – *Then a cloud covered the tent of the congregation, and the glory of the LORD filled the tabernacle. And Moses was not able to enter into the tent of the congregation, because the cloud abode thereon, and the glory of the LORD filled the tabernacle. And when the cloud was taken up from over the tabernacle, the children of Israel went onward in all their journeys: but if the cloud were not taken up, then they journeyed not till the day that it was taken up. For the cloud of the LORD was upon the tabernacle by day, and fire was on it by night, in the sight of all the house of Israel, throughout all their journeys.*

> 1 Kings 8:10-11 – *And it came to pass, when the priests were come out of the holy place, that the cloud filled the house of the LORD, so that the priests could not stand to minister because of the cloud: for the glory of the LORD had filled the house of the LORD.*

The cloud of God's manifest presence is still over His church today; however, that cloud has not been able to fully manifest His Presence in the church as it has yet to do: it is not visible to the natural eye. The Lord has revealed to this author that there is a problem in the church that hinders the cloud of His Glory from being seen and His divine presence from being fully experienced.

What the Lord revealed, during a time of prayer, was that there are two clouds over the church at the present time. Both clouds have been in place for centuries. The top cloud is the Cloud of His Glory. Beneath it is another cloud. This other cloud obscures our view of the Cloud of His Glory, (His presence). This lower cloud is a cloud of dust and dirt. This dust cloud is the only one that can be seen, and it covers the entire church.

This cloud of dust is composed of airborne earthly dirt which settles on everything and must be swept away before we can see the Cloud of His Glory. I inquired of the Lord during the time of this revelation, "What is the dust and where did it come from"?

The Lord graciously answered by reveling that the dust is stirred up by the wind. He showed that the wind is the preaching of man, (many are "windy" saying much more than they should); and the dust is the doctrine of man and his traditions. Man is made of the dust of the earth, and the wind stirs up that dust and blows it around into the churches; so much so that it covers everything.

When man puts his own ideas and limited understanding into his teaching and preaching, the result produces the doctrines of man and not the pure doctrines of God. It is man blowing his own dust and dirt around presenting it as being from God when it is not.

> Ephesians 4:14 – *that we henceforth be no more children, tossed to and fro, and carried about with every wind of doctrine, by the sleight of men, and cunning craftiness, whereby they lie in wait to deceive;*

The dust cloud that covers the church consists of the many conflicting doctrines of men that is now present in various churches. This dust obscures our ability to clearly see the Glory of God; instead we see so much else, particularly that which of man and of this world. This dust cloud may not have been generated deliberately by man, but rather is a product of ignorance of God and His Word, clinging to false beliefs and traditions; some of which were introduced by pagan and demonic sources - infiltration by the spirit of antichrist.

How do we house clean and get rid of all this man generated dust? We know from nature that rain settles the dust. The next move of God that we expect is called the "latter rain". This will be a time of the Holy Spirit's washing the church with the pure Word, cleansing it of the false doctrines and traditions of man in preparation for His coming. Consider the following prophetic word:

> Hosea 6:2-3 – *After two days* (a day as a thousand years is two thousand years since His resurrection and formation of the church) *will He revive us: in the third day* (the millennium) *He will raise us up, and we shall live in His sight. Then shall we know, if we follow on to know the LORD; His going forth is prepared as the morning; and He shall come unto us as the rain, as the latter and former rain unto the earth.*

> James 5:7-8 – *Be patient therefore, brethren, unto the coming of the Lord. Behold, the husbandman waiteth for the precious fruit of the earth, and hath long patience for it, until he receive the early and latter rain. Be ye also patient; stablish your hearts: for the coming of the Lord draweth nigh.*

> Zechariah 10:1 – *Ask ye of the LORD rain in the time of the latter rain; so the LORD shall make bright clouds, and give them showers of rain,*

Pray for the latter rain, the last day outpouring of the Holy Spirit; because rain settles the dust and washes it away. This is a spiritual rain that is needed!

> Joel 2:23 – *Be glad then, ye children of Zion, and rejoice in the Lord your God: for He hath given you the former rain moderately, and He will cause to come down for you the rain, the former rain, and the latter rain in the first month.*

The apostle Peter quoted further from this passage in Joel on the Day of Pentecost because it applies right up to the coming return of Lord.

Acts 2:16-20 – *But this is that which was spoken by the prophet Joel; And it shall come to pass in the last days, saith God, I will pour out of my Spirit upon all flesh: and your sons and your daughters shall prophesy, and your young men shall see visions, and your old men shall dream dreams: and on my servants and on my handmaidens I will pour out in those days of my Spirit; and they shall prophesy: and I will shew wonders in heaven above, and signs in the earth beneath; blood, and fire, and vapour of smoke: the sun shall be turned into darkness, and the moon into blood, before that great and notable day of the Lord come.*

This latter rain refers to the work of the Holy Spirit which began on Pentecost, nearly two thousand years ago, and will continue up to the return of Jesus. The work of the Holy Spirit, who is "the Spirit of Truth" brings the dust clearing spiritual rain; the washing of the Word of God.

John 16:12-14 – *I have yet many things to say unto you, but ye cannot bear them now. Howbeit when he, the Spirit of truth, is come, he will guide you into all truth: for he shall not speak of himself; but whatsoever he shall hear, that shall he speak: and he will shew you things to come. He shall glorify me: for he shall receive of mine, and shall shew it unto you.*

The Holy Spirit will "clear the air" of the false doctrines and the traditions that man and demons created. He is the necessary one who will remove all the dust and dirty doctrines of man so that the church can "worship in Spirit and Truth".

John 4:23-24 – *But the hour cometh, and now is, when the true worshippers shall worship the Father in spirit and in truth: for the Father seeketh such to worship him. God is a Spirit: and they that worship him must worship him in spirit and in truth.*

The Lord's presence is to be manifested in the church when assembled together as well as in the individual temple of your body. His glory is to be seen in each place of His habitation; this will even be world-wide.

Habakkuk 2:14 – *For the earth shall be filled with the knowledge of the glory of the LORD, as the waters cover the sea.*

John 14:6 – *Jesus saith unto him, I am the way, the truth, and the life: no man cometh unto the Father, but by me.*

When God reveals truth or a doctrine to man, he seeks to understand it with his limited human intelligence. This often negates the Word of God because it must be spiritually understood and received by faith.

1 Corinthians 2:14 – *But the natural man receiveth not the things of the Spirit of God: for they are foolishness unto him: neither can he know them, because they are spiritually discerned.*

Trying to understand and fulfill God's Word with the natural mind brings His sovereignty down to man's humanity. For this reason we have a seriously fragmented church. We are not "one" as our Lord prayed in John 17, but we are grievously divided. And what is it that divides us? Our doctrines – (our dust); not His doctrines!

The Lord, by His Spirit, has restored many truths to the church in the past few decades. These are not new truths even though they appear to be new to us; this is because we were not walking in them previously. The church has lost many truths because of the interference of man and his limited understanding and denominational stubbornness.

When man receives a new truth, he either intellectualizes it or he begins to miss-apply it by implementing it through his own fleshly weakness and natural understanding.

Such doctrines as divine healing, discipleship, authority, lordship, deliverance and casting out demons, all came from God by inspiration of the Holy Spirit. The abuses, excesses and messes created by these doctrines, (or dust), are not God's doing, but man's miss-application of what God gave to the church.

As any housewife knows, dust settles in everything; and so it is with this dust of man's doctrines. There is no place where this dust is not covering everything in various depths; masking or dirtying up the Word and work of God in churches.

From nature, we also learn that dust is a result of dryness, the lack of rain. You can't stir up dust when it is wet. Spiritual dryness occurs between periods of the Holy Spirit's waves of refreshing and outpouring. It is during the in between periods of spiritual dry spells that man starts to incorporate his own ideas or interpretations and begins to stir up the dust.

As mentioned previously, the next move of God will restore fully the gift ministries of apostle and prophet. Apostles are the "guardians of doctrine" as wise master builders. Prophets will put their fingers on the errors in the church, give warning of the consequences of such errors, and admonitions to seek God with a whole and pure heart; and "worship in spirit and in truth". Both will work to clear the air of the dust by restoring the sound doctrines of God.

It seems that many times we receive a new revelation from the Lord and set out immediately to proclaim it: we do so in error and the divisive results become obvious. We need to be patient with a new revelation from the Lord until we receive a confirmation from other trusted sources. Even then we should not jump to proclaim it until He says "when and where" to do so. This will prevent much harmful effects caused by man's presumption and zeal and will help keep the dust from being stirred up.

The ministry of the apostles and prophets will be the final perfecting, finishing, completing and equipping of the saints in preparation for His return and to rule in His kingdom. They will finish the house of God, the temple not built with human hands – His dwelling place.

The dust cloud will be eliminated and the Cloud of His Glory, with the manifestation of His Presence will fill His Holy Temple, His church, and all those that are His. Then the earth shall begin to see the Glory of the Lord.

Chapter 12

ONE CHURCH –
THE TRUE CHURCH

Jesus prayed for His followers and also for what He knew would become His church after He ascended back to heaven.

> John 17:20-23 – *Neither pray I for these alone, but for them also which shall believe on me through their word; that they all may be one; as thou, Father, art in me, and I in thee, that they also may be one in us: that the world may believe that thou hast sent me. And the glory which thou gavest me I have given them; that they may be one, even as we are one: I in them, and thou in me, that they may be made perfect in one; and that the world may know that thou hast sent me, and hast loved them, as thou hast loved me.*

How can the church be one as Jesus prayed; especially in view of the discord, fragmentation and doctrinal differences that divides it today? How can the church be one when its many factions follow so many different personalities as leaders?

> 1 Corinthians 3:1-4 – *And I, brethren, could not speak unto you as unto spiritual, but as unto carnal, even as unto babes in Christ. I have fed you with milk, and not with meat: for hitherto ye were not able to bear it, neither yet now are ye able. For ye are yet carnal: for whereas there is among you envying, and strife, and divisions, are ye not carnal, and walk as men? For while one saith, I am of Paul; and another, I am of Apollos; are ye not carnal?*

How will the church become one? Will it be accomplished openly for all the world to see, or will it only become one in the spirit realm where the world cannot see? The answer is recorded in John 17:21 - *that the world may believe;* and again in verse 23 – *that the world may know.*

This tells us that the one church will literally and physically be one body before Jesus returns for it. This will be the testimony to the world of God's love as stated further in verse 23 – *and hast loved them, as thou hast loved me.*

God's love will be in the one true church and the world will see it, marvel at it, and even hate it. The world will hate this church because it cannot comprehend the God-kind of love that will be manifested in it. His love in His church will be His light in this world of darkness as it reveals His glory: but those in darkness cannot comprehend it and take offense to it.

> 1 John 4:5 – *In him was life; and the life was the light of men. And the light shineth in darkness; and the darkness comprehended it not.*

As described in Chapter One, the other church fell back into the sea of humanity, back into the darkness; that is except for those who were truly seeking the Lord and accepted Jesus Christ as the only way in. The sea of humanity is drowning in the spiritual darkness by not acknowledging the "light" that came for their benefit.

The true church in these last days will be much like the first church; it was in one accord in faith and unity, looking out for each other for their mutual benefit. How did this accord or oneness develop? They were one because all of the attention of the entire church was directed to Jesus Christ. In Him they were one! None looked upon himself or his own things, purpose, plans, ambitions, etc.   The oneness they experienced was in focusing on the centrality of Christ. Diversity can exist and function in beautiful harmony when all attention is focused on Him.

> 1 Corinthians 12:12-20 – *For as the body is one, and hath many members, and all the members of that one body, being many, are one body: so also is Christ. For by one Spirit are we all baptized into one body, whether we be Jews or Gentiles, whether we be bond or free; and have been all made to drink into one Spirit. For the body is not one member, but many. If the foot shall say, Because I am not the hand, I am not of the body; is*

it therefore not of the body? And if the ear shall say, Because I am not the eye, I am not of the body; is it therefore not of the body? If the whole body were an eye, where were the hearing? If the whole were hearing, where were the smelling? But now hath God set the members every one of them in the body, as it hath pleased him. And if they were all one member, where were the body? But now are they many members, yet but one body.

For years many in church leadership have tried to bring about unity among the churches in the ecumenical movement which was promoted by the Roman Catholic Church. Another attempt in recent decades has been to unify the Charismatic and Full Gospel elements of the Body of Christ around the banner of "signs and wonders" or the "Word of Faith" group which also failed. All such efforts have failed because the basis for the attempted unity has been something other than faith in Jesus Christ. Such efforts will continue to fail because they leave out certain other parts of the Body of Christ that differ in some doctrine or tradition. There will be no unity of the faith until all five of the Gift Ministries, that Jesus established, are allowed to fully function. Their work is for:

Ephesians 4:12-13 – ... *the perfecting of the saints, for the work of the ministry, for the edifying of the body of Christ: till we all come in the unity of the faith, and of the knowledge of the Son of God, unto a perfect man, unto the measure of the stature of the fulness of Christ.*

Excluding the essential Gift Ministries denies the Holy Spirit the use of those that He wants to work through to perfect or complete the church as the one unified body.

As mentioned previously, the Holy Spirit wants to use all five of His end-time gift ministers to complete the saints, forming them into the image of Christ. The work of the apostles and prophets is particularly important for this task to place the focus on Jesus Christ and to correct the errors and false doctrines that have led so many churches astray. They will see to it that the absolute true gospel will go into all the world to produce the Father's desired results.

Romans 8:29 – *For whom he did foreknow, he also did predestinate to be conformed to the image of his Son, that he might be the firstborn among many brethren.*

The work of the apostles, in particular, is for Christ to be formed in all believers; as was the work of the apostle Paul.

Galatians 4:19 – *My little children, of whom I travail in birth again until Christ be formed in you,*

The result of their work as directed by the Lord will be a glorious church, without spot or wrinkle of any blemish: it will be filled with His Glory.

Colossians 1:27 – *to whom God would make known what is the riches of the glory of this mystery among the Gentiles; which is Christ in you, the hope of glory.*

With the character and nature of Christ fully formed in each believer then the church will be manifested as the children of God. Scripture says that all of creation is looking forward to this time.

Romans 8:18-19 – *For I reckon that the sufferings of this present time are not worthy to be compared with the glory which shall be revealed in us. For the earnest expectation of the creature waiteth for the manifestation of the sons of God.*

Then the true church will be prepared for His coming since it has fully conformed itself unto His image and likeness.

1 John 3:1-3 – *Behold, what manner of love the Father hath bestowed upon us, that we should be called the sons of God: therefore the world knoweth us not, because it knew him not. Beloved, now are we the sons of God, and it doth not yet appear what we shall be: but we know that, when he shall appear, we shall be like him; for we shall see him as he is. And every man that hath this hope in him purifieth himself, even as he is pure.*

The condition of the church as it now appears does not properly represent Christ and the children of God. When His character and nature is fully manifested in His people it will be evident by His love being on full display for all to see. Love, (charity and caring), is the full level of spiritual maturity that reveals Him; but obviously we are not there yet as we have to make changes and repent of our self-centeredness.

> James 4:8-10 – *Draw nigh to God, and he will draw nigh to you. Cleanse your hands, ye sinners; and purify your hearts, ye double minded. Be afflicted, and mourn, and weep: let your laughter be turned to mourning, and your joy to heaviness. Humble yourselves in the sight of the Lord, and he shall lift you up.*

As we lay down our lives and self-centered wills and humble ourselves, we are to seek Him above all else becoming dependent upon Him. He then will be able to direct us by His Spirit drawing us closer to Him. As we avail ourselves to Him as His Holy habitation, He will fill His temple, the church and His saints with His presence.

Then the world will see and recognize the church as His Holy habitation. This is because believer's own identities will be lost as they take on His identity. Our priorities and desires will change from earthly and material to heavenly and the things of His kingdom. As stated in scripture, our own life's identity will be hid in Him.

> Colossians 3:1-4 – *If ye then be risen with Christ, seek those things which are above, where Christ sitteth on the right hand of God. Set your affection on things above, not on things on the earth. For ye are dead, and your life is hid with Christ in God. When Christ, who is our life, shall appear, then shall ye also appear with him in glory.*

Thus we will take on His identity and we will be one in Him and with Him. It is Jesus Christ manifesting in His saints that will make us one fulfilling the Lord's prayer.

> John 17:20-26 – *Neither pray I for these alone, but for them also which shall believe on me through their word; that they*

all may be one; as thou, Father, art in me, and I in thee, that they also may be one in us: that the world may believe that thou hast sent me. And the glory which thou gavest me I have given them; that they may be one, even as we are one: I in them, and thou in me, <u>that they may be made perfect in one</u>; and that the world may know that thou hast sent me, and hast loved them, as thou hast loved me. Father, I will that they also, whom thou hast given me, be with me where I am; that they may behold my glory, which thou hast given me: for thou lovedst me before the foundation of the world. O righteous Father, the world hath not known thee: but I have known thee, and these have known that thou hast sent me. And I have declared unto them thy name, and will declare it: that the love wherewith thou hast loved me may be in them, and I in them.

As Christ is formed in us through the work of all of the five gift ministries, we become one in Christ. Individuality will no longer be important to anyone because all have humbled themselves and begin to "prefer one another" or esteem others higher than themselves as His Love in us matures.

Philippians 2:1-5 – *If there be therefore any consolation in Christ, if any comfort of love, if any fellowship of the Spirit, if any bowels and mercies, fulfil ye my joy, that ye be likeminded, having the same love, being of one accord, of one mind. Let nothing be done through strife or vainglory; but in lowliness of mind let each esteem other better than themselves. Look not every man on his own things, but every man also on the things of others.*

All who abide in Him will exalt Him. As this happens, no man, no assembly, no denomination, no particular doctrine, nor tradition or dogma and nothing else will have any meaning but Him in this one true church.

It seems hard to imagine what His last day church will be like since we have not seen anything like it in recent history. But with God, all things are possible and He will form the true and holy habitation, His true church, as we yield to Him.

Ephesians 4:24 – *and that ye put on the new man, which after God is created in righteousness and true holiness.*

Christ will be seen in His people: His glory will be seen in them, on them, and through them: it will be the Light of His Glory! The church will be one, and it will be glorious. He will be pleased and proud to have it as His Body. This is the Lord's doing, not by man's efforts. Have you ever noticed that churches built by man often are known by the name of their pastor? Thus many pastors consider the church that they pastor as "their" church, or call it "my" church, instead of His.

We must recognize what is the church of man, and what is the church of our Lord Jesus Christ in these last days; there is a difference. Which church are you part of? Which church do you want to be part of? The church man is building or the church Jesus Christ is building?

Ephesians 2:20-22 – *of the household of God; and are built upon the foundation of the apostles and prophets, Jesus Christ himself being the chief corner stone; in whom all the building fitly framed together groweth unto an holy temple in the Lord: in whom ye also are builded together for an habitation of God through the Spirit.*

Another manifestation of the true church is that it will stand against the carnal corruption and evil influences of the devil that are promoted by sinful leadership in governmental politics, the entertainment industry, mega corporations, the media and all the witchcraft and occult organizations. The other church will just go along to get along, and will not put up any resistance to the immorality and corruption being advanced by Satan and his forces. In fact some portions of the other church will embrace the current corrupt and immoral trends of "woke" community that are being promoted; they refuse to take a stand against such! The other church does not recognize or engage in spiritual warfare against evil forces of the devil.

Ephesians 6:10-18 – *Finally, my brethren, be strong in the Lord, and in the power of his might. Put on the whole armour of God, that ye may be able to stand against the wiles of the devil. For we wrestle not against flesh and blood, but against principalities, against powers, against the rulers of the darkness of this world, against spiritual wickedness in high places. Wherefore take unto you the whole armour of God, that ye may be able to withstand in the evil day, and having done all, to stand. Stand therefore, having your loins girt about with truth, and having on the breastplate of righteousness; and your feet shod with the preparation of the gospel of peace; above all, taking the shield of faith, wherewith ye shall be able to quench all the fiery darts of the wicked. And take the helmet of salvation, and the sword of the Spirit, which is the word of God: praying always with all prayer and supplication in the Spirit, and watching thereunto with all perseverance and supplication for all saints.*

Jesus said that His church will stand against the evil of the enemy which the other church will not oppose. Jesus also declared that the gates of hell shall not prevail against His church, but will obviously envelope the other church and even find favor within it.

Matthew 16:16-18 — *He saith unto them, But whom say ye that I am? And Simon Peter answered and said, Thou art the Christ, the Son of the living God. And Jesus answered and said unto him, Blessed art thou, Simon Bar-jona: for flesh and blood hath not revealed it unto thee, but my Father which is in heaven. And I say also unto thee, That thou art Peter, and upon this rock* (Peter's confession), *I will build my church; and the gates of hell shall not prevail against it.*

Thus the world will hate the true church because it stands for righteousness and opposes that which is wicked and corrupt in the world and of the devil. However, the world does embrace the other church because it conforms to the world. Consider which is more important to you, being loved by the world, or being loved and cherished by God the Father, and Jesus Christ His Son? Which church do you prefer to be part of; the other church, of His true church?

Chapter 13

THE REASON FOR THE VISION OF CHAPTER 1

This chapter will sound shocking to many Christians, but please carefully consider the message. The vision was the result of a prayer asking the Lord to help me feel the joys of the Christmas Season. In the vision I saw Jesus standing at the head of His army of believers. He had His sword drawn and stood with a fiery look in His eyes as He was going to deal with an evil enemy.

Then I heard the Spirit of the Lord say to my spirit, "Don't look down at a babe in a manger; look up at the King of Glory". It was when I looked up in my spirit that I saw Him; dressed for battle. Then I realized that it was the celebration Christmas that so offended Him that He wants to fight against.

Consider what the Christmas celebration represents. It is filled with various fantasies of things that do not exist, of which draw attention away from Christ Jesus. Then you have an imaginary figure referred to as Santa Claus, (more like Satan Claus), who does supernatural things. This myth, along with several other imaginary creatures, gets children to focus their attention on what is totally false, and most likely is demonic. What is ironic is the story, "The Night Before Christmas" was written by a Presbyterian minister; obviously he was part of the other church and that left Jesus totally out of the picture.

A major problem with all these myths, traditions and lies is that they are projected on children who come to believe in such falsehoods. Then when they are told the truth about Jesus Christ they have a hard time accepting Him as fact when all the other stories told them they find out were untrue.

God, the Father, and Jesus Christ, despise (or hate) Christmas. Such a celebration is found nowhere in the Bible, and was never observed by the early church. So how did this corrupt celebration become established in the church? Christmas is a product of the biggest "other" church when it "Christianized" the pagan celebration of Saturnalia bringing it into the church as a sanctioned ritual called the "Mass for Christ": thus Christ's mass, or Christmas.

Saturnalia was the pagan worship of the sun god at the Winter Solstice because of the increase in the length of daylight returning. Since this celebration was of pagan origin it was open to demonic input to what is now called Christmas. Eventually more and more traditions were added to the celebration like the story of St. Nicholas. Then more extreme fairy tale fantasies were added until we have what today is observed as Christmas. Notice that Christmas in not really a "Christian" holiday because almost everyone in the western world celebrates it. Thus it is more of a secular holiday and seems to worship material things and fairy tales. Yes, God hates it!

Consider the fallacies of how Christmas is celebrated. First of all, Jesus was not born on December 25th. He was born in late September or early October during the Fall Festivals that God ordained as His Holy days: Trumpets, Atonement and Tabernacles. It is not likely that Jesus was born in a barn or stable, as commonly portrayed, because it would have violated Hebrew laws of cleanliness. Likewise there probably were no animals present as that would also violate their laws of cleanliness.

The manger that was used as the baby's crib was a feeding trough that hay was placed in to feed the sheep. Again, according Hebrew strict laws on cleanliness, sheep were not to eat hay that was on the ground where they relieved themselves. The reason that a manger was available to use as a crib is because the sheep were out in the fields with their shepherds and not in the sheepfolds where they are kept during the winter months. Jesus was likely born in a sukkot, a booth prepared for the celebration of Tabernacles, since there were many available as that festival day approached.

The actual timing of Jesus' birth can be determined based on the priestly duties of Zachariah, along with his wife Elizabeth, Mary's cousin. Elizabeth gave birth to John the Baptist six months prior to Jesus' birth. As a priest, Zachariah was of the division or "course' of Abia.

> Luke 1:5-7 – *There was in the days of Herod, the king of Judæa, a certain priest named Zacharias, of the course of Abia: and his wife was of the daughters of Aaron, and her name was Elisabeth. And they were both righteous before God, walking in all the commandments and ordinances of the Lord blameless. And they had no child, because that Elisabeth was barren, and they both were now well stricken in years.*

Abia's division of the priesthood served from May-June. So, that's when the angel appeared to Zachariah advising him of his coming birth of his son and what to name him.

> Luke 1:8-13 – *And it came to pass, that while he executed the priest's office before God in the order of his course, according to the custom of the priest's office, his lot was to burn incense when he went into the temple of the Lord. And the whole multitude of the people were praying without at the time of incense. And there appeared unto him an angel of the Lord standing on the right side of the altar of incense. And when Zacharias saw him, he was troubled, and fear fell upon him. But the angel said unto him, Fear not, Zacharias: for thy prayer is heard; and thy wife Elisabeth shall bear thee a son, and thou shalt call his name John.*

When Zacharias concluded his service, he went back home and Elizabeth conceived, thus she became pregnant in the month of June.

> Luke 1:23-24 – *And it came to pass, that, as soon as the days of his ministration were accomplished, he departed to his own house. And after those days his wife Elisabeth conceived, and hid herself five months,*

Six months later Mary was visited by Gabriel who made the announcement of her divine conception.

> Luke 1:26-31 – *And in the sixth month the angel Gabriel was sent from God unto a city of Galilee, named Nazareth, to a virgin espoused to a man whose name was Joseph, of the house of David; and the virgin's name was Mary. And the angel came in unto her, and said, Hail, thou that art highly favoured, the Lord is with thee: blessed art thou among women. And when she saw him, she was troubled at his saying, and cast in her mind what manner of salutation this should be. And the angel said unto her, Fear not, Mary: for thou hast found favour with God. And, behold, thou shalt conceive in thy womb, and bring forth a son, and shalt call his name JESUS.*

Then Mary goes to visit her cousin Elizabeth, who is now in her sixth month of pregnancy.

> Luke 1:36, 39 – *And, behold, thy cousin Elisabeth, she hath also conceived a son in her old age: and this is the sixth month with her, who was called barren. … And Mary arose in those days, and went into the hill country with haste, into a city of Juda; and entered into the house of Zacharias, and saluted Elisabeth.*

Jesus was conceived when the angel appeared to Mary in December, six months after John the Baptist was conceived. These recorded events give us a time reference for the birth of Jesus. Thus it appears that Jesus was conceived in late December, on or during Hanukkah, "The Festival of Lights. The apostle John calls this feast by its former name, "The Feast of Dedication".

> John 10:22-23 – *And it was at Jerusalem the feast of the dedication, and it was winter. And Jesus walked in the temple in Solomon's porch.*

Jesus kept this festival, and He is called "the light"; also "the light of the world"; which He is. Since Jesus was conceived in December, and given the normal 180 days of human gestation, he would have been born in late September or early October. What happens in September or October? It is the celebration of God's Holy Days that begin with the Feast of Trumpets, followed by the Day of Atonement, followed by the Feast of Sukkot! "The Feast of Booths", also called "The Festival of Tabernacles".

Consider that the God of the New Testament is the very same God of the Old Testament. He gave forth prophesies in the Old Testament that were fulfilled in the New Testament. What Christians fail to realize is that God used the Old Testament "Feasts" to portray and foretell the major prophetic events that would occur in the New Testament?

- Hanukkah - Jesus was conceived in late December, possibly or probably during Hanukkah – Feast of Dedication.
- Sukkoth - Jesus was born September-October, during fall Holy days.
- Passover - Jesus was crucified during Passover, at the same day that the lamb was slain.

- Unleavened Bread - Jesus was in the tomb during this feast.
- First Fruits - Jesus was resurrected during The Festival of First Fruits
- Feast of Weeks - Jesus sent the Holy Spirit at Pentecost (Feast of Shavuot)
- Trumpets - Jesus is coming again - could it be during Rosh Hashanah? (Feast of Trumpets – note that trumpets were used to announce the coming or entrance of the King.)

Another fallacy of the Christmas story is the three wise men, referred to as the "maggai". First of all scripture does not say there were just three, and they were not present as is typically represented in the average "manger" scene.

> Matthew 2:1-2, 7-8 – *Now when Jesus was born in Bethlehem of Judæa in the days of Herod the king, behold, there came wise men from the east to Jerusalem, saying, Where is he that is born King of the Jews? for we have seen his star in the east, and are come to worship him. ... Then Herod, when he had privily called the wise men, enquired of them diligently what time the star appeared. And he sent them to Bethlehem,*

They didn't even appear until nearly two years later when they entered the house where the young child was. They did not go to Bethlehem but followed the star that led them in a different direction.

> Matthew 2:9-11 – *When they had heard the king, they departed; and, lo, the star,_which they saw in the east, went before them, till it came and stood over where the_young child was. When they saw the star, they rejoiced with exceeding great joy. And when they were come into the house, they saw the young child with Mary his mother, and fell down, and worshipped him: and when they had opened their treasures, they presented unto him gifts; gold, and frankincense, and myrrh.*

These wise men, or maggai, were actually Hebrew descendants of Daniel and other Hebrews that served as maggai in the lands of Babylon and Persia, and made their journey from there.

Please understand that all of the Hebrew people did not return to Israel after the seventy years of Babylonian captivity. There was a massive Israeli community throughout the Persian Empire as revealed in the story of Ester who became queen of the Persian Emperor. She interceded to the king on behalf of all the Israelites in the empire who Haman wanted to annihilate. This was about 150 years after fewer than 50,000 Israelites returned to Israel from their seventy year Babylonian captivity.

These scholarly Hebrew maggai were familiar with the scriptures and prophecies about the coming Messiah. It took them a period of time to recognize the star and its meaning, then to organize their journey to Israel. After meeting with Herod they were directed to Bethlehem, but instead, the star directed them to Nazareth, to the house of Joseph where they met the young child and presented their gifts and probably told of the Old Testament prophesies about the child; he that was born King of the Jews.

The Bible does not instruct us to celebrate Jesus birth, though celebrating birthdays is a common practice for much western civilization. However the Bible does instruct us to celebrate and acknowledge His death till He comes. How many in the church actually do this?

> 1 *Corinthians* 11:23-26 – *For I have received of the Lord that which also I delivered unto you, That the Lord Jesus the same night in which he was betrayed took bread: and when he had given thanks, he brake it, and said, Take, eat: this is my body, which is broken for you: this do in remembrance of me. After the same manner also he took the cup, when he had supped, saying, This cup is the new testament in my blood: this do ye, as oft as ye drink it, in remembrance of me. For as often as ye eat this bread, and drink this cup, ye do shew the Lord's death till he come.*

God hates Christmas; and this is what He was showing me in the vision. The vision went on to show that Christmas, and many other false doctrines and traditions, were generated by the other church; the church built by man in which demons are eager to enter and dwell in so as to corrupt the Word of God, the message of the gospel, and His love for us. The other church has created a facade, an imitation, with another gospel and form of Jesus.

There is another fallacy that the other church has embraced as a tradition, and that is the Easter celebration which perverts the true account of Jesus' crucifixion and resurrection. Jesus was not placed on the cross to die for our sins on Good Friday. He was in the grave for three days and three nights: you don't get three days and three nights between sunset Friday and after sunset Saturday when He arose. This concept is the result of failure to understand Hebrew time periods as ordained by God. "Evening and morning are the next day"; meaning that the next day begins at sunset; as established by God in Genesis 1.

In the year that Jesus was crucified, Passover began on a Thursday which began at sunset on Wednesday. So Jesus had to be off of the cross by sunset on Wednesday because Thursday began after sunset. Jesus was crucified on Wednesday, which the Jews called the Day of Preparation, the day they killed the Passover Lamb.

> John 19:3 – *The Jews therefore, because it was the preparation, that the bodies should not remain upon the cross on the sabbath day, (for that sabbath day was an high day,) besought Pilate that their legs might be broken, and that they might be taken away.*

Jesus became THE PASSOVER LAMB for all of mankind!

> 1 Corinthians 1:7b – ... *For even Christ our Passover is sacrificed for us.*

The next day, Thursday being Passover was the high Holy Sabbath, not the weekly seventh day Sabbath. Jesus rose from the grave after sunset Saturday night, (after the weekly Sabbath), which began the first day of the week. So you get three nights from our Wednesday night, (which to the Jews begins Thursday), to Friday, and three days from Thursday to Saturday. Jesus arose after sunset Saturday, (the weekly Sabbath), which to the Jews begins the first day of the week. He was gone from the tomb when Mary arrived before daylight.

> John 20:1 – *The first day of the week cometh Mary Magdalene early, when it was yet dark, unto the sepulchre, and seeth the stone taken away from the sepulchre.*

Note that it was still "dark", not yet sunrise; Jesus arose right after sunset on what we consider Saturday night.

Easter is a pagan celebration of the goddess of sex and fertility, thus the eggs and bunny rabbits. Even the word "Easter" comes from a pagan source; it is a derivative of the name of the Saxon goddess of sex and fertility, Eastre. Most of the ancient cultures worship this goddess but under different names: Astarte, Isis, Ishtar, Venus, Diana, Eastre, etc. In addition, Lent and Ash Wednesday are not found in scripture as they are man-made traditions found in the other church.

It is not surprising that such a problem exists today in various churches as the apostle Paul had to address the same such issues in his day; and he had strong words for such.

> Galatians 1:6-8 – *I marvel that ye are so soon removed from him that called you into the grace of Christ unto another gospel: which is not another; but there be some that trouble you, and would pervert the gospel of Christ. But though we, or an angel from heaven, preach any other gospel unto you than that which we have preached unto you, let him be accursed.*

Consider the angel Moroni who declared a false gospel to Joseph Smith that created the Mormon Church.

> Colossians 2:6-8 – *As ye have therefore received Christ Jesus the Lord, so walk ye in him: rooted and built up in him, and stablished in the faith, as ye have been taught, abounding therein with thanksgiving. Beware lest any man spoil you through philosophy and vain deceit, after the tradition of men, after the rudiments of the world, and not after Christ.*

The other church may use His name and elements of His Word, but beware of what they add or delete that clouds the truth of the gospel of the Lord Jesus Christ.

As revealed in the vision, the false other church will be exposed for what it is, and it falls back into the sea of humanity from which it came. It will cease to exist, at least in the eyes of the Lord and His true church. Then the world will be able to see the one true church of the Lord Jesus Christ because He is seen as the head of it, and it will be recognized by its true character and nature, (as described in Chapter Fourteen). The church that man built will come to be as nothing. Whose church do you want to be in? His, or the other Church that man built?

Chapter 14

CHURCH LEADERSHIP

Is There Something Missing?

To lead means going before; out in front; and also means to be an example or role model. Too few church leaders do this; instead they follow the pattern of heads of corporations and businesses in dictating and delegating. Some of the greatest military leaders of history were out in front leading their troops, not simply standing behind spouting orders.

Jesus Christ, the Head of His Church, was out in front showing his disciples what to do and how to do it. He set the example.

> Matthew 16:24 – *Then said Jesus unto his disciples, If any man will come after me, let him deny himself, and take up his cross, and follow me.*

What Jesus was saying, in part was, "leave your old way of doing things behind and follow my lead and example. I know the way; this is how to live and minister God's love to others; this is how it's is done." The apostle Paul declared a similar thing; being the example to follow.

> Philippians 3:17 – *Brethren, be followers together of me, and mark them which walk so as ye have us for an ensample.*

> 2 Thessalonians 3:7-9 – *For yourselves know how ye ought to follow us: for we behaved not ourselves disorderly among you; neither did we eat any man's bread for nought; but wrought with labour and travail night and day, that we might not be chargeable to any of you: not because we have not power, but to make ourselves an ensample unto you to follow us.*

A similar admonition came from the apostle Peter when he wrote to the church leaders.

> 1 Peter 5:3 – *feed the flock of God which is among you, taking the oversight thereof, not by constraint, but willingly; not for filthy lucre, but of a ready mind; neither as being lords over God's heritage, but being ensamples to the flock.*

One of the reasons that the church of today has lost its "turning the world upside down" influence is because much of its leadership is no longer setting the proper example. Instead, they seem to be more intent on "pontificating" orders and orchestrating programs, or simply heading up their respective church or clerical services. Thus they cease to have a positive life changing or redeeming impact in their communities. Many today seem to be more intent on conforming their church to the ways of society, the world and the carnal lusts of the flesh. This leads to the condition that the apostle Paul described will exist in the last days.

> 2 Timothy 3:1-5 – *This know also, that in the last days perilous times shall come. For men shall be lovers of their own selves, covetous, boasters, proud, blasphemers, disobedient to parents, unthankful, unholy, without natural affection, trucebreakers, false accusers, incontinent, fierce, despisers of those that are good, traitors, heady, highminded, lovers of pleasures more than lovers of God; having a form of godliness, but denying the power thereof: from such turn away.*

Too few church leaders stand against the corruption of political correctness and the social progressives. They likely fear to speak out against such because doing so may cause them to lose their government sanctioned tax exempt 501.C.3 status; (which they really don't need anyhow because the United States Code declares churches to be tax exempt).

Proper church leadership will build believers up in their faith; bringing them to full spiritual maturity by equipping them with the Gifts of the Holy Spirit as well as the Fruit of the Spirit. They are to train them to minister to others with love and compassion; administer healing to those in physical need; and how to assist those of the church family in financial need along with the widows, orphans and homeless; then how to engage in witnessing to their local community with the gospel.

Also greatly needed is to be able to recognize and engage with others whom God has called and gifted with various forms of ministry; which so many today exclude and thus deny what God has provided for the development of the saints.

> Ephesians 4:7-8 – *But unto every one of us is given grace according to the measure of the gift of Christ. Wherefore he saith, When he ascended up on high, he led captivity captive, and gave gifts unto men.*

Many in church leadership today fail to recognize all the ministry gifts that Christ has provided to build His church. They say such ministries are not for today, but the Lord never put an expiration date on them. They need to be fully recognized and allowed to function in order to bring the church to the full state of spiritual maturity that is needed. (This subject is repeated again because it is so important.)

> Ephesians 4:11-13 – *And he gave some, apostles; and some, prophets; and some, evangelists; and some, pastors and teachers; for the perfecting of the saints, for the work of the ministry, for the edifying of the body of Christ: till we all come in the unity of the faith, and of the knowledge of the Son of God, unto a perfect man, unto the measure of the stature of the fullness of Christ:*

The failure to have all five ministry gifts in operation allows the enemy, with his false prophets, teachers and preachers to bring in all manner of false doctrines, rituals and traditions into the church – just as we see now.

> Ephesians 4:14-16 – *that we henceforth be no more children, tossed to and fro, and carried about with every wind of doctrine, by the sleight of men, and cunning craftiness, whereby they lie in wait to deceive; but speaking the truth in love, may grow up into him in all things, which is the head, even Christ: from whom the whole body fitly joined together and compacted by that which every joint supplieth, according to the effectual working*

in the measure of every part, maketh increase of the body unto the edifying of itself in love.

Jesus gave us these five ministry gifts for the *perfecting* (completing) of building His church. He never intended for one man to do the entire work as pastors have been attempting to do for the past few centuries. All are to work together by respecting and acknowledging each other's gifting and allowing them to work as needed. When specific gift ministries are need to operate, recognize them and allow them to operate – "*by that which every joint supplieth*".

For example: when healing is needed, allow the ones with the gifts of healing to minister. If teaching is needed, allow the ones with the gift of teaching to minister. If a prophetic word is needed, allow the prophets to minister. This is because the pastor does not have it all, nor is he supposed to, as addressed by Paul. It appears that most pastors fear to allow other gift ministries to function, afraid that they will take over their church or their position. They fail to realize it is not their church, but Christ's, and it is He who has established His gift ministries; but most pastors cannot recognize the Lord's called and gifted ones, or allow them to function in their calling.

> 1 Corinthians 12:27-30 – *Now ye are the body of Christ, and members in particular. And God hath set some in the church, first apostles, secondarily prophets, thirdly teachers, after that miracles, then gifts of healings, helps, governments, diversities of tongues. Are all apostles? are all prophets? are all teachers? are all workers of miracles? have all the gifts of healing? do all speak with tongues? do all interpret?*

This brings up another issue; that of false prophets, teachers and preachers which Jesus and Paul warned would be present in the last days. True discernment is lacking in church leadership. This discernment is needed to recognize what, or who, is of God and who is not. Discernment is one of the gifts of the Holy Spirit, and also comes from close and intimate fellowship with the Lord which makes it easier to recognize those who are, and are not of God.

Paul then goes on to address the most effective way to minister to others – by love and compassion.

1 Corinthians 12:31 – *But covet earnestly the best gifts: and yet shew I unto you a more excellent way.*

Having the God kind of love for others, as Jesus did, and as He commanded, is the most effective means of ministering to those in need.

1 Corinthians 13:1-3 – *Though I speak with the tongues of men and of angels, and have not charity, I am become as sounding brass, or a tinkling cymbal. And though I have the gift of prophecy, and understand all mysteries, and all knowledge; and though I have all faith, so that I could remove mountains, and have not charity, I am nothing. And though I bestow all my goods to feed the poor, and though I give my body to be burned, and have not charity, it profiteth me nothing.*

If a church leader or minister cannot minister in this way, he needs to get out of the ministry because he is not effective; and he is not honoring the Lord Jesus Christ in true ministry to His church! Make room for those called and gifted to do so!

Remember, Jesus set the example to follow; He came to serve, not to be served or to receive honor as so many pastors seem to desire today. This was illustrated when Jesus washed the disciple's feet as recorded in John 13.

John 13:12-17 – *So after he had washed their feet, and had taken his garments, and was set down again, he said unto them, Know ye what I have done to you? Ye call me Master and Lord: and ye say well; for so I am. If I then, your Lord and Master, have washed your feet; ye also ought to wash one another's feet. For I have given you an example, that ye should do as I have done to you. Verily, verily, I say unto you, The servant is not greater than his lord; neither he that is sent greater than he that sent him. If ye know these things, happy are ye if ye do them.*

Please recognize that the word "minister" means "servant"!

Matthew 20:25-27 – *But Jesus called them unto him, and said, Ye know that the princes of the Gentiles exercise dominion over them, and they that are great exercise authority upon them.*

> *But it shall not be so among you: but whosoever will be great among you, let him be your minister; and whosoever will be chief among you, let him be your servant:*

Another important factor in church leadership is encouraging the people to pray. Jesus exemplified this so much to His disciples that they asked Him to teach them to pray.

> Luke 6:12 – *And it came to pass in those days, that he went out into a mountain to pray, and continued all night in prayer to God.*

> Luke 11:1 – *And it came to pass, that, as he was praying in a certain place, when he ceased, one of his disciples said unto him, Lord, teach us to pray, as John also taught his disciples.*

Prayer is so important that the word "pray" is listed 511 times in scripture, and the word "prayer" is listed 131 times.)

The apostle Paul told those whom he wrote to that he prayed earnestly for them. In his teaching on spiritual warfare, he identifies the need to be equipped with the full armor of God and that prayer is a necessary element.

> Ephesians 6:18 – *praying always with all prayer and supplication in the Spirit, and watching thereunto with all perseverance and supplication for all saints;*

Prayer is the key to opening the doors of ministry to the lost.

> Matthew 9:37-38 – *Then saith he unto his disciples, The harvest truly is plenteous, but the labourers are few; pray ye therefore the Lord of the harvest, that he will send forth labourers into his harvest.*

Prayer is also needed to have a moral and sound form of government.

> 1 Timothy 2:1 – *I exhort therefore, that, first of all, supplications, prayers, intercessions, and giving of thanks, be made for all men; for kings, and for all that are in authority;*

that we may lead a quiet and peaceable life in all godliness and honesty. For this is good and acceptable in the sight of God our Saviour; who will have all men to be saved, and to come unto the knowledge of the truth.

Perhaps the reason why there is so much corruption and moral decline in America is due to the failure of the church and its leaders to seriously and earnestly pray for our nation and its leadership.

Church leaders should emphasize the importance and need for prayer; leading by example. This writer has observed that many churches no longer have a mid-week prayer service as I was involved with decades ago. Those churches that did have that service used it as another opportunity to preach with only a brief time of prayer following the message. Thus the preaching was the real reason for the meeting and not a concerted effort in corporate prayer.

I remember participating in a ministry that conducted "Prayer Breakfasts"; but then again a time of prayer seemed to be an after-thought as the main event was having a message preached to the group. This group was expanding to the point that I was asked to establish a prayer breakfast in my part of town. When I did, I determined to focus on the need for prayer as our primary purpose, and leave the preaching to other venues and church services. When the directors discovered what I was doing I was removed as the leader of this unit. It appeared that they were more interested in promoting preachers rather than prayer warriors and intercessors. The need for prayer became a side-line and not the objective. It appears to be the same in many churches today.

The church needs the right kind of leaders, those who pattern their ministry after Jesus Christ, His disciples and apostles, as in the early church. Think about this for your Church Leadership!

Chapter 15

HOW TO IDENTIFY
THE TRUE CHURCH

By Its Love

1 John 3:2 – *Beloved, now are we the sons of God, and it doth not yet appear what we shall be: but we know that, when he shall appear, we shall be like him; for we shall see him as he is.*

Love will be the means of identifying the church of the Lord Jesus Christ, because it will look like Him manifesting His character and nature. His character and nature is the Fruit of the Spirit that needs to be seen in His church. The very first Fruit listed is love – the God kind of LOVE.

Galatians 5:22-23 – *But the fruit of the Spirit is love, joy, peace, longsuffering, gentleness, goodness, faith, meekness, temperance: against such there is no law.*

These qualities of Christ's nature are the means of identifying His people, those that compose His church.

1 John 3:10 – *In this the children of God are manifest, and the children of the devil: whosoever doeth not righteousness is not of God, neither he that loveth not his brother.*

It should be easy to identify between the followers of Jesus, (His church), and those that are deceived and follow the devil, with all that is false and not of God. They are unrighteous and have a selfish love of themselves, and for the things of this world.

266

1 John 2:15-16 – *Love not the world, neither the things that are in the world. If any man love the world, the love of the Father is not in him. For all that is in the world, the lust of the flesh, and the lust of the eyes, and the pride of life, is not of the Father, but is of the world.*

When people are asked, "What is the opposite of love", they usually answer, "hate". The word "hate" means to despise or dislike, but it does not properly identify as the opposite of "love". Since the God kind of love means "giving" and "caring", then the opposite of love is "selfishness"; which means looking out for one's self. This character trait results in carnal lusts. As listed in the scripture above, the lustful self is all about the big "I": "I" will; "I" want, and "I" am. More specifically, it consists of lust of the flesh (or I will); lust of the eye (or I want); and pride of life, (or I am). These lusts are the three areas of human vulnerability that Satan is successful in tempting that leads to sin.

The true church is to be "selfless", having denied self as Jesus said.

Luke 9:23 – *And he said to them all, If any man will come after me, let him deny himself, and take up his cross daily, and follow me.*

The other church has not denied the "self" and can be likened to the Laodicean Church of Revelation 3; they were more interested in material goods, the things of this world; thus they were self-centered, refusing to deny self or take up their cross daily which made them lukewarm.

Revelation 3:16-17 – *So then because thou art lukewarm, and neither cold nor hot, I will spue thee out of my mouth. Because thou sayest, I am rich, and increased with goods, and have need of nothing; and knowest not that thou art wretched, and miserable, and poor, and blind, and naked:*

Their focus was on what they loved, and it wasn't Jesus or the Father. Jesus told them to repent! Their desires made Jesus want to vomit them out which would mean their demise as a church because they looked more like the world than His church. They were more representative of the other church in the vision of chapter one that fell back into the sea of humanity since that is where their heart was.

Even the church at Ephesus was warned to repent and return to its first love or else Jesus would remove it from being His church.

> Revelation 2:5 – *Remember therefore from whence thou art fallen, and repent, and do the first works; or else I will come unto thee quickly, and will remove thy candlestick out of his place, except thou repent.*

Thus LOVE is what the Lord is looking for as evidence of the true church and His genuine believers. Such is the true church of Jesus Christ as it will be giving and caring, showing love for God as well as love for others as is commanded by God; just as it will be in heaven. Love for God, and love for others identifies it as doing His will. Love is the message that God initiated from the beginning of His commands to man.

> *1 John 3:11 – For this is the message that ye heard from the beginning, that we should love one another.*

Since this is the message of God from the beginning, let's look at what He declares was to be the evidence of His people: it is in the Ten Commandments.

- *Thou shalt have no other god before me.*
- *Thou shalt make no idols*
- *Thou shalt not take the name of the Lord Thy God in vain*
- *Keep the Sabbath Day Holy*
- *Honor thy father and thy mother*
- *Thou shalt not murder*
- *Thou shalt not commit adultery*
- *Thou shalt not steal*
- *Thou shalt not bear false witness against thy neighbor*
- *Thou shalt not covet*

Note that the first four commandments are about loving God; the next six commandments are about loving others. Thus the Ten Commandments are about love; not the man kind of love, but the God kind of love; the agapeo which is giving, caring and compassion; also referred to as charity.

Many today claim that the Ten Commandments of the law are no longer valid since Jesus fulfilled the law. They fail to realize that this command for us to love is written in our hearts by His Spirit, including the rest of the Ten Commandments.

> Hebrews 10:16 – *This is the covenant that I will make with them after those days, saith the Lord, I will put my laws into their hearts, and in their minds will I write them;* (also in Hebrews 8:10).

God's laws and commands, like His Word, do not change, do not fail, and do not end; that is because His Word is eternal.

> Luke 21:33 – *Heaven and earth shall pass away: but my words shall not pass away.*

Therefore the command to love is eternal and will be fulfilled and maintained forever!

> Romans 13:8-10 – *Owe no man any thing, but to love one another: for he that loveth another hath fulfilled the law. For this, Thou shalt not commit adultery, Thou shalt not kill, Thou shalt not steal, Thou shalt not bear false witness, Thou shalt not covet; and if there be any other commandment, it is briefly comprehended in this saying, namely, Thou shalt love thy neighbour as thyself. Love worketh no ill to his neighbour: therefore love is the fulfilling of the law.*

> 1 John 3:23-24 – *And this is his commandment, That we should believe on the name of his Son Jesus Christ, and love one another, as he gave us commandment. And he that keepeth his commandments dwelleth in him, and he in him. And hereby we know that he abideth in us, by the Spirit which he hath given us.*

Here we see that the God kind of love fulfills the law, (Ten Commandments) as well as the words of the prophets. Consider that if everyone in the world lived with the God kind of love that there would be absolutely no crime, and no injustice. No one would lie, cheat, steal or have an adulterous affair. Instead there would be abundant grace, mercy and harmony.

We need to understand that the very foundation of the kingdom of God is love. Why, because God is LOVE!

> 1 John 4:7-8, 11-12 & 16 – *Beloved, let us love one another: for love is of God; and every one that loveth is born of God, and knoweth God. He that loveth not knoweth not God; for God is love … … Beloved, if God so loved us, we ought also to love one another. No man hath seen God at any time. If we love one another, God dwelleth in us, and his love is perfected in us. … And we have known and believed the love that God hath to us. God is love; and he that dwelleth in love dwelleth in God, and God in him.*

As already stated, the God kind of love gives, and is about caring and sharing; thus it is also called *charity*. In 1 Corinthians 13, referred to as the love chapter, the word charity is used in the place of love.

> 1 Corinthians 13:1-3 – *Though I speak with the tongues of men and of angels, and have not charity, I am become as sounding brass, or a tinkling cymbal. And though I have the gift of prophecy, and understand all mysteries, and all knowledge; and though I have all faith, so that I could remove mountains, and have not charity, I am nothing. And though I bestow all my goods to feed the poor, and though I give my body to be burned, and have not charity, it profiteth me nothing.*

Of all the qualities of God's character and nature, the greatest quality is love; God wants to see that same quality of love in us showing that we are His children, and the Church of the Lord Jesus Christ.

> 1 Corinthians 13:13 – *And now abideth faith, hope, charity, these three; but the greatest of these is charity.*

> John 15:13 – *Greater love hath no man than this, that a man lay down his life for his friends.*

John 3:16 – *For God so loved the world, that he gave his only begotten Son, that whosoever believeth in him should not perish, but have everlasting life.*

1 John 3:16 – *Hereby perceive we the love of God, because he laid down his life for us: and we ought to lay down our lives for the brethren.*

Therefore those who provide leadership in the true church of the Lord Jesus Christ will show forth the Fruit of the Spirit; just as Jesus said; that is how you shall recognize them. And they will work to produce that same fruit in believers.

Matthew 7:20 – *Wherefore by their fruits ye shall know them.*

Please be advised, the leadership in the other church are likely under the influence of the spirit of antichrist, not the Lord Jesus Christ. The spirit of antichrist is very lustful which is why you will see all manner of corruption and worldliness in the other church, fulfilling fleshly lusts.

1 John 2:18-19 – *Little children, it is the last time: and as ye have heard that antichrist shall come, even now are there many antichrists; whereby we know that it is the last time. They went out from us, but they were not of us; for if they had been of us, they would no doubt have continued with us: but they went out, that they might be made manifest that they were not all of us.*

Thus they formed the other church! They created the doctrines in the other church that are of men and demons; doctrines and traditions that are contrary to the truth of the Lord Jesus Christ. These sort of leaders are among those that Jesus described:

Matthew 7:22 -23 – *Many will say to me in that day, Lord, Lord, have we not prophesied in thy name? and in thy name have cast out devils? and in thy name done many wonderful works? And then will I profess unto them, I never knew you: depart from me, ye that work iniquity.*

These have the love for the things of the world and seek to satisfy their own lusts for position, material things, power and control over others. The true church has love for God, and possesses the love of God toward others. Those who love the world are aligned with Satan, the god of this world.

> 2 Corinthians 4:3-4 – *But if our gospel be hid, it is hid to them that are lost: in whom the god of this world hath blinded the minds of them which believe not, lest the light of the glorious gospel of Christ, who is the image of God, should shine unto them.*

Those who are unredeemed have the devil's character and nature which manifests as wicked carnal behavior. The devil hates those in whom the Spirit of Christ dwells and so he attacks them through those who follow him, just like Satan went after Job. Satan is cruel, and so are those who unwittingly are his servants. Such cruelty is the opposite of Love, thus we can identify between the children of God, (Christ's true Church), and the children of the devil.

> 1 John 3:11-13 – *For this is the message that ye heard from the beginning, that we should love one another. Not as Cain, who was of that wicked one, and slew his brother. And wherefore slew he him? Because his own works were evil, and his brother's righteous. Marvel not, my brethren, if the world hate you.*

The wicked will be at war with, and persecute, the righteous in this life until Jesus returns to destroy them and set up His righteous kingdom and government.

> 1 John 3:10 – *In this the children of God are manifest, and the children of the devil: whosoever doeth not righteousness is not of God, neither he that loveth not his brother.*

Obviously there is much that needs to be done by those truly called as Christ's servants and who are led of the Lord by His Holy Spirit. The building of His church is not yet finished and it must be made ready for His return. The God kind of love is the Holy identifier and must be seen in His Church! It is the Fruit by which it shall be recognized!

John 15:1-8 – *I am the true vine, and my Father is the husbandman. Every branch in me that beareth not fruit he taketh away: and every branch that beareth fruit, he purgeth it, that it may bring forth more fruit. Now ye are clean through the word which I have spoken unto you. Abide in me, and I in you. As the branch cannot bear fruit of itself, except it abide in the vine; no more can ye, except ye abide in me. I am the vine, ye are the branches: He that abideth in me, and I in him, the same bringeth forth much fruit: for without me ye can do nothing. If a man abide not in me, he is cast forth as a branch, and is withered; and men gather them, and cast them into the fire, and they are burned. If ye abide in me, and my words abide in you, ye shall ask what ye will, and it shall be done unto you. Herein is my Father glorified, that ye bear much fruit; so shall ye be my disciples.*

It is the life (zoe) of Christ flowing in and through His people that produces this divine Fruit that God is looking for in His children! Thus the true church is revealed and the other church is exposed.

This author has spoken to believers since the 1970's that the church that Jesus is returning for will be much like the early church as it began. It will be filled with the glory, the power and the love of Christ manifesting in them. The true church will go "full-circle", back to its original form to the point where the believers were first called "Christians" in ancient Antioch.

Acts 11:26b – ... ... *And it came to pass, that a whole year they assembled themselves with the church, and taught much people. And the disciples were called Christians first in Antioch.*

They were called "Christ's ones", or Christians, because Christ was seen in them. Their love will also be evident for one another as their care for each other will show; there will be no partisanship, division or sectarianism.

Acts 4:32-35 – *And the multitude of them that believed were of one heart and of one soul: neither said any of them that ought of the things which he possessed was his own; but they had all things common. And with great power gave the apostles witness of the resurrection of the Lord Jesus: and great grace was upon them all. Neither was there any among them that lacked: for as many as were possessors of lands or houses sold them, and brought the prices of the things that were sold, and laid them down at the apostles' feet: and distribution was made unto every man according as he had need.*

The power of the Lord's presence will also manifest among this church of the last days as at the beginning. How can I say this with confidence? Because of the scripture given at the beginning of this chapter.

1 John 3:2 – *Beloved, now are we the sons of God, and it doth not yet appear what we shall be: but we know that, when he shall appear, we shall be like him; for we shall see him as he is.*

The church Jesus is coming for will look and act just like Him! He will be seen in His people! Obviously we are not there yet; but as we earnestly seek Him – HE WILL BE!

Finally, the ultimate thing that God wants is for you to love Him with the kind of love that He has for you. This is because Love is the very foundation of the kingdom of God.

Matthew 22:37 – *Jesus said unto him, Thou shalt love the Lord thy God with all thy heart, and with all thy soul, and with all thy mind.*

1 Corinthians 13:12 – *And now abideth faith, hope, charity, these three; but the greatest of these is charity –* (LOVE).

CORRUPT BELIEFS
AND PRACTICES
THAT BECAME PART
OF THE OTHER CHURCH

Historically recognized "church fathers" had a hand in introducing the corruption that has grown. (Understand that church history was written by these "church fathers" in order to reflect the doctrines and dictates of the Roman Church and has little bearing on real church history.)

Clement: declared himself Bishop of Rome; approximately A.D. 95, endorsed the clergy and the position of High Priest and Deacons as having authority over the laity.

Ignatius: Bishop of Antioch; approximately A.D. 117, fine tuned the hierarchical system by removing any and all types of ministry or service from laymen and placing all under the control of the clergy.

Irenaeus: Bishop of Lyon, France; approximately A.D. 130-212, established "apostolic succession" meaning anyone involved in ministry had to be ordained by the established order and under their "covering" (control).

Tertullian: Bishop of Carthage, approximately A.D. 160-230, re-enforced the role of clergy by a centralized Order, or point of authority (control) as "know it alls" and that the laity are unlearned and ignorant people that must obey the Order.

<u>Cyprian</u>:	Arch Bishop of Carthage, approximately A.D. 237-247, declared that the Church, its traditions and rulers had precedence over people, not Jesus Christ or the Word of God.
<u>Augustine</u>:	Bishop of Hippo, approximately A.D. 395-430, championed loyalty to Roman Catholicism and the laity-smothering Constantinian "establishment" church. He merged the state (Rome) with the church thus giving the church an army and the power of the state to enforce its beliefs, doctrines and edicts. He felt the state needed the church to transform society, and the church needed the state to enforce that transformation. Thus began the executions for heresy.

Based on the beliefs, practices and theology of these respected church fathers, they regarded themselves to be above the Bible and to be the final authority. To them the Bible means whatever they say it means, and they were never wrong; and God help those who oppose or resist their decrees.

The following is a list of things that these so-called infallible authorities incorporated as institutions into the Mother church:

YEAR	TRADITION
140	Pope Hyginus establishes clergy as a superior order distinct from laity
150	Sprinkling replaced immersion for baptism
200	Clergy given title of "Priest"
200	Origen brings in Greek oratory and performance modeled after Plato
211	Prayers for the dead endorsed by Tertullian
250	Recognition of the continued virginity of Mary
250	Infant baptism initiated (became institutionalized in A.D. 416)
258	Holy water documented by Cyprian
270	Monasticism (the shuttering away of persons for sanctification)
320	Utilization of wax candles and incense as part of worship service
320	Pastors became "professional", salaried by the state
375	Veneration of angels and dead "saints"
375	Use of images and icons as objects of worship
378	Damascus I becomes Pope.

380	Christianity becomes "state" religion and is imposed on all citizens
394	Establishment of the Mass
402	Innocent I calls himself "Ruler of the Church of God"
405	List of forbidden books made
420	Purgatory proposed
431	Mary elevated as the "Mother of God"
451	Leo I takes title of Pope and confers it on all previous bishops of Rome posthumously.
476	Indulgences received for the dead
500	Priests don gaudy costumes and funny hats that show rank
526	Extreme unction
590	Purgatory confirmed
600	Pray to Mary, angels and dead saints
709	Kissing the Pope's foot
787	Veneration and worship of images and relics
819	Feast of the assumption of Mary
858	Wearing of papal crown begins with Nicolas 1
859	Papal claims to temporal powers by employing forged documents
869	Western (Rome) and Eastern (Constantinople) churches divide
995	Canonization of "dead saints"
1045	Gregory VI bought office of Pontiff by paying Pope Benedict to resign
1074	Celibacy established for Priests
1080	Reading the Bible forbidden in common language, (the beginning of reading restrictions of the Bible)
1184	Inquisition begins - millions executed in the name of heresy
1190	Selling of indulgences (a fund raising scheme for the church)
1208	The Rosary - prayer beads
1215	Transubsatantiation - the communion wafer and wine turn into the body and blood of Christ by incantation of priest
1220	Adoration of the wafer (host)
1245	Limbo invented for dead, unbaptized infants
1300	Stained glass becomes part of church architecture

1342	Treasury of Merits - credits for good deeds now can be transferred
1414	The cup forbidden to laity at communion, only Priests can drink wine
1484	Innocent VIII orders extermination of Waldenses (opposition believers group)
1546	Council of Trent - Pope has power over all the earth; church tradition has authority equal to scriptures; seminaries instituted
1547	Rejection of justification by faith alone (reaction to Luther's doctrine)
1564	Immorality caused by nude statues so fig leaves order to be retrofitted
1572	Solemn mass for St. Bartholomew's Day massacre of Huguenots
1854	Immaculate Conception instituted (Mary born sinless)
1870	Papal infallibility established
1931	Mary named "mediatrix" (gives favors not granted by God and quicker than Jesus
1950	Assumption of Mary to heaven
1954	Mary named "Queen of Heaven" and enshrined

What remains of this Roman abomination that can still be found in the Protestant churches? The hierarchical rule that the Lord Jesus Christ, himself said he hates - (referred to as "the deeds of the Nicolaitans" in Revelation 2:6). The so-called holy days of the Roman Church: Christmas, Lent, Good Friday, Easter, All souls/saints day (Halloween). The church building with its platform (sacristy) and pulpit; pews; choirs and sermons - just to list a few items.

10 CHARACTERISTICS OF RELIGIOUS CHURCH SYSTEMS JESUS WARNS US AGAINST - August 16, 2014 by Joseph Mattera (copied from the Internet)

Every church and/or organization has a corporate culture with norms, rules and expectations that pressure participants to conform. Some cultures are good and some bad.

That being said, there are particular attributes that characterize false religions or become the norm during religious decline in a true faith such as Christianity.

The Old Testament prophets such as Isaiah, Micah and Amos decried religious ritual that was without true righteousness, humility and love for neighbor (Is. 1:10-17; 58; Amos 5:21-24; Mic. 6:8). The line of prophets arose starting in the 8th century B.C. primarily because Israel had a tendency to focus more on adhering to the temple ritual worship of the Levitical system than the ethical lifestyle required by the Law of Moses as found in the Ten Commandments. For this, the prophets pronounced judgment upon the nation, and God dispersed the people and, on two occasions, let enemies destroy their temple.

We have the same issue in today's church, irrespective of the denomination or expression of the body of Christ. The following are 10 of the characteristics of false religious systems as taught by Jesus in Matthew 23:

1. There are onerous rules and regulations some call legalism (Matt. 23:1-3). In the contemporary church, there are numerous man-made traditions and requirements that never arose from the Word, which have become an unnecessary burden upon believers. For example, in many Pentecostal churches the emphasis is on outward holiness related to attire, makeup, the cutting of hair, jewelry and other regulations. I have spoken to numerous young people who stopped attending church because these regulations made them feel weird in front of their unchurched friends. Fundamentalists in the past forbade any form of entertainment, including watching movies, listening to the radio, watching television, etc. These are legalistic efforts to bring holiness that have resulted in numerous churches losing their next generation.

2. The church leaders serve to receive prestige from men (vv. 5-7). God makes it clear in His word that some religious leaders love the praise of men more than the praise of God (John 12:42-43). The judgment of God is against the leaders who are constantly posturing themselves within their denomination to attain the highest seats of authority and places of honor among men. Truly, some of the greatest people of God in the earth today are hidden from the public eye.

3. The leaders crave titles and moving up the ranks of hierarchical religious systems (vv. 8-11). Today's church is replete with people who use titles to validate their ministries. I can't tell you how many people I have met with the title apostle, bishop, doctor or archbishop on their business cards who have very little influence in the church and secular world. Truly God doesn't care about an apostolic title; God looks more at apostolic function and fruit. I have found that, the more a person speaks about their academic achievements and ecclesial titles, the more insecure they are as a person and about their ministry accomplishments. I say this as a person who has been consecrated both a bishop and apostle and who flows in circles with leaders who use these titles. There is nothing wrong with these titles (both are biblical) as long as we don't flaunt them, crave them and depend upon them for validation and/or to hide that we do not have real apostolic function and fruit. Many of the greatest leaders in the church world do not insist upon people referring to them with a title.

4. The leaders have an entitlement mentality (vv. 11-12). I believe in the biblical principle of serving the people of God as a prerequisite to being qualified to function in the same ministry as they do. For example, Joshua

was called the servant of Moses; Elisha served Elijah; David served Samuel and Saul, and the 12 apostles served Jesus.

That being said, there has also been abuse of this principle since many people desire to become leaders partially because it enables them to be waited upon. I believe younger ministers should serve older, more mature ministers out of honor and proper protocol, but at the same time older ministers should not demand it or become abusive if they do not receive it. We do not receive titles in the kingdom so we can be waited upon but so that we can have greater opportunity to serve in the church.

The more mature a Christ follower is, the more they will celebrate service as the highest form of ministry and leadership. God resists those leaders who emotionally abuse and/or lord it over those under their care (1 Pet. 5:3).

5. The leaders become a stumbling block to others seeking the kingdom (vv. 13-15). It has been evident the past 30 years in both the evangelical and Roman Catholic churches that leaders can become huge stumbling blocks instead of assets to the kingdom. Whether it is lavish lifestyles, sexual misconduct, abuse of power, or other forms of narcissism, many believers have been turned off from Christianity by those who are supposed to represent it. Truly those who handle the Word of God will receive the most scrutiny at the judgment seat of Christ (James 3:1).

6. The leaders value and love money and wealth more than anything else (vv. 16-17). While I do not believe church leaders should live in poverty, nor do I believe they should receive salaries from their churches that are greatly disproportionate to the average income of their congregation and/or community. The religious leaders Jesus denounced seemed to value gold more than the glory and honor of God. Leaders should never serve primarily for money but for the love of God and His people (1 Pet. 5:2).

7. The weightier matters of the Word are neglected (vv. 23-24). Although I believe and practice the principles of tithing, fasting, church attendance and the like, they should never be an excuse for me to think I have fulfilled all of my Christian duties. Jesus says here that we ought to continue to tithe but also include in our lifestyle the practice of treating others with justice, mercy and faithfulness. For example, if we tithe but treat our spouse poorly, neglect the poor in our midst, or mistreat others, our tithe will not do us any good. Then we are just like the Pharisee Jesus describes in Luke 18:10-14.

8. Ritual is valued more than inner transformation (vv. 25-28). In the church we all have our traditions and rituals; whether it is the high-church liturgies of the Roman Catholic, Orthodox or Anglican churches, and/or the more informal gatherings of the Pentecostals and evangelicals. The tendency for human beings is to fall into a routine and equate our routine with true worship. Jesus told the Samaritan woman that she worshipped what she did not know (John 4), which means that people can worship in ignorance and/or without a true experience with God.

    Whether it is the sacraments of denominational churches or the shouting, shaking and tongue talking of the Pentecostals, human nature has a tendency to fall into habit patterns of outward worship bereft of the life-changing dynamic of encountering the living God. We do not have to do away with these rituals, sacraments and traditions but should integrate them with true heartfelt worship and passion for our Lord.

9. They honor the departed saints without living like them in the present (vv. 29-32). I have found that it is much easier to study about revival than to actually work hard for it. It is much easier to study church history than it is to make history. Every denomination and expression of the church has its Christian heroes of the past, but very few denominations, churches and adherents attempt to emulate the life, passion and sacrifice of the saints of old (for example: Ignatius, Tertullian, Cyprian, Augustine, Luther, Calvin, Francis, Whitefield, Wesley, Edwards, Finney, Spurgeon, Moody, Hudson Taylor, John G. Lake, Wigglesworth, Maria Woodworth-Etter, Francis Schaeffer and more).

    Jesus wants us to honor the prophets of old by living like them, not merely by building and revering their tombs.

10. They reject the prophets and wise men who confront their false systems (vv. 33-37). Those who are captivated by a religious system will never listen to those speaking for God who are not of their denomination and/or do not have acceptable academic credentials. Sound familiar? The Pharisees and Sadducees rejected Jesus (John 7:14-18) and Peter (Acts 4:13) for the same reason. It is not an accident that in Luke 3:1-2 it shows that the Word of God came to John in the wilderness and not to an already established institutional leader. Thus, God bypassed the litany of prominent political and religious leaders and their systems (3:1) because they were so corrupt.

    When a leader is captivated by their religious system or dead institution they become blind to the pure Word of the Lord. God has to bypass them and speak prophetically through those outside the dead institution. Those who are humble and have ears to hear (as Nicodemus in John 3) will recognize and receive the people God sends to them, irrespective of their institutional affiliation.

Truly, God cannot be contained in a temple, an institution, a denomination or any one religious system. He is Lord of all and will seek after those who worship Him in spirit and in truth (John 4:23-24). May God help us to avoid these 10 judgments!

Printed in the United States
by Baker & Taylor Publisher Services